St. Benedict's Toolbox

The Nuts
and Bolts
of Everyday
Benedictine
Living

Jane Tomaine

To Dorothy
"Place your hope in God alone."

Peace & blessings,
Jane Tomaine

MOREHOUSE PUBLISHING

Morehouse Publishing is an imprint of Church Publishing, Incorporated.
Morehouse Publishing, P.O. Box 1321, Harrisburg, PA 17105
Morehouse Publishing, 445 Fifth Avenue, New York, NY 10016

Quotations from the Rule of Benedict so designated are from *RB1980: The Rule of Benedict in English* (Collegeville, Minn.: The Liturgical Press, 1981). Permission granted by The Liturgical Press.

Scripture quotations in this book, unless otherwise indicated, are from the New Revised Standard Version Bible, copyright © 1989 by the Division of Education of the National Council of Churches of Christ in the U.S.A. Used by permission. All rights reserved.

Prayer book quotations are taken from The Book of Common Prayer (1979) of the Episcopal Church of the USA, The Church Hymnal Corporation.

For more information, ideas, tools, and readings see www.stbenedictstoolbox.org.

Cover art by Dorothy Thompson Perez
Design by Beth Oberholtzer

Library of Congress Cataloging-in-Publication Data

Tomaine, Jane.
    St. Benedict's toolbox : the nuts and bolts of everyday Benedictine living / Jane Tomaine.
      p. cm.
    Includes bibliographical references (p.) and index.
    ISBN 0-8192-2152-X (pbk. : alk. paper)
    1. Benedict, Saint, Abbot of Monte Cassino. Regula. 2. Benedictines—Rules. 3. Monasticism and religious orders—Rules. 4. Spiritual life—Christianity. I. Title: Saint Benedict's toolbox. II. Title.
BX3004.Z5T66 2005
255'.106—dc22

                               2004026838

Printed in the United States of America

06 07 08 09 10   6 5 4

Contents

To John

Preface

Ever since I was a child, one of my favorite pastimes is working on jigsaw puzzles. As I find each piece and fit it into place, a beautiful scene begins to take shape. A tree begins as a speck of green, forms gradually, and emerges as a majestic pine. A hand gains a body and face to become a person. Piece by piece the work is completed. How like a jigsaw puzzle is the work of God in our lives! Like the pieces of a puzzle, God places the seemingly disparate pieces of our lives into a picture that, for a time, only God knows. All along the way, through the circumstances of our lives and the choices we must make, God says to us, "Here, my child, take this piece; place it here. Now this piece. Now another. And another," until some form or pattern begins to emerge that we can see.

My acquaintance with the Rule of Benedict came in 1997, while attending a continuing education course on congregational culture at The General Theological Seminary in New York City, an Episcopal institution. The Rule immediately spoke to me. It was centered in Christ and the Gospels, rooted in relationships, and practically oriented—no vague, euphoric clouds here. Benedict was a practical, no-nonsense person who was in love with God. I resonated with his main points: to put Christ at the center of life, to remain connected with people, to listen for God in everything, and to follow God's will. Benedict advocated a mindful, holistic approach to life that is rooted in relationships to God, to others, and even to ourselves. And so, as is my pattern when encountering a subject of interest, I immediately purchased books about the Rule. I can't remember whether or not I read them right away, but I do know they stood faithfully on my bookshelf and waited patiently to be rediscovered in the fullness of time.

Two years later, again while at General, this time enrolled in the two-year Congregational Development Institute, I was reacquainted with the Rule. I bought more books and my interest moved into active mode. I introduced the Rule to my women's spirituality group at church through

Elizabeth Canham's book *Heart Whispers* and John McQuiston II's contemporary paraphrase of the Rule *Always We Begin Again*. In 2001, I entered a Doctor of Ministry program at the Theological School of Drew University in Madison, New Jersey. One of the requirements for the degree was to lead a major project with a team of parishioners. After exploring a range of subjects, the team and I decided to introduce the Rule of Benedict to the entire parish. We were convinced that the Rule had something important to say, especially to those of us who led frantic, fast-paced lives. This introduction was accomplished in a seven-week program that we entitled "The Benedictine Season." During this time we made changes in our liturgy à la Benedict and provided several educational opportunities for parishioners to delve into the Rule. The regular Sunday lectionary was set aside for one that I created to correspond with the key points of Benedict's Rule. At the suggestion of the team, I wrote a book for parishioners that both introduced the teachings of the Rule and offered ways to apply the ideas to daily life. A year later after I'd completed the thesis requirement for the degree, I decided to send the book to Morehouse Publishing. Their interest has brought this book to you.

That you are reading these words indicates that you already have either an interest in or a curiosity about the Rule of Benedict (or maybe you've been corralled into reading this book by someone else). Whatever the reason, I pray that you'll find Benedict a rich and wise spiritual guide, accessible to we modern folk who are on the ancient path to God and to fullness of life. May this book and the Rule help you see more clearly the picture of you that God is forming through the jigsaw pieces of your life.

Acknowledgments

Few are the endeavors in life that are completed alone. I would like to express my heartfelt thanks to some of those people who have helped me in this project.

I'm grateful to the members of the Benedictine Project Committee at St. Peter's Episcopal Church in Livingston, New Jersey—Cynthia Brady, Tara Gieger, Peggy Holloway, Scott Lodge, Michael McGrane, Ruth Portela, and Nancy Tiensch—whose creativity sparked the ideas for the "Benedictine Season" program at our church and inspired me to write a book about the Rule for our parishioners. And thanks go to Janice Woodruff, whose computer savvy contributed to the design and layout of the book that I wrote for my parish and to *St. Benedict's Toolbox*. I am indebted to Robert Gallagher, developer of the Congregational Development Institute, who first introduced me to the Rule of Benedict in 1997, at a continuing education week at The General Theological Seminary in New York City and reacquainted me with the Rule in 1999, at the Congregational Development Institute.

Several friends read the manuscript of *St. Benedict's Toolbox* prior to submission to the publisher. I thank them for their efforts in culling through the draft, giving me suggestions, corrections, and encouragement. Thanks go to the Reverend Peter deFranco, priest in the Diocese of Newark, who read the manuscript from his perspective as a former Cistercian monk, and also to three other readers who graciously contributed their time and helpful suggestions: Sr. Shane Margaret Phelan of the Episcopal Community of Saint John Baptist in Mendham, New Jersey, and my dear friends Dee Rogers and Mary Beth Starrett.

My pastoral supervisor, Dr. Patricia Briegs, and my former supervisor and doctoral advisor, Dr. William Presnell, were both sources of support and practical advice throughout both the "Benedictine Season" and the creation of this book.

My spiritual director, Sr. Margaret Brackett of the Sisters of Mercy, guided me in Ignatian spirituality for fourteen years and introduced me to *lectio divina* and praying the psalms.

My editor, Nancy Fitzgerald, left me an incredible message a year ago saying that Morehouse was interested in publishing the book that I had sent to them. For her meticulous work on the manuscript, her valuable suggestions, and her help and consideration throughout the whole and truly collaborative process, I am thankful.

I'm especially grateful to my dear friend of thirty-some years, Mary Beth Starrett, who has been a beacon of encouragement and a close spiritual friend; and to my husband, John, for lifting my spirits so many times and for his wise counsel, his patience, his support, the dinners he made, and his love.

And finally, last but not least, I thank my dear friend Benedict, who continues to point me in the direction of Christ and to guide my own spiritual journey.

Welcome to *St. Benedict's Toolbox*

Fifteen centuries ago a young man turned his back on his studies and on the worldly city of Rome and ventured forth into the Italian countryside in search of something more important than education, more valuable than position, and more precious than wealth. Motivated by a force whose power surpassed any of these, this young man was driven by his quest for God. As he searched, his wisdom, understanding, and compassion grew. Others on the same quest gathered around him. He guided them and they learned from him. He pointed the way to Christ through the Gospels. His name was Benedict of Nursia.

While most of us will never live alone in a cave for three years as this man did, or establish monastic houses in Italy, or write a Rule, you and I also seek God. We search for the joy that cannot fade. We long to banish the sense of dis-ease that can permeate our lives. We crave the peace that comes when we rest in God's arms. We want to be good disciples of our Lord, Jesus Christ. We desire to be channels for God's grace and love in a world that is cold and disinterested.

And so we ask St. Benedict to be our guide. As you read this book you'll become acquainted with this remarkable yet humble man through the words of the monastic Rule that he wrote for his fellow sixth-century monks. The wisdom of this Rule still speaks profoundly to us today. As you and I learn about and practice parts of this Rule, St. Benedict becomes our loving spiritual father, too. I can't imagine a better spiritual father in zeal, compassion, humility, wisdom—and even in his sense of humor!

And so, I welcome you to this journey with St. Benedict. As he would bid the monk at the gate to say to a visitor, so I say to you: "Your blessing, please."[1]

The Format of This Book

St. Benedict's Toolbox: The Nuts and Bolts of Everyday Benedictine Living is designed to teach about the Rule of Benedict and to help you, the reader, (and me, the writer!) bring what we learn about this sixth-century monastic Rule into everyday twenty-first-century life. As you read, you'll discover just how much of his Rule can increase the quality of our lives by giving us "tools" that we can use to, in Benedict's words, "open our eyes to the light that comes from God."[2]

In this book you'll find that longer chapters unpacking the Rule alternate with shorter pieces called "Interludes." Interludes offer a change of pace to the reading. They're either stories or reflections on some aspect of the Rule and generally relate to a topic from the previous chapter. If you wish, take a moment to scan the table of contents.

Each chapter first presents various aspects of the Rule. Then, at the end of the chapter, you'll find the Toolbox, which contains three to eight "tools" to help you apply what you learned to daily life. These tools are varied in their content and application. Some offer instruction on prayer and other spiritual disciplines. Some ask you to reflect on your life in light of what you learned about the Rule. Others give suggestions for maintaining healthy relationships in your life. Still others address how you spend your time, how you view your work, and how you might live a more Christ-centered life. Each tool in the Toolbox has three parts:

1. Purpose: A brief statement about what the tool is designed to do.
2. Background: An explanation of the rationale for the tool—(for example, how it ties into the Rule of Benedict and how it might be important to your spiritual life or to your relationships).
3. The Tool: A step-by-step guide to using the tool.

Before continuing you might wish to take a look at one or two tools to see the format.

You don't need to use all the tools as you read this book. Choose the ones that seem interesting to you or those that will help you develop your spiritual, relational, and personal skills and abilities. You may begin to use certain tools as you read this book and then, later, come back and try new ones.

In the Appendix on page 188, you'll find a complete list of tools by chapter. If you have access to the Internet, I invite you to log on to www.stbenedictstoolbox.org. There you'll find a chart to help you keep track of the tools you're using, as well as a chart that cross-references each tool to a subject: prayer, listening for God, relationships, work, and so on. The charts can be downloaded.

How to Use This Book

I recall years ago when I first read the books in *The Lord of the Ring* series. They were so interesting and engaging that I literally galloped through them, especially the last half of the final book of the trilogy. *Please don't read this book in the same way!* I hope you will find this book interesting and pray that it engages you, but this book is designed to be read more slowly, giving time to both digest and practice what Benedict teaches. The best way to use this book is to take one chapter at a time: *read* the chapter, *reflect* on what you've read, and finally *respond* by using the Toolbox.

The pace at which you read this book and use the tools in the Toolbox is up to you. Go at a pace that makes sense for you. It's important that you give yourself time to digest the informational portion of each chapter and to use one or more of the tools that are at the end of each chapter.

Here are some reading options:

- Read a chapter at the beginning of each week. Choose one or more of the tools to use throughout that week.
- Read a chapter and set your own time interval for that chapter. Use the tools for that chapter during that time interval.
- If you're reading this book in a group, decide together how long to spend on each chapter.

Some thoughts about the tools:

- When you finish reading each chapter and you're ready to decide on which tools to use, pray for the guidance of the Holy Spirit.
- Choose tools that are interesting to you and stretch you, but don't take on too much at once. Benedict was clear about this in the Rule: people need to be challenged but not overwhelmed.
- It's best to choose one or two tools in a chapter at a time. You can always go back and try other tools later.
- When you go on to a new chapter, keep using tools from the previous chapters.
- As you continue reading through the book, go back to the Toolbox in earlier chapters and try other tools.
- If a tool isn't working for you, try a different one. Then go back later and see if the first tool might now offer you something helpful.

Don't throw in the towel if something initially seems too difficult. Growth is never easy. Try using part of a tool. You might also try breaking a tool into smaller steps; then celebrate as you accomplish or work on each one.

Keep in mind as you read that one of the main goals of this book is to deepen your relationship with God. It's to be a spiritual journey and not an exercise to finish as quickly as possible. Like the Bible, the Rule of Benedict offers a lifetime of insight and guidance that's not absorbed quickly.

Keeping a Journal

I know a woman who has kept a personal journal for years. At the day's end she picks up her pen, takes out her journal, and records the events of the day. She's remarked to me that there have been many times that she's gone back and reread portions of old journals to understand her journey.

Journaling can be meaningful and interesting, especially when you're learning new ideas and behaviors that can become a part of—and even change—your life. As you read about the Rule, it can be helpful to write down ideas and suggestions that you find especially important. The tools from the Toolbox in each chapter are designed to impact various aspects of your life, so it may be helpful to record what happens and how you feel as you use these tools. I find that when I journal it helps me to clarify my thoughts and to reflect on my experiences. I always journal my prayer time, recording what happened, how my mood might have changed, how I felt, and any new insights that I may have gained in prayer.

You can write in a notebook, on loose-leaf paper, in a special journal that you can purchase at stationery stores, or even on your computer. Take a few minutes each day to write down your thoughts and record your experiences.

Here are some "Rules" for journaling:

- First and most important, there are *no* rules!
- Journaling is only for you, so you can abbreviate, write in incomplete sentences, or use other techniques that are personal and of your own invention.
- You don't have to write perfectly and neatly.
- You don't need to use perfect grammar.
- You can draw pictures if you wish.
- Record your feelings. This is important. Be honest.
- Do your best to journal every day, even if you make only a brief entry.

Journaling is possible even for those who feel they are not skilled writers. Journaling is for your eyes only; no one else need see what you write. If you feel "writer's block" and don't know how to begin, just start your pen moving with anything. There have been days that I've begun with words like, "Well, I really don't know what to write today" or "Well, nothing really happened." The truth is, when we "show up," God can act! I think it's like taking a walk when we're tired. We don't want to do it and start by dragging our feet, wishing it all was over. But once we get going we not only pick up the pace, we also feel much better.

Have your journal handy as you use the Toolbox. You can jot down thoughts and answers to some of the questions posed in the Toolbox. If you find yourself moving into another topic as you write, go for it. The Holy Spirit is probably moving you into another important area, using what you were writing before as a springboard into something else.

After you've been journaling for a while—perhaps for several weeks or months—go back and read your earlier entries. Doing this periodically will help you gain insights about your life, about your relationship with God, and about where God might be leading you.

Framing Your Journey in Prayer

As you continue, pray each time you begin to read and before you decide on a tool or use a tool. Let prayer become the interlocking thread that holds it all together.

Take a moment now and pray to remain open to the guiding of the Holy Spirit as you read through this book and use the tools in the Toolbox. I'll pray too for you, dear reader.

Let us begin.

> Let us get up then, at long last, for the Scriptures rouse us when they say: *It is high time for us to arise from sleep* (Rom 13:11 RB). Let us open our eyes to the light that comes from God, and our ears to the voice from heaven that every day calls out this charge: *If you hear his voice today, do not harden your hearts* (Ps 95 RB).
>
> From the Prologue to the Rule, Verses 8–10 *RB1980*
> (Please see p. 20 below.)

 TOOLBOX

The Beginning of the Journey

Welcome to the first tool!

Tool #1: Becoming Aware of Where You Are Right Now

Purpose of the Tool. To understand what we personally bring of ourselves and our history to the exploration of the Rule of Benedict.

Background on the Tool. What we bring *to* an experience greatly impacts what we take *from* that experience. And what we bring is as varied as patterns in a kaleidoscope. We bring ourselves and our personal histories with all their richness and diversity. We bring our thoughts about the past, our recent experiences, and our hopes for the future. We also bring particular desires about our relationship to God and to those with whom we share our life. All these impact how and what we learn.

The Tool

Take a moment to identify the three key things that you are bringing by answering these three questions. Identify the one or two most pronounced things in each category. If you've decided to use one, write out the answers in your journal.

1. Who am I? (Answer whatever first comes to you. No need to call in Freud!)
2. What is going on in my life? (The key things that are happening right now.)
3. What is the desire of my heart for this study? (What would you most like to experience or achieve?)

Now keep your responses in mind for a few moments while we continue.

Whenever I begin a study such as this book offers, I think about the liturgical season of Advent. Each Sunday in Advent we light candles on the Advent Wreath, until all are burning brightly and the season's Holy Light reaches the darkest corners of our hearts. On Christmas Eve, with the central candle, the Light of Christ, burning brightly on the wreath, we sing carols and celebrate the Eucharist. A holy calm touches and restores. The Rule of Benedict draws us to this same light, for the focus of the Rule is how to live a Christ-centered life. Holy calm all year-round, even in the midst of a fast-paced life, is available to us for the asking.

Where the Rule will touch you the most will depend on your personal characteristics, the events of your life past and present, and the desires that you hold. Keep them in mind when you read, as you reflect on the Rule and apply the ideas to your life.

May God bless your journey.

The Rule of Benedict
A Tool for Christian Living

> *The aim of the Rule is to teach us to follow*
> *Christ and to follow him in love. . . . The Rule,*
> *we discover, teaches us on every page to love*
> *Christ, to remain in His company in times of*
> *consolation and joy as well as in times of trial,*
> *in the way that He wills.*
> —SIGHARD KLEINER, O.C. [1]

We are ready to begin a journey that calls us into a deeper relationship with God, who continually reaches out to bring us an awareness of the Divine Presence in our lives. Yet, in the rush of daily life, with its many challenges, joys, and worries, we can lose sight of this Presence. Too often we fail to draw upon the rich resources that God offers us each hour of every day. Instead we can feel alone, frustrated, or angry. We forget that we have been marked as Christ's own in our baptism. We turn aside from his grace and from the call to be his followers.

Our Christian Imperative: The Baptismal Covenant

The service of Holy Baptism found in The Book of Common Prayer of the Episcopal Church reminds us of our continuing call to discipleship. Each time an infant, a child, or an adult is received into Christ's Body, the Church, and is marked on the forehead with the sign of the cross as Christ's own forever, we are given an opportunity to renew our own Baptismal Covenant. We ask for God's help to begin again in following the Way of Jesus Christ. We first renew our beliefs in God as Creator, Redeemer, and Giver of Life through the Apostles' Creed. We follow this with five core questions that provide the framework for our life in Christ.

1. Will you continue in the apostles' teaching and fellowship, in the breaking of the bread, and in the prayers?

2. Will you persevere in resisting evil, and, whenever you fall into sin, repent and return to the Lord?
3. Will you proclaim by word and example the Good News of God in Christ?
4. Will you seek and serve Christ in all persons, loving your neighbor as yourself?
5. Will you strive for justice and peace among all people, and respect the dignity of every human being?[2]

To each of these we answer, "I will, with God's help." (The complete Baptismal Covenant is found on pages 304–5 in The Book of Common Prayer of the Episcopal Church.)

You may belong to a different denomination of the Christian faith. Each denomination has an understanding of the meaning of baptism within its tradition. I encourage you to find a copy of the service of Baptism for your church and catechism of your faith tradition. When the Baptismal Covenant of the Episcopal Church is discussed in this book you will be able to reference your own covenant.

Although we desire to follow Jesus Christ and live into our Baptismal Covenant however that covenant or statement of discipleship is expressed, much gets in the way of our good intentions. Life is often out of balance as we're stretched one way and then another. We become distracted from what's really important to us, not finding enough time for family and friends, for ourselves, and for God. Technology blurs clear boundaries between work and home, community, and solitude. With computer, cell phone, and fax, we can be on call "24/7." Events control us, expectations control us, culture controls us. Changes in jobs, changes in the circumstances of our lives, the challenge of raising children, or caring for aging parents, the focus on competition in our schools—all these and more can make us feel overwhelmed and powerless to cope with and manage the volume of activities each day.

This has spiritual consequences. We're not always able to look at life and see the good. Instead we look at the world through glasses that see life as half-empty. We focus on what isn't right, is yet to be, or is still missing. We find ourselves, and even our children, not living *in* the present, but living *for* the future. We can't stop long enough to reflect on why we're not satisfied. We long for a way to make sense of it all. We come to church seeking a connection with God, yet life is out of control. In a world where children need pocket planners to keep track of their schedules, where life is more about success than about the richness of relationships, and where a complex consumer society screams for our attention, we long for a way to break free.

The challenge before us is to find a way to live that is less fragmented and more fulfilling, a way that will allow us to find a stabilizing center for life, a way that will enable us to live into our full potential as children of God. With the psalmist we cry, "How could we sing the Lord's song in a foreign land (Ps 137:4)?"

Sitting at the Feet of the Lord and the Great Commandment

In the Gospel of John, Jesus said, "If you continue in my word, you are truly my disciples; and you will know the truth, and the truth will make you free" (8:31–32). How do we continue in Christ's word? What is this truth that will make us free? I believe the answers can be found in this familiar story:

> [Jesus] entered a certain village, where a woman named Martha welcomed him into her home. She had a sister named Mary, who sat at the Lord's feet and listened to what he was saying. But Martha was distracted by her many tasks; so she came to him and asked, "Lord, do you not care that my sister has left me to do all the work by myself? Tell her then to help me." But the Lord answered her, "Martha, Martha, you are worried and distracted by many things; there is need of only one thing. Mary has chosen the better part, which will not be taken away from her." (Luke 10:38–42)

Martha's problem wasn't that she was busy, but that she was distracted by her busyness and worry. Does this sound familiar? It does to me! Instead, our Lord entreats us to listen like Mary. To hear what God is saying to us requires us to make a choice.

We must choose to sit at the feet of the Lord.

We sit at the feet of the Lord and *listen*. We listen so that we can continue in the Word and find the truth in him that will make us free (John 8:21–32). Our choice to sit at his feet will be fruitful for we have been given this promise:

> Ask, and it will be given you; search, and you will find; knock, and the door will be opened for you. For everyone who asks receives, and everyone who searches finds, and for everyone who knocks, the door will be opened. (Matthew 7:7–8)

Our lives will be transformed as we seek to love and to follow Jesus and his teachings. And the cornerstone of this teaching is about love and relationships.

> One of the scribes came near and heard them disputing with one another, and seeing that he answered them well, he asked him, "Which commandment is the first of all?" Jesus answered, "The first is, 'Hear, O Israel: the Lord our God, the Lord is one; you shall love the Lord your God with all your heart, and with all your soul, and with all your mind, and with all your strength.' The second is this, 'You shall love your neighbor as yourself.' There is no other commandment greater than these." (Mark 12:28–31).

As Christians we are to love God first, then love neighbor as ourselves. This is the Word that we will hear when we sit at Jesus' feet with Mary. Because he will be at the center of our hearts and minds as we fulfill the roles and the responsibilities that God has given us, our relationships to God, to others, and to ourselves will be deepened and transformed. We will bear fruit through our service to Christ. We will sing our Lord's song, bringing the truth we find in our relationship with him into a fragmented world. The question then is this:

How do we sit at the feet of our Lord so that we may fulfill the promises that we make in our Baptismal Covenant and live Jesus' commandment to love God and neighbor as self?

Finding a Guide

A number of years ago I used to sew almost all my own clothes. Skirts, blouses, suits, pants, and shorts would be churned out in varieties of fabric, color, and style. I'd sewn since I was twelve years old, first helped by a wonderful, elderly neighbor my brother Jim and I called Auntie Sue. By the time I was an adult, my efforts were yielding pretty good results. I knew what to do and I was careful. However, my sewing really improved after I purchased a book on how to sew. It was one of those *Reader's Digest* "how-to" books. Every sewing technique imaginable was meticulously illustrated and thoroughly explained. (For those of you unfamiliar with sewing, hang in there, or watch *Sewing with Nancy* on cable TV!) While I knew, for example, how to apply a collar to a blouse—sew right sides together, trim the seam, turn, press, and tack by hand—the book provided better ways to improve and enhance what I was doing by showing me details and making suggestions. First stay-stitch the garment and clip to the stitching, trim the collar interfacing, baste on the collar, sew the seam on the machine, trim and grade the layers so that no two are the same length and the collar is the widest, press the seam flat first and then press it open. And so on. What a difference these additional instructions made! The *Reader's Digest* book became the tool that moved my sewing from competent to almost professional.

While the message that Jesus gives us is simply stated—to love one another—you and I undoubtedly could use a tool to help us hone our skill to translate this commandment into everyday life. We need reminders of who we are to be and how we are to act or not act toward one another. We need ways to see the many times and places where God is present in our lives so we may draw on this holy Presence. We also need guidance as we search for God.

The *Reader's Digest* how-to book was the tool I used to enhance my sewing abilities. On an infinitely greater scale, the Rule of Benedict can be the tool that you and I choose to help us fulfill our Baptismal

Covenant and Jesus' commandment to love. Benedict's Rule is a tool that meticulously and thoroughly details how to sow (sew?) the seeds of kindness and Christlike love in all our relationships.

A Thumbnail Sketch of the Rule of Benedict

First let me briefly explain the Rule of Benedict. In the sixth century, Benedict of Nursia designed what he termed "a little rule" to help the monastic communities he founded to better love God, self, and one another by providing some guidelines on how to live a spiritual life in community. The Rule covers the essentials of worship, work, study, prayer, personal conduct, the use of time, relationships, leadership and authority, hospitality, and possessions. It fosters a way of life that is rooted and grounded in Christ, providing a tool to help us find a center of stability so needed in today's world. As Joan Chittister wrote in *Wisdom Distilled from the Daily: Living the Rule of St. Benedict Today*, the Rule is designed "for ordinary people who live ordinary lives. . . . It was written to provide a model of spiritual development for the average person who intends to live life beyond the superficial or the uncaring."[3]

Please don't be intimidated by the word "Rule." Benedict's Rule isn't a series of steps that must be followed "or else," or a list of "to-dos" that list makers like myself love to check off. The word *rule* comes from the Greek term *canon*, which originally meant "trellis." This is a wonderful image for us. A trellis is a tool that helps a grapevine become more productive—without it, the branches of the vine will grow into a tangled mass and bear less fruit.

We are the branches in the vine that is Christ (John 15:5). We need a structure to guide our lives so that we may also bear much fruit. The Rule becomes a trellis to which we can attach ourselves, guiding us toward Gospel living. David Steindl-Rast, a brother in the Order of St. Benedict, explains that the Rule of St. Benedict is a way we can "put ourselves into a frame of mind that will lead us to live life in its fullness."[4] For me, this frame of mind is what Paul called "the same mind that was in Christ Jesus" (Phil 2:5). I'm firmly convinced that the Rule of Benedict can help us to be more mindful, more faith-filled, and more joyous because, in very simple language, Benedict gives us specific ways to live with Christ in our heart.

In Closing

It is my hope and prayer that the Rule of Benedict will become a tool to guide you so that you will walk confidently in the path of your Baptismal Covenant and strengthen your relationship with God, with yourself, and with others. These are the overarching goals of *St. Benedict's Toolbox*. To accomplish this, the book offers the following as additional goals:

- To know that God is intimately involved in your daily life.
- To listen for God in all aspects of your life, from Scripture to daily occurrences and relationships.
- To apply Benedict's teaching on the Rule to make the often chaotic and fragmented twenty-first-century life less chaotic and fragmented! (Yes, it *can* be done!)
- To discover ways to maintain healthy relationships with others and a healthy and balanced view of self.
- To use the tools in the Toolbox to reflect on your life and to practice ideas from the Rule.

In *The Rule of Benedict: Insights for the Ages*, Joan Chittister wrote that to live the Rule involves not a set of mechanics but a "change of heart and a turn of mind."[5] May this journey with Benedict change our hearts and minds, as we who yearn for life take on the mind of Christ and sing his song to the world.

Let us begin!

> Clothed then with faith and the performance of good works, let us set out on this way, with the Gospel for our guide, that we may deserve to see him *who has called us to his kingdom* (1 Thess 2:12).

FROM THE PROLOGUE TO THE RULE, VERSE 21 RB1980

 **TOOLBOX**
Introduction

Our Benedictine journey has three key goals: (1) living into our Baptismal Covenant, (2) following Jesus' Great Commandment, and (3) meeting the challenge of living as a Christian in today's world. Here are three tools to help you begin to reflect on these goals.

As you begin these or any of the tools found in this book, pray for the guidance of the Holy Spirit.

Tool #1: **Living the Baptismal Covenant**

Purpose of the Tool. To provide an opportunity to review how you apply the Baptismal Covenant to your life. If you're not a member of the Episcopal Church, you may substitute the Baptismal Covenant or statement on baptism from your church or denomination.

Background on the Tool. One of the goals of this book is to provide you with some ways to deepen your ability to live into your Baptismal

Covenant. It will be helpful for you to know which areas are already strong and which could use some honing.

The Tool

Read the Baptismal Covenant that follows and answer the questions. Write your answers in your journal or note them briefly here. If you're using a Baptismal Covenant or a statement on baptism from a different denomination or church, the reflection questions still apply.

1. Will you continue in the apostles' teaching and fellowship, in the breaking of the bread, and in the prayers?
2. Will you persevere in resisting evil, and, whenever you fall into sin, repent and return to the Lord?
3. Will you proclaim by word and example the Good News of God in Christ?
4. Will you seek and serve Christ in all persons, loving your neighbor as yourself?
5. Will you strive for justice and peace among all people, and respect the dignity of every human being?[6]

Which of the actions described in the above questions come most easily for you?

Which of the actions are hardest for you to do?

Which of the actions challenge you?

Are there any areas you wish to know more about?

As you read through this book, keep in mind how you answered these questions. Look for ways that the Rule can help you to live your covenant with God.

Tool #2: A Review of My Relationships

Purpose of the Tool. To give you an opportunity to assess various aspects of your relationship to God, to others, and to yourself.

Background on the Tool. In the Rule, establishing strong relationships with God, with others, and even with oneself is highly important. Relationship and community building are key teachings. Assessing how you view your relationships can help you look for specific teachings in the Rule that can strengthen these relationships.

The Tool

The tool is a simple questionnaire to answer using a sliding scale of 1 to 5. *Be honest in your answers.* Circle the number that best fits where you are and not where you think that you should be! Using the scale shown here, please rate the statements below.

	1	2	3	4	5
	almost never	not often	some-times	often	almost always

MY RELATIONSHIP WITH GOD

	1	2	3	4	5
1. I take time for daily prayer.	1	2	3	4	5
2. I see God at work in the lives of those around me.	1	2	3	4	5
3. I hear and respond to God's direction in my life.	1	2	3	4	5
4. I take time to be quiet with God.	1	2	3	4	5
5. My relationship to God is strong.	1	2	3	4	5
6. I use the Bible as a resource for prayer.	1	2	3	4	5

MY RELATIONSHIP TO MYSELF

	1	2	3	4	5
7. I take time for myself each day.	1	2	3	4	5
8. There are many different parts to my life, such as family, friends, work, leisure, rest, and so on. Although at times one area may need to take precedence over another, I believe that *all* of these need to receive appropriate attention.	1	2	3	4	5
9. I am able to give each part of my life this appropriate attention.	1	2	3	4	5
10. There are times when I want to run away, literally or figuratively.	1	2	3	4	5
11. Living in the "present moment" is being attentive to what is happening now without being distracted by past regrets or future anxieties. I find that I am able to live in the present moment.	1	2	3	4	5
12. My life feels fragmented.	1	2	3	4	5

MY RELATIONSHIP WITH OTHERS AND WITH THE WORLD AROUND ME

	1	2	3	4	5
13. I spend quality time with my family and friends.	1	2	3	4	5
14. I am concerned about the world beyond myself and my family.	1	2	3	4	5

15. I am forgiving of others.	1	2	3	4	5
16. In a difficult situation I am able to remain open to others.	1	2	3	4	5
17. In a conversation I can listen with full attention.	1	2	3	4	5
18. I see Christ in other people.	1	2	3	4	5

When you have finished, look over your answers. As you review your answers, consider answers of 3 or below to indicate areas that you could focus on during your study of the Rule. For example, if you scored 3 on question #6, "I use the Bible as a resource for prayer," you might want to learn and use *lectio divina*, a form of prayer introduced in chapter 2 that uses Scripture. You may wish to circle the questions that will be a special focus for you during this journey with Benedict.

Tool #3: Mary or Martha?

Purpose of the Tool. To give you an opportunity to assess whether you are more like Mary or more like Martha in your daily life.

Background on the Tool. Martha was focused on actively serving the Lord, Mary on listening to the Lord. Both mirror two important poles of our daily lives—serving others and replenishing our emotional and spiritual "well." As you work through this book, it will be helpful for you to know which of these modes of living is most comfortable for you.

The Tool

Answer the following questions.

- Do you spend the greater part of your day doing things for others or for yourself?
- Do you take time for yourself each day? How much time? Are you ever able to sit down and read, or talk with a friend?
- How much time do you take each day for prayer, reading Scripture, or meditation?
- Are you comfortable with the amount of time that you have for yourself?
- Are you always on the move from morning until night? Does your schedule leave you exhausted?
- If you could, how would you change the way you spend most days?

When you reflect on the answers to the questions, is there a trend toward always "doing," jumping from one task to the next without a break? If so, you may be more of a Martha. A trend toward taking time for reflection is more what we see in Mary. But sometimes we can take *too much* time for ourselves and neglect our responsibilities for others. I like to think that Mary did both—time for herself and her relationship with God and time to help others.

Being like Martha does not necessarily mean we have no relationship with God. And being more like Mary doesn't mean we do nothing for others. Yet, we may find that we're more comfortable in one role than in another. Whichever is our comfort role, we need to take some time to develop its opposite. If you are more like Martha, with an outward focus, pay close attention to what Benedict and the Toolboxes suggest regarding prayer, time alone, and balance in life. If you are more like Mary, comfortable with an inward focus, pay close attention to what Benedict and the Toolboxes suggest regarding community, relationships, and service to others.

If you find yourself most often in the action mode with hardly time to catch your breath, then the sections of the book that encourage reflection and quiet will nurture your inward self. If you find yourself most comfortable being alone, spending a considerable time alone, and/or taking time to nurture your spiritual life, then pay attention to the teachings that have us reaching out to others.

The beauty is that the Rule of Benedict provides us with a balanced approach to life that tends to needs of both the inward and the outward person.

⌒ *Interlude* ⌒
Listening for God in the Daily

There is no event so commonplace
but that God is present within it.[7]

In his book *Now and Then*, author and Presbyterian minister Frederick Buechner writes about the importance of looking for the presence of God in our lives. Buechner says that if "you keep your eye peeled to it and your ears open, if you really pay attention to it, even . . . a limited and limiting life will open up onto extraordinary vistas." He continues:

> Taking your children to school and kissing your wife good-bye. Eating lunch with a friend. Trying to do a decent day's work. Hearing the rain patter against the window. There is no event so commonplace but that God is present within it, always hiddenly, always leaving you room to recognize him or not to recognize him.[8]

What a wonderful way to live, this recognition of God in everything! Think of how this would enrich our daily life were we to seek, to really look for, and to trust in the presence of God in even the smallest detail of our lives. We would find comfort in the midst of pain, an even greater joy in happiness, and reserves of energy to do the tasks that fall to us each day, knowing that God is with us as we work. Over and over we would come face to face with our blessedness. On this we would ground our lives: God is present in my life; God has not left me alone; God loves me and Christ is with me.

Benedict knew that recognizing the presence of God in one's life is what lifts the darkness and brings us to the joy of becoming who God would have us to be. In the Prologue to the Rule, Benedict quotes the following verse from John's Gospel: "Walk while you have the light of life, that the darkness of death may not overtake you (12:35 RB)." He knew also the urgency to pursue the light of God and that this pursuit leads to life in all its wholeness and fullness. In fact, in verse 13 of the Prologue he changed "walk" to "run"!

You and I need to pursue this light with the same urgency, for our lives truly depend on it. Christ will help us walk from the darkness of depression, hopelessness, lack of confidence, disappointment, or whatever our own personal darkness may be. We can live in peace, for finding God in our daily lives is bound to change the way we view both situations and people. Again and again we'll discover new paths through old situations. Perhaps we might even amend old habits and actions, knowing that the Holy One is a part of everything we do, a witness to the person we choose to be at every moment.

The beauty of listening for God in ordinary daily life is that each day can become a vibrant creation when we trust that God is always present, when we look for God in every aspect of our lives, especially in the commonplace and ordinary. We see God as we listen to our life and recognize that each of us is precious to God. Life itself is a gift and holds endless promise when we open ourselves to living with the Holy One, our Creator. Only God knows the treasures that are in store for us. Only God can foresee the grace that we can be for others when our eyes are on God. As Buechner succinctly states,

> Listen to your life. See it for the fathomless mystery that it is. . . . In the boredom and pain of it no less than the excitement and gladness: touch, taste, smell your way to the holy and hidden heart of it because in the last analysis, all moments are key moments, and life itself is grace.[9]

Putting the Ideas into Practice

How do we learn to listen for God? The two key ingredients are trust and thanksgiving. First we *trust that God is in the midst of our lives*, to be found not only in the good of our lives, in moments of joy and exulta-tion, but in the difficult and sad times of our lives as well. And so we look and listen for God's presence everywhere and at all times. We listen for God in both embrace and conflict, in large and in small, in what seems significant and in what seems mundane. It doesn't matter, for God is in all these places.

The second ingredient is that we *give thanks for all*. Thanksgiving flows from trust: when we begin to see that God cares for even the small concerns of our lives, thanksgiving is a spontaneous response. As we rec-ognize and interpret the events of our lives as imbued with the provi-dence and loving mercy of God, we can live with lighter, thankful hearts, knowing that we're upheld by an infinite and loving power.

TOOLBOX
God in All Things

Finding God in all things is a theme of Benedictine spirituality. Our response to this reality of God present everywhere is one of profound thanksgiving. Think of this: we are never alone and left hapless to man-age life by ourselves!

It takes spiritual skills to find God in the ordinary stuff of daily life and to be thankful for everything. Some of us have these skills naturally; others need an intentional way to learn and to practice. This section is designed to help you begin to listen for God in all things. I've also included a tool to help us remember to be thankful. We truly are thank-ful people, it's just that sometimes life gets in the way and we forget to say so.

Tool #1: Listening for God in a Task

Purpose of the Tool. To help you begin the practice of listening for God in daily life.

Background on the Tool. Recognizing God's presence in all of life may be a new concept to you. Or it may be one that you have heard about but have difficulty accepting. Frederick Buechner writes that we need to keep our eyes peeled and our ears open and really pay attention to what's going on around and inside us. This kind of awareness and understand-ing takes both practice and faith. I like to think that the practice can help us increase our faith.

The Tool

- Pick a task that you can perform regularly. It can be anything from driving a car to preparing a meal to making particular telephone calls. If you wish, write it down on the line provided below.
- Then, each time you do this task, put on a heart of love and listen for God.

To help you get started, as you begin the task think about how God might be present in the task, in the people involved, and within you. Ask that God be revealed to you in the task that you're doing.

When you're ready, expand this practice to other tasks.

The task I will begin with is _____.

Tool #2: Some Ways to Give Thanks

Purpose of the Tool. To encourage the practice of thankfulness.

Background on the Tool. John McQuiston II, an attorney from Memphis and author of *Always We Begin Again*, a contemporary paraphrase of the Rule of Benedict, places thankfulness at the core of Benedict's Rule. He writes:

> The first rule is simply this:
>
> live this life
> and do whatever is done,
> in a spirit of Thanksgiving.[10]

He goes on to say that whoever participates in life with thanksgiving will receive life's full promise.

Never underestimate the power of thankfulness!

The Tool

The following represent just a few ways to practice the power of thanksgiving.

- *Do a nightly thanks review.* Several years ago I gave each person in my congregation a very small spiral notebook and suggested that at the end of each day they record three to five things for which they were thankful. I offer this suggestion to you. My guess is that, over time, your daily list will expand as you put on the glasses of thankfulness as you view the world.
- *Take a Thankfulness Walk.* This is a gentle way to offer prayers of thanksgiving.[11] In it we focus on our senses and let what we experience become our prayer of thanksgiving.

- Begin with your sight. As you walk, look around. Give thanks for the ability to see. Give thanks for what you see. Pray for those who cannot see. Then move to your hearing. Give thanks for your ability to hear. Listen to the sounds around you. Give thanks for each and offer prayers for those who cannot hear.
- You may then move on to smell, touch, and taste or stay with just one of the senses, as long as you're able to be alert to what you are praying.
- *Be a spontaneous giver of thanks.* When something wonderful happens, give thanks. When something bad happens, try to give thanks, too. The latter is difficult. We may not be able to do this right away. Give thanks for the people who are helping you through a difficult time.

PART I
Getting Started

Before we explore the Rule of St. Benedict and how it can apply to our lives, we're going to briefly look at the history of Benedict and the Rule in chapter 1. Then in chapter 2 we'll look at a form of prayer, based on Holy Scripture, that Benedictines and other Christians have used for centuries. I introduce this prayer early in our journey so that you can learn and practice this prayer while you're reading *St. Benedict's Toolbox*.

The Rule of Benedict
Relevant and Appropriate

*The Christ-centredness of the Rule and of the life
to which it gives rise is overwhelming. Christ
stands at the head of every avenue. . . . Christ
is the beginning and the end, the ground of my
being and the goal of my seeking. With Christ all
things become possible; without Christ nothing
makes sense.*

—ESTHER DE WAAL[1]

Who was Benedict? What is his Rule all about and why was it written? How does Benedictine spirituality relate to who we are as Christians? As Episcopalians or United Methodists, Presbyterians or Roman Catholics? Does Benedict's teaching have value to us today? We'll explore these questions in this chapter, as we look at Benedict and his times, explore the Rule and its main teachings, and consider its impact on Christian tradition.

A Time of Uncertainty and Turmoil

Benedict was born into a world of turbulence and violence. The fall of Rome in 410 CE, seventy years before his birth, had shocked the civilized world. The onslaught of "barbarian" tribes brought about the official end of the Western empire in 476, with the deposition of Romulus, the last emperor. After an extended peace under conqueror Theodorix, king of the Ostrogoths, Italy was again ravaged by war. The sixth century was an age characterized by danger, mass injustice, dislocation of population, and the apparent collapse of almost all high culture.[2] Not even the Church was spared disruption as theological controversies raged. Distracted church leaders had to contend also with political turmoil. It seemed that there wasn't a sovereign or ruler who wasn't either an atheist, a pagan, or a heretic.[3] It was into this chaos that Benedict brought the promise of an ordered, Christ-centered life.

Benedict Forms Communities

St. Benedict was born around the year 480 in the Umbrian province of Nursia in Italy. His biography, attributed to Pope Gregory the Great, describes Benedict's family as one of high station. They sent him to Rome to study, but the young man quickly abandoned the life of a scholar and left the city he felt was too corrupt. Several years later he went to an area near the town of Subiaco, where he lived for three years as a hermit in a hillside cave. There he was "discovered" by others who recognized his holiness and wisdom. He founded the monastery of Subiaco, which still exists today, along with eleven other monasteries on this hillside. Benedict left the area when he was threatened by a local priest who was jealous of Benedict. The story is that the priest, Florentius, attempted to poison Benedict through the gift of tainted blessed bread.

Leaving the hatred behind, Benedict traveled to Monte Cassino in the imposing mountains of the central Apennines in Italy. Tearing down pagan temples within the walls of an ancient fortress, he formed a new community and remained there for the rest of his life. We believe that Benedict wrote the Rule for the monks of Monte Cassino. His sister, Scholastica, established herself nearby with her own community of nuns, and it was said that the two met once a year. Benedict died in 547. Forty years after his death, the monastery at Monte Cassino was destroyed by the Lombards.* Today the relics of St. Benedict may be found at the abbey of St. Benôit-sur-Loire in France.

Pope Gregory's biography of Benedict is filled with wondrous accounts of miracles and stories about the saint. While we may question the accuracy of these accounts, we may heed the love and reverence they show toward Benedict. Here's one story.

> During a time of famine the severe shortage of food was causing a great deal of suffering in Campania. At Benedict's monastery the entire grain supply had been used up and nearly all the bread was gone as well. When mealtime came, only five loaves could be found to set before the community. Noticing how downcast they were, the saint gently reproved them for their lack of trust in God and at the same time tried to raise their dejected spirits with a comforting assurance. "Why are you so depressed at the lack of bread?" he asked. "What if today there is only a little: Tomorrow you will have more than you need." The next day about thirty hundredweights of flour were found in sacks at the gate of the monastery, but no one ever discovered whose services almighty God had employed in bringing them. When they saw what had happened, the monks were filled with gratitude and learned from this miracle that even in their hour of need they must not lose faith in the bountiful goodness of God.[4]

---

*The Lombards were a Germanic tribe that began in southern Sweden and worked their way south, invading Italy and establishing rule there in the sixth century CE.

The Creation of the Rule

At the time that Benedict wrote the Rule, monasticism was three hundred years old. He inherited a tradition that required monks to do fantastic feats to achieve holiness: from fasting for two months to sitting on poles or in trees for days or months at a time. This tradition had developed as a substitute for martyrdom after Christianity had become the state religion under Constantine in the fourth century. Rigorous, yes, but practical for ordinary people like us? We would respond with a resounding "No!" and Benedict would agree, for he established a different way of achieving holiness and connection to God. Find God by being in relationship with one another, he said. Achieve holiness by being normal. Base your faith on the changelessness of God and of God's love and empowerment.[5] Relate in a healthy way to yourself, keep that relationship in its proper proportion and recognize that your role as a Christian is to love God and to serve others.

Benedict incorporates ideas from several other rules. He stresses the importance of being in a community and not living either in isolation or as a wanderer. In this he followed two fourth-century monastics who also formulated Rules—Basil in Asia Minor and Pachomius in Egypt—and Benedict adapted a famous rule known as the "Rule of the Master." Pachomius, who lived from around 292 to 348, originated the communal form of monastic life. At one time his monastery contained no less than fourteen hundred monks who lived together "with common practices and exercises, according to fixed rules, and under the guidance or government of a director."[6] It is this model that Benedict brought to the Western Church. Benedict emphasized living together in one physical place and remaining solidly faithful to that place and to the people in that place. This is one reason why the Rule is so pertinent to our lives. All of us already live "in community." In fact we are a part of many communities: family, marriage, friendships, committed relationships, church families, the workplace, religious organizations, neighborhoods, and cities.

Benedict wrote his Rule for the monks of his own monastery. He had no thought or idea of establishing a monastic rule that you and I, over fifteen centuries later, would consider valuable for our own lives. Yet, within a century or two after his death in 547, Benedict had become the patriarch of Western monasticism and his Rule the most influential in the Western Church. By the high Middle Ages, most of the monasteries of the West had adopted his rule.

Benedictine monasteries became beacons of light and learning in a world of violence. As the communities grew during the medieval period, they became the extensive complexes that we are familiar with today. One hundred or more monks would live in a monastery that would have a great church on its property. When pilgrims and visitors came to these places of worship, the monasteries interacted with the world. Abbots, who were the leaders of the monasteries, often became political figures with great power.

Pressures from the world outside brought change and great wealth. Over time the monasteries became lax in fulfilling the way of life as directed in the Rule. Yet there have always been individuals who sought to truly live the Rule of Benedict. In the eleventh century the Cistercians were established as an offshoot of the Benedictine houses. They sought to bring about reform and a return to following the original Rule, with an emphasis on contemplation.

What Is the Rule of Benedict?

Imagine you're holding your checkbook, or, better yet, take your checkbook out and look at it. Imagine a book about an inch larger in length and width and about one-quarter inch thick. This is the size of Benedict's Rule—with standard-sized print!

Benedict's Rule, originally written in Latin, includes a Prologue and seventy-three chapters. Most modern translations divide these chapters into numbered "verses" for easy referencing of the content. In *St. Benedict's Toolbox*, I use several translations of the Rule as well as my own paraphrase of verses. References to the Rule show both chapter and verse. For example, verse 10 of the Prologue is cited as "Prologue 10" and chapter 42, verse 5 is shown as "42.5." When I quote the *RB1980* translation of the Rule, "RB" will precede the chapter and verse citation: "RB 42.5." Abundant Scripture quotes found within verses of the Rule are italicized and cited as book, chapter, and verse followed by RB if the translation varies from the New Revised Standard Version: for instance, "1 Pet 4:11 RB."

Each chapter of the Rule has a title that explains the content of that chapter: for example, "The Tools for Good Works," "The Sleeping Arrangements of the Monks," "The Reception of Guests," and "Distribution of Goods according to Need." Benedict gives directions for the way monks should live together in his community. Here are some of the broad topic areas he addresses in his Rule:

> *Liturgical Instructions for the Divine Office*, or *Opus Dei* ("the work of God"). These are the eight daily community prayer services that compose the main occupation of the monks. (The Divine Office is covered in chapter 6 of this book.)
>
> *Roles, Responsibilities, and Procedures for Community Members.* Benedict provides qualifications and "job descriptions" for leaders as well as for other selected jobs within the monastery. He also includes directions for such things as sleeping arrangements, meals, food, clothing, work, discipline, and the process for joining the monastery.

How to Live Together in Community. An important part of the Rule involves interpersonal relations: how monks should treat one another and conduct themselves to promote peace and harmony in the community.

Spiritual Direction. Benedict encourages his monks—and us—to take our relationship with God seriously and to actively nurture it. He provides directions for such disciplines as prayer, study, Lenten practices, and living with humility before God.

The Rule has theme words: roots, belonging, community, fulfillment, sharing, space, listening, and silence.[7] The Rule also addresses questions from "How do I relate in love to other people?" and "How do I find meaning in what I must do each day?" to "What are the priorities of a Christian life?"

In a Prologue and seventy-three chapters, Benedict explains how we can live a Christ-centered life with others. Noted Anglican author Esther de Waal summarizes beautifully the content of the Rule:

It is all about love.
It points me to Christ.
Ultimately the whole meaning and purpose of the Rule is simply, [in Benedict's own words] "Prefer nothing to the love of Christ."[8]

The center of the Rule is Christ, the cornerstone is Scripture, and the focus of the Rule is how to live in loving relationship with God, self, and others. That's why the Rule is so relevant for all Christians. The way to live, Benedict states in his Prologue, is by following the Gospels (Prologue 21), especially Jesus' main directive to love one another.

Benedict sees that the way to holiness is through other people. While we might agree that it's easy to be a saint alone, Benedict knew that people are relational creatures, desiring relationships with others as well as with God. While stressing the importance of being in community, Benedict felt that there also needed to be a balance between being alone and being with others.

The Rule is practical and down-to-earth, and easy to read. Benedict's gentleness and understanding flow through the words. "Therefore," he writes in the Prologue, "we intend to establish a school for the Lord's service . . . we hope to set down nothing harsh, nothing burdensome. The good of all concerned, however, may prompt us to a little strictness in order to amend faults and to safeguard love" (RB Prologue 45–47). In her book *Living the Rule Today*, Sr. Joan Chittister likens the Rule to a railing that you can cling to while climbing the stairs. We all need some kind of railing to hold onto in this life: one that supports both our physical and spiritual journeys, one that will better help us to live out our Baptismal Covenant and follow Christ in our daily lives.

Last but not least, the Rule is very much about living an ordinary life well. Thomas Merton, monk, priest, and spiritual writer, said the essence of the Rule is "doing ordinary things quietly and perfectly for the glory of God."[9] I encourage you to purchase a copy of the Rule of Benedict for reference as you read this book. (See the section on suggested reading for suggested editions of the Rule, p. 200.)

The Benedictine Influence on Anglicanism

The Benedictine tradition dominated the spiritual landscape of pre-Reformation England, and had a profound influence on the development of Anglican spirituality. Marked by moderation and good sense, Benedictines discouraged extremes of outlook or behavior. With the Incarnation as its starting point, Benedictine spirituality seeks to draw out the invisible divine presence in the visible world and "a deep, single-minded attachment to the person of Jesus Christ."[10] For those of us who are Episcopalians and have inherited English spirituality, our roots are Benedictine.

Anglicans identify themselves not through a doctrine or catechism but through worship. If you want to know what most Anglicans believe, read The Book of Common Prayer. The importance of worship to our Christian life is a Benedictine concept that was passed down to us over the centuries. Though the Rule itself is brief, Benedict explains, in meticulous detail, the order of worship, the psalms, the canticles, and the responses to be used in the Divine Office. This monastic tradition, also called the "Hours" or the "Daily Office," brought the monks together eight times a day for corporate prayer, beginning long before dawn and continuing into the evening. During the Reformation of the sixteenth century, many Reformed churches dismissed the idea of corporate prayer (also known as the "Daily Office") as too "papist." However, Thomas Cranmer restored the Daily Office to the people and to its place in the Church when he included Morning and Evening Prayer—"matins" and "evensong"— in the first Book of Common Prayer in 1549. This tradition has continued in the daily offices of Morning and Evening Prayer in our own Book of Common Prayer today. Our prayer book also provides "descendents" of the early Offices in a noonday prayer service as well as a late-evening service called "Compline." Though these services weren't in the early Anglican prayer books, they were restored in the twentieth century.

Anglican liturgical prayer books are specifically Benedictine. Anglican writer Martin Thornton points out that the spirituality of the Rule is built on three key moments: the Eucharist, the Divine Office, and personal prayer—the very same priorities as our prayer book.[11] And authors Peter Anson, a Roman Catholic, and A. W. Campbell, an Anglican, who studied religious communities in the Anglican Communion, note that the Anglican Church is a kind of generalized monastic community. The Book of Common Prayer has preserved the foundations of Christian monastic prayer, but simplifies it for contemporary use.[12]

Community, so important in the Rule of Benedict, is also important in the Anglican tradition. In what Robert Hale calls a *leitmotif* (a dominant or recurring theme), "the church terms itself the Anglican *Communion*; its key liturgical text that unites the faithful is the Book of *Common* Prayer; and the traditional Anglican designation of the central, unifying sacrament is Holy *Communion*."[13] To be in community is an essential part of Benedictine life and thought. It's easy to see why many Anglicans are so comfortable with the Rule of Benedict!

The Benedictine Influence on Christian Church Tradition

The Christian church and all its many denominations and individual churches share their roots in the early church formed by the apostles. Monastic communities grew from these roots, too, taking an active role in forming and transmitting Christian tradition and practice. Whether or not your branch of Christianity preserves the liturgical practices of the monastic houses of the Anglican and Roman Catholic traditions, all of us share, in various forms, the practice of prayer and contemplation that is rooted in monastic tradition.

If you're not Anglican or Roman Catholic, I encourage you to explore the influences of the Rule of Benedict within your own tradition. The last tool in the Toolbox of this chapter will help you make connections between your tradition and that of the Rule (see p. 27).

The Relevance of the Rule

Benedict called his monastery "a school of the Lord's service" (Prologue 45) for those who wished to become monks and renounce their own wills. But you and I are invited, too. Benedict's "little school" can help us seek God in our lives.

Those of us who worship in the Anglican tradition are already, in one sense, "Benedictines": our worship, tradition, and spirituality have been profoundly influenced by Benedictine practice and thought. So Benedict's teaching can reinforce and enhance who we are as Anglican Christians. Yet people from many and varied branches of the Christian church have written of the deep influence of Benedict and his Rule on their lives. What they say about the power of the Rule, not only for spiritual matters but for total life formation, speaks beyond any denominational boundaries to anyone who seeks to live a Christlike life.

Episcopal priest, author, and retreat leader Elizabeth Canham describes her love of Benedict's Rule and its practical application to her life:

I fell in love because this man spoke of a life in a hospitable community, of simplicity, balance, and an ordered way of living designed to create an environment that fosters freedom to grow fully into the persons God created us to be.[14]

Wil Derkse, a Dutch Benedictine oblate (someone associated with a monastery or convent who hasn't taken vows as a member), writes of the practical application of the Rule:

I have experienced that the Benedictine spirituality is a veritable treasure-trove of old and yet new insights which may be incarnated anew, concerning good leadership, informed decision-making, fruitful communication, good human resource management, salutary conflict resolution, a careful management of one's possessions, a blessed lifestyle which provides space. An attractive aspect is that Benedictine spirituality directs itself so distinctly toward what needs to be done here and now, at this moment.[15]

Esther de Waal wrote of the meaning that she has found in following the teaching of Benedict. She follows Benedict "to discover how to be human now today, tomorrow and for the rest of my life."[16] The Rule is relevant to any age, she says, because it "continually points beyond itself to Christ himself."[17] Not century-specific, it is Christ-focused, helping us live according to the Gospels, which is why the Rule is so important for us today. For Benedict, the Rule was a means to this end. As Christ is brought into hearts and minds century after century and generation after generation, so, too, the Rule offers relevant guidance and inspiration for all times. Sr. Joan Chittister offers this testimony of the Rule's relevance:

The Rule of Benedict is a guide to the great ideas and questions of life in every age. . . . Instead of a power that is exploitative, [Benedict] calls for a power that is open and developing. He calls for an obedience that says, "I am not my own God. God is God." He treats the question of human dignity in the face of a world that is highly oppressive. He talks about community in a time when individualism is rampant.[18]

Basil Hume, a Roman Catholic cardinal who led a Benedictine monastery for twenty years in England, wrote of our society's dilemma: "our great skill and power . . . on the one hand," but "our inability to get things right on the other."[19] He believed the greatest folly of all—and the cause of the dilemma—was "to forget that above us and beyond us there is a voice that calls us all the time to a change of heart, and to a new beginning."[20] For him, the Rule was the way to open our hearts and lives to the divine light. Benedict "speaks of conversion in a period when we are faced with a narcissism so deep that one-third of the world consumes two-thirds of the goods of the world and we don't even have the grace to blush. He speaks of simplicity to a human nature bent on acquisition and consumerism. He talks about stewardship in the face of rampant unmindedness of the resources of people and the earth. He talks about union with God when people are concerned only with the secular."[21]

As followers of Jesus Christ, we want to move beyond self-absorption, and we want our lives to mean something—to God, to ourselves, and to others. The Rule provides a way to do this within the context of the Gospels and with Christ at the center. Basil Cardinal Hume said that the Rule "makes it possible for ordinary folk to live lives of quite extraordinary virtue."[22]

Listening to the Ordinary

Benedict begins the Prologue to his Rule with these words:

> Listen carefully, my son [and daughter], to the master's instructions, and attend to them with the ear of your heart (RB Prologue 1).

To listen is the main message of Benedict's Rule: to listen for God, to listen to God, and then to respond to God's call in love. This is a special kind of listening—it is listening "with the ear of your heart." We listen in prayer. We listen to Scripture. We listen to the people, to the situations, to the joys and the struggles that make up our lives.

The Rule of Benedict asks us to listen for and to find God in the ordinary, daily stuff of life. We don't have to be fancy—pole sitting isn't required. God is before us and within us, waiting to be found. The challenge is that every day we have so many things to do, and the crush of work can leave us hurrying through one task to move on to the next. But is it possible instead to do our work on one level yet reflect with our mind and heart on where God is in the task? Can we allow the task before us to reveal itself as an opportunity to find God?

Earlier I posed the question "How we can sit at the feet of the Lord with Mary and listen?" One way is to cease rushing through the tasks and demands of life, always thinking ahead to the next thing or to tomorrow or worrying about yesterday. Instead, we can try to focus on where we are right now and become fully present to God in our tasks, our interactions with others, our work, and our play. This is a powerful way to sit at the feet of the Lord with Mary and listen. We put on the mind of Christ and dare to look for God in the most mundane activities. We live in the present moment, focused on what we're doing. We put on a heart of love and do our work for love of God and others.

As yeast causes dough to rise so that it can be baked and served to nourish, so, too, the practices that Benedict encourages in his Rule act as "leaven in the loaf."[23] We're transformed from within so we can nourish not only ourselves but those around us, near and far.

TOOLBOX
The Rule of Benedict: Relevant and Appropriate

This Toolbox is designed to give you an opportunity to interact with the material you've just read. While most tools in the Toolbox give you actual ways to apply Benedict's teaching in the Rule, the tools on the following pages address several areas that may impact your learning.

Tool #1:   Questions about the Rule and Its Application to My Life

Purpose of the Tool. To give you an opportunity to write down any questions that you might have after reading the brief introduction to the Rule.

Background on the Tool. As you read about the Rule, some questions may have surfaced about the Rule or about how it may apply to your life. By identifying these you can look for answers as you continue reading.

The Tool

On a separate sheet of paper or in your journal, write down questions that surfaced as you read the introduction to the Rule.

Tool #2:   Identifying Words with Negative Connotations

Purpose of the Tool. To uncover hidden resistance to words or concepts that are foundational to this study of the Rule of Benedict.

Background on the Tool. Some words and concepts in Benedictine spirituality can initially raise the hackles of twenty-first century Americans, who are known for their rugged individualism, independence, competitiveness, and focus on goals. Words like *stability, obedience, rule, vows, ordinary,* and even *monastery* or *monastic* may be less comfortable to us than words like *self-expression* or *self-development.* Best to get these out in the open to clear the way for the Benedictine interpretation!

The Tool

Looking back through this chapter, list any words or concepts that you think might have a negative connotation in the twenty-first century.

Now, put a check by any that may be a "red light" for you.

Read and think about each word that you checked. Ask yourself the following questions about each of the words:

- What do I feel when I say the word?
- What is the meaning of the word as I think about it now?
- What is the negative connotation for this word or concept? For example, does it imply a loss of individuality, independence, or autonomy? Does it feel dangerous somehow?

Now, as you continue, keep an open mind to discover the Benedictine interpretation of these words. Remember that Benedict *is* advocating that we set aside our individual agendas for the sake of nurturing and strengthening our relationships. Can we do it?

Tool #3: The Influence of St. Benedict on Church History and Tradition

Purpose of the Tool. To encourage those readers who are not Anglican or Roman Catholic to explore the influence of Benedict and/or monasticism in their church's history and tradition.

Background on the Tool. Learning is always more meaningful if we can find points of connection with our life: that's what *St. Benedict's Toolbox* is all about. Discovering the influence of Benedict's Rule on your church's tradition may make the Rule more meaningful to you.

The Tool

Here are some suggestions for finding out if and how Benedict, his Rule, and monasticism may have impacted the history and liturgical practice of your church.

- Locate books about the history of your denomination. Use the index in each to find references to Benedict and/or monasticism.
- Do the same as the above for your liturgy.
- Talk to your priest or minister about the influence of Benedict and monasticism.
- Explore spiritual practices that are encouraged by your church or denomination. Keep these close at hand as you learn about the Rule to recognize influences or synergies.

⁓ *Interlude* ⁓
Paying Attention to the Breadcrumbs

How can we seek and find God's plan for our life? Spirituality writer Debra Farrington suggests that one of the best ways is found in the story of Solomon in 1 Kings. When confronted with a dilemma, Solomon prayed for a "hearing heart," to help him judge wisely.[24] This is precisely what Benedict recommends in the Prologue to his Rule: his monks are to attend to his instructions with the ear of their heart so that they can find God's will in even the smallest and most ordinary circumstance of life.

For the ancient Hebrews, the heart was the center of everything physical, intellectual, emotional, and spiritual. "What Solomon sought—and what we seek too—is for God to use our bodies, feelings, minds, spirits [and other people] to show us the right path, not just for big decisions but all the time."[25] We need to use "our hearing heart" everyday, Farrington writes, to exercise this way of hearing in the small things so that we'll be better able to hear in the big things. The hearing heart is attentive to all the ways God is present in our lives, and notices the "metaphorical breadcrumbs" God leaves for us to follow.[26] Farrington suggests how you and I can develop this hearing heart so that we see all those breadcrumbs:

> Learn to notice the gifts God gave you and watch the way your own life story is developing if you want to know more about God's will for you. God may not put a burning bush in your path, but there will be plenty of other clues about what God may want you to do or be.[27]

I find great comfort in the idea that knowledge of God's will often comes gradually. If I believed otherwise, I might waste my whole life waiting for a stunning, one-time event like the apostle Paul had on the road to Damascus, where "a light from heaven flashed around him" (Acts 9:3–4) and the Lord spoke to him. Though this kind of conversion will probably not happen to most of us, this doesn't mean that God has abandoned us. As you and I look back on our lives, we can see plenty of clues as to where God has been leading us. Once as I struggled with finding God's will and plan for me, my pastoral supervisor offered some simple advice: "Look back over your life," she said. "You'll see the threads there that led to today."[28]

In one of what I call my "former lifetimes," as an instructor of service representatives for Indiana Bell, I wrote a training manual that gave exercises and job tips to help the reps do their job better. The realization recently hit me that this is exactly what I'm doing now with this book— only the subject matter is different. I'm helping you—and me—take steps to become better followers of Jesus Christ, using Benedict's Rule to help us fulfill our Baptismal Covenant and to love God, neighbor, and self.

As you and I look back over our lives, questions like the following can help us to recognize the breadcrumbs that God had placed along the way for us to follow: "What happened? Who were we with? What happened next? What did it feel like?" As we answer these questions, we can explore related threads woven through our experience. We can identify the gifts God has given to us—our talents as well as our spiritual gifts such as joy, love, humor, compassion, perseverance, generosity, and self-control— and how we have used these gifts. That can lead us to questions like this: "Is God, through the breadcrumbs of my life right now, drawing me in another direction, or the same direction? What is the next logical step?" Remember that the breadcrumbs are there not only for the big directions in life. They're placed by a loving God to help us with the challenges of the ordinary yet holy work we do every day.

As we follow the breadcrumbs we also pay attention to our bodies, which may have even more to tell us. Stress responses such as shallow breathing or tenseness can be clues in discerning the wrong path from the right one.[29] When we have made a right decision, our bodies will tell us through calmness and steadiness. A friend tells me that her back is her right-or-wrong indicator: when her lower back aches she knows she needs to take another direction. My guess is that all of us have some kind of body signal of right or wrong: tightness in the throat, tension in the neck, or the inability to concentrate. Be aware of the connection between daily events and decisions and your body.

The hearing heart also needs to be with others. In a time when many monastics lived a hermit's life of isolation, Benedict advocated living in community where monks could support one another as each sought God. Others can help us along the path to holiness, too, as we seek God's plan. People in our communities—at home, church, workplace, or school—can help us to see our lives from a different perspective or can confirm that we're moving in the right direction. We need to seek out people who can guide us as we discern what is happening in our lives. All are God's messengers who can expand our hearing beyond our own predispositions and desires. We can assist others in the same way, for life is not to be lived for ourselves alone, but for God and in service to others.

Finally, prayer and study are important tools that can help us develop and nurture a hearing heart. We approach prayer in openness to hear what God is saying to us. We read Scripture with openness, knowing that God will speak to us through the Word. *Lectio divina*, or divine reading, is a Benedictine form of prayer that uses Scripture as a resource for conversation with God and is an important way to develop a hearing heart. In the Book of Isaiah, God says to the prophet and to you and me, "Incline your ear, and come to me; listen, so that you may live" (Isa 55:3).

Just follow the breadcrumbs!

TOOLBOX
Awareness in the Journey

We often have difficulty making decisions about what to do, where to go, or what path to take. It's even harder when we haven't thought about where we've been and where we are now. These tools can help you become more aware of these issues.

Tool #1: Following the Breadcrumbs

Purpose of the Tool. To help you look for the breadcrumbs in your life, either short term or long term.

Background on the Tool. Breadcrumbs are those markers and events in our lives that draw us along God's path. Paying attention to these helps us discover that God is always present, leading and guiding. Reflecting back on our experiences will help us see how God was present then and how God continues to be present now.

The Tool

First, identify the major events of your life. Write them on a separate piece of paper or in your journal.

Now, ask yourself these questions: What happened? Who was I with? What were my feelings? What did I learn? What happened next?

In looking back over these events, can you see any threads? These are the "constants" that may underlie your experiences. Were there skills that you used throughout or skills that you developed?

Now think about your life today.

- How do your past experiences relate to who and where you are today? Are you using some of the same skills today?
- What are the breadcrumbs that you see as you look back over the last several months or years?
- Is God, through the breadcrumbs of your life, drawing you in another direction, or perhaps the same direction?
- Looking at the breadcrumbs, what might God's path be for you now? What is the next logical step?

Remember, you are not alone in all this. God gives the meaning. Benedict wrote this in his Prologue to the Rule:

> What can be sweeter to us than this voice of Christ as he invites us, dearest sisters and brothers? See how, in his loving mercy, the Lord points out to us the Way of Life (Prologue 19–20).[30]

Tool #2: Living Reflectively

Purpose of the Tool. To encourage you to take time for reflection during the day.

Background on the Tool. In the Prologue to the Rule, Benedict encourages us to keep our eyes and our ears open in order to see and hear where God is calling us every moment of the day (Prologue 9), both in the little things and in the big, important things. To do this we need to develop the skill of living reflectively, in awareness of what we're doing or have done. Living reflectively is another way to hear God's voice among the many that compete for our attention.

The Tool

Develop the skill of observation. Mentally step outside yourself throughout the day and gently assess your attitudes and actions. Do the same when in conversation with others. Before going to bed, think about the day, looking gently at who you were and what you did throughout the day.

This skill of self-observation takes a long time to develop. I know I'm not there yet! Will you join me in working on this practice?

CHAPTER 2

The Prayer of *Lectio Divina*
Listening to God in Scripture

> *In* lectio *we do not seek so much to enlighten the mind or to move the will. Rather we seek the immediate experience of God. We seek to be present to God, who is present in his inspired Word, and let him speak directly to us. It is a direct, immediate encounter with our Friend, our Guide, our teacher, whom we love.*
> —M. BASIL PENNINGTON[1]

In the Prologue to the Rule, St. Benedict encourages us to listen with the ear of our hearts. This is a deep kind of listening that is open and attentive. It is a listening that enables us to hear the God who is present in all of life, the God who reaches out to heal, to strengthen, to inspire, and to show where our help is needed. One of the best ways to listen to God is through Holy Scripture in a form of prayer called *lectio divina* (pronounced "lek'-see-oh deh-vee'-na").

Lectio divina, which means "holy (or divine) reading," is an ancient form of prayer that uses Scripture as a way to hear God's word for us. At one time all Christians practiced this form of prayer. The art was preserved in the many Benedictine monasteries and convents around the world where time has always been set aside each day for this "holy reading."

Why Pray with Scripture

The Holy Scriptures are an amazing gift. They offer us not only our spiritual history but the richness of Jesus—who he was, how he related to people, the miraculous things that he did, what was important to him, and who he is for us—and the wisdom and the energy of Paul. Through the words of Scripture, God reaches out to strengthen, heal, teach, and challenge. Scripture shows us the way to live and how we're to relate to

God and to one another. The sheer beauty of its poetry and expression is yet another gift of Scripture. It's no wonder that Benedict rooted the Rule so firmly in the Word of God. The beauty of *lectio divina* is that it offers the gift of Scripture as a way to unite us with God and to recognize that we are personally loved by God.

The Prayer of *Lectio Divina*

To prepare for this prayer—or any type of prayer—quiet down so you can hear God's soft voice. Take a minute to focus on your breathing to calm and prepare yourself to listen. Then, continue with a prayer to the Holy Spirit for openness to the Spirit's guidance.

We Read the Passage Slowly: Lectio

The name used for this step is *lectio*, which is Latin for "reading." We read Scripture slowly. *Lectio divina* calls for a different way of reading. We tend to read a newspaper or a novel quickly, but *lectio* uses a slower pace that encourages us to savor each word instead of hurrying to the end. Let me offer a comparison. Think of whatever it is that you love to eat. Is it a great pasta dish or a rich and hearty stew, or perhaps one of those "sinful" desserts with apt names like "Death by Chocolate?" If you're like me, when you take the first bites, you take joy in the taste, chewing slowly, savoring flavors. (Yum!) That's the approach of *lectio*: we read slowly, savoring the words, for through these words God will speak to us and nourish our souls. As we slowly read, a word or phrase may catch our attention. This is God speaking to us.

It's helpful to read or whisper aloud, allowing us to both speak *and* hear God's Word. We can keep the pace slower when we read out loud, so that we're better able to hear God's quiet voice. Remember, we don't rush through a great meal. (At my house our holiday meals last six hours—a marathon of cooking and eating!) The Word of God is food to be savored slowly.

Trusting that God will speak to us through Scripture, we open ourselves to listen. M. Basil Pennington, a well-known author on prayer, explains that we "allow the Word to nourish us as the words are read not for information but rather for transformation."[2]

As we slowly read, a word or a phrase may catch our attention. For example, a text might speak to a situation or person we're struggling with in our own lives, or we might suddenly feel a sense of peace or hope. Sometimes I find that a phrase makes me think, "This is the same thing that's happening to me" or "That's exactly what I'm feeling" or "That's not what I'm doing now but maybe it's what God wants me to do." Whenever a word or phrase stands out for you, *even in the smallest way,* stop! Remember that God doesn't generally shout at us.

We Meditate on the Word or Phrase: Meditatio

The second step is *meditatio*, Latin for "meditation." In this step we take in the word or phrase that grabbed us and ruminate on it, letting the text penetrate our being through repetition and reflection. The image of an animal quietly chewing its cud was used in antiquity as a symbol of the Christian pondering the Word of God.[3] We must "take in the word—that is, memorize it—and while gently repeating it to ourselves, allowing it to interact with our thoughts, our hopes, our memories, our desires."[4]

This repetition or chewing of the word or phrase was first explained in a fifth-century text by John Cassian. The "novice-master of western monasticism," Cassian encouraged monks always to be in this stage of *meditatio*:

> All do the work assigned to them, all the while repeating by heart some psalm or passage of Scripture. Thus they have no opportunity or time for dangerous schemes or evil designs, or even for idle talk, as mind and heart are ceaselessly occupied with spiritual meditations.[5]

While Cassian felt that *meditatio* was helpful in the discipline of monks, I find it's helpful for ordinary people, too. As we chew on the text given to us by God, we explore what the word or phrase is saying to us and how it connects with our lives: the experiences, challenges, problems, opportunities, and emotions.

We Talk with God: Oratio

In the next step, *oratio*—Latin for "prayer"—we talk with God. St. Cyprian said, "In Scripture, God speaks to us, and in prayer we speak to God."[6] We carry on a conversation as if with a friend for, indeed, God *is* our friend. The wonderful thing about a good friend is that we can say anything, being totally honest, sharing our troubles, our most painful experiences, and our deepest joys. We talk to God about how we see the word or phrase of Scripture connecting with our lives, and ask God to show us this connection even more clearly.

In this dialogue with God we may find ourselves being changed. A nagging worry may lessen or a joy may increase. We may experience gratitude or a renewal of hope and trust in God.

You may be wondering how to know when to move from reflecting on the passage into this third step. In *Too Deep for Words: Rediscovering Lectio Divina*, Thelma Hall reminds us that God will take care of this for us.

> It is when [the] love of God touches our heart that we are drawn into the next level: *Oratio*, or prayer. All else has been preliminary, for this is the real beginning of prayer.[7]

Oratio is "prayer of the heart" into which we are drawn by God. When we connect our lives to Scripture and find wisdom, hope, and strength, we realize that this is prayer given to us by God.

We Are Silent: Contemplatio

Finally, in *contemplatio* or "contemplation," we stop *doing* and simply *be*, resting without words in God's embrace. We still our hearts and our minds and are silent.

At some point we may become restless or distracted. That's our clue to continue the slow reading or, if appropriate, to end our prayer with a prayer of thanksgiving.

As you go through your day, take the word or phrase with you. Write it down if that works for you. Repeat it throughout the day as a form of prayer and connection to God.

Some Prayer Tips

Remember that you don't need to finish the whole psalm or selection of Scripture. If you don't even move beyond the first sentence, line, or word, that's fine. For those of us who have an "I've-got-to-finish-it-all-and-I've-got-to-finish-it-right-now" personality, this open-ended approach can be a real challenge. But whether we "finish" a passage or not isn't the point. Fr. Luke Dysinger, a Benedictine monk, reminds us that "*lectio divina* has no other goal than spending time with God through the medium of His word. The amount of time we spend on any aspect of *lectio divina* depends on God's Spirit, not on us."[8] This is wonderful news: you and I aren't in charge, God is! So we can relax and simply accept the way God chooses to reveal God's self. Father Dysinger writes, "Do not expect lightning or ecstasies."[9] So don't be discouraged if "nothing" seems to happen in your prayer. And never judge your prayer or your ability to pray. *Lectio divina*, or any prayer for that matter, has much to do with trust. We trust that God hears us. We trust that God has something to say to us and will let us hear it. We trust that God will help us to pray. And we know our trust isn't in vain for we know that God is faithful.

A Sample of *Lectio Divina*

The interlude for this chapter presents a brief example of *lectio divina* from my own experience. I've included it to give you an idea of how the four steps work. I encourage you to read this interlude found on pages 40–42 before you try *lectio divina* or use any of the tools in the Toolbox. Set aside some time for *lectio divina* at least three days a week. Listen to God with the ear of your heart.

TOOLBOX
The Prayer of *Lectio Divina*

This Toolbox provides you with information to help you learn how to pray the prayer of *lectio divina*, or Holy Reading. It includes format and resources.

Tool #1: A Format for Holy Reading (*Lectio Divina*)

Purpose of the Tool. To guide you in the practice of the prayer of *lectio divina.*

Background on the Tool. To provide you with a format to follow for Holy Reading. See Tool #3 for a selection of scriptural resources.

The Tool

The format for Holy Reading is organized under an acronym to help you recall the suggested order: stay on T-A-R-G-E-T! This format can be used with any form of prayer.

Text: Have text of Holy Scripture marked and ready.

Alone: Be alone where you can be uninhibited in your response to God's presence.

Relaxed: Stay relaxed and peaceful. Harmony of body and spirit. If you are not calm, take a minute to listen to your breath.

God's Presence: Acknowledge God's presence and ask for God's grace and the presence of the Holy Spirit.

Enter Prayer:

Read the Passage—Lectio

Slow and attentive. When something strikes you, STOP. This is when you experience a new meaning, feel peace, experience God's love, or struggle with or are disturbed by what the words are saying. This is God speaking to you directly through Scripture. Do not move on.

Meditate—Meditatio

Repeat the word or phrase. Memorize it through repetition. *Explore the relationship* of the word or phrase to your life. How does the word or passage resonate with you? In what way does it touch your life? Let thoughts surface that connect the text to your life.

Converse with God—Oratio

Converse with God about the word or passage and what it has triggered. Think of God in the second person ("you"). Tell God what you are thinking and feeling. Be honest! What do you want of God? What help do you need?

Be Silent—Contemplatio

Rest in God's presence. Be silent and without words. *Move on* when you're ready. (Note: Praying Scriptures has nothing to do with "getting through" passages; it has everything to do with letting the meaning of each single word sink into your life.)

T hanksgiving   After your prayer, reflect on the prayer experience. Journal if you wish.

Take the word or phrase with you and repeat it as you perform your daily activities.

Tool #2: Establishing a Practice of Holy Reading

Purpose of the Tool. To help you set up a regular practice of the prayer of *lectio divina*.

Background on the Tool. We all need help in beginning new things and establishing new habits.

The Tool

- Make a commitment to pray the prayer of *lectio divina* this week.
- Decide which days you'd like to offer this prayer to God. For example, begin with two days a week.
- Use the tools that follow as resources for your prayer. Start with five or ten minutes at a time.
- Do your best to meet your promise to yourself and to God.
  (Note: I've found this form of prayer to be my mainstay. I use it even when I am tired: a slow, gentle reading, placing myself in God's hands works!)

I encourage you to keep a prayer journal. You jot down what Scripture verses you used and write out the text of any verse/s that moved you for future prayer. Also write down what happened in prayer such as "Was tired and unfocused. Felt peace when read this verse." This journaling is also a form of prayer. One monk has called it *scripto divina*, or "holy writing."

Tool #3: Scriptural Resources for Holy Reading

Purpose of the Tool. To provide you with an initial list of resources.

Background on the Tool. There are many scriptural texts to use for Holy Reading. Begin with this list or feel free to choose your own. Keep a list of Scripture that you've found meaningful.

The Tool

The Psalms are perhaps the best place to start when learning this type of prayer. Some suggestions include the following:

PSALMS

Psalm 16	"Protect me, O God, for in you I take refuge"
Psalm 23	"The Lord is my shepherd"
Psalm 27	"The Lord is my light and my salvation"
Psalm 42	"As a deer longs for flowing streams"
Psalm 51	"Have mercy on me, O God, according to your steadfast love"
Psalm 63	"O God, you are my God, I seek you"
Psalm 84	"How lovely is your dwelling place, O LORD of hosts!"
Psalm 91	"You who live in the shelter of the Most High"
Psalm 95	"O come, let us sing to the LORD"
Psalm 96	"O sing to the LORD a new song"
Psalm 98	"O sing to the LORD a new song"
Psalm 103	"Bless the LORD, O my soul"
Psalm 104	"Bless the LORD, O my soul"
Psalm 139	"O LORD, you have searched me and known me"
Psalm 143	"Hear my prayer, O Lord"

OTHER SCRIPTURE

Isaiah 11	"A shoot shall come out from the stump of Jesse"
Isaiah 35	"The wilderness and the dry land shall be glad"
Isaiah 40	"Comfort, O comfort my people"
Isaiah 43	"When you pass through the waters"
Isaiah 55	"Ho, everyone who thirsts"
John 14–16	"Do not let your hearts be troubled"
Romans 8:1–39	"There is therefore no condemnation . . ."

Or take one of the Gospels and read through it slowly.

Keep an ongoing list of passages you've found meaningful. Jot them down here or record them in your journal.

Tool #4: Using a Daily Lectionary

Purpose of the Tool. To provide you with other resources for Holy Scripture.

Background on the Tool. There are other ways to find scriptural texts. Worship or prayer books often provide a lectionary that gives daily Scripture readings from the Psalms, the Hebrew Scriptures, the Epistles, and the Gospels.

The Tool

The Book of Common Prayer of the Episcopal Church provides a two-year cycle of readings that follows the Church year. Instructions for how to use this lectionary begin on page 934 in the prayer book.

If you belong to another denomination, check worship and prayer books for similar daily readings. You can also use Sunday Scriptures as a source throughout the following week.

Tool #5: Using Nonscriptural Texts

Purpose of the Tool. To provide you with other ideas for resources you can use for *lectio divina.*

Background on the Tool. Many other texts can be used for Holy Reading. We're blessed with access to the writings of countless numbers of faithful witnesses to Jesus Christ and to the power of the Holy Spirit working in people's lives.

The Tool

In addition to Scripture, which is my primary material for *lectio divina,* I've been drawn to the works of spiritual writers such as Julian of Norwich, Teresa of Avila, Brother Lawrence, Henri Nouwen, Anthony de Mello, Joyce Rupp, Esther de Waal, and Joan Chittister. Visit your church library or a good bookstore, or ask your church friends which writers have been meaningful for them. Check out the books listed in the bibliography of this book for more ideas. Using nonscriptural texts is very much in keeping with Benedict's Rule, for in chapter 73 he lists several books that provide guidance on the road to perfection: the *Conferences* of the holy catholic Fathers, their *Lives* and *Institutes,* and finally the rule of St. Basil, which was mentioned earlier in this book. Just keep in mind that you're not reading for knowledge but for God's voice speaking directly to you.

⌒ *Interlude* ⌒
A Sample Prayer of *Lectio Divina*

This interlude offers a sample of a *lectio divina* on Psalm 23, to give you an idea of how the prayer may go. The Scripture from the New Revised Standard Version (NRSV) of the Bible is in italics. You'll notice that I didn't finish the psalm. The goal isn't to finish, but to stop when a word or passage strikes you and then to explore what God might be saying through that word or passage. Our thoughts, questions, and feelings are all ways that God can speak to us.

I follow the format for prayer given in Tool #1 of the Toolbox for chapter 2. I've chosen a text—Psalm 23—and have it marked and ready before me. I'm alone and relaxed. After sitting quietly a few minutes, listening to my breathing, I acknowledge God's presence and offer a prayer for the guidance of the Holy Spirit: "Loving God, I come before you for your honor and glory and for my sanctification. I pray for the grace to respond to the presence of the Holy Spirit in this prayer. Help me hear your Word for me this day."

Read the Passage Slowly: *Lectio*

I then begin to slowly read the psalm that I have chosen for the prayer time.

The Lord is my shepherd . . .
I shall not want . . .

The second line resonates with me, especially the word "want," so I stop reading.

Meditate: *Meditatio*

I repeat the phrase over again several times.

I shall not want . . . I shall not want . . . I shall not want.

I explore the connection of the phrase with my life, realizing how many times over the last few days my wanting motivated my actions. Some desires were good, like wanting to help a friend by listening to her struggle raising two boys. Some things I wanted were focused on myself. I think, "If I want all these things is God really my shepherd? Am I spending too much time trying to meet these wants instead of letting God guide my life?"

Talk with God: *Oratio*

I begin to talk with God about what struck me in the passage.

Loving God, I say you are all I need but, in fact, I am always wanting so many things. I want to have meaningful work to do. I want to be able to finish that work. I want things to go well and become frustrated when they don't. I want people to do certain things or act in certain ways. I want to feel more close to you in prayer. I want things to go smoothly. I want to feel useful. I want some time to myself to relax. I want people to listen to me. See? I want and want and want.

How do I learn to want just you? How do I learn to let some things go that seem so important to me and just trust that you will provide me with what I need, *really* need?

I continue talking with God about this issue of wanting.

Be Silent: *Contemplatio*

When I feel there is no more I can say, I stop and listen to God. I open my heart and am silent before God. I use deep breathing to stay focused. For a time I am quiet and still.

After a time I feel restless and find myself thinking about things other than my prayer. I recognize the sign to move on.

The Steps of *Lectio Divina* Begin Again

I begin to slowly read once more (*lectio*).

> *He makes me lie down in green pastures . . .*
> *He leads me beside still waters . . .*
> *He restores my soul . . .*
> *He leads me in right paths for his name's sake . . .*

I stop reading at the last line and move into the second step (meditation). The passage reminds me that my life is not just for me: it is for God and for others. I then realize how I might learn to want just God and let other things go. I can truly let God guide my life along the right paths.

After reflecting a bit longer I move into the prayer, the third step (*oratio*) and begin again to converse with God.

> Here is a clue, dear God: if I am able to embrace that my life is for you, I will want what you want for me. Help me to do that. Help me to expand my view of life, my view of what is important. You have guided me again and again . . . always and in all ways. My memory is so short. Forgive me for that. Help me to be on the lookout today for ways that you are guiding me and, through me, guiding others.

I then move into silence and rest in the presence of God in the last step of the prayer form (contemplation).

When once again I feel restless I begin reading again.

Even though I walk through the darkest valley . . .
I fear no evil
For you are with me . . .

I repeat the last line and give thanks that God is indeed with me.

Your rod and your staff—they comfort me . . .

At this point I realize that, although I'm reading the text, my mind is wandering and that my prayer time is drawing to a close.

I give thanks for what God has shown me in my *lectio divina* and move to my closing prayers.

I hope that this example gives you an idea of how simple holy reading is. It's conversation with a God who loves us and wants us to know the nearness of God's Presence.

Putting the Ideas into Practice

Take a favorite psalm or passage of Scripture and use the Toolbox for this chapter beginning on page 36 to guide your prayer of *lectio divina.*

PART II

The Benedictine Vows: The Core of the Rule

When men and women commit to religious life under the Benedictine Rule, they take three vows that convey the core of the Rule. The vows are stability—to stay put—obedience—to listen and respond to God's direction—and conversion of life—to remain open to transformation. Those of us outside a convent or monastery might think of the vows as *values*.[1] We can embrace the values of stability, obedience, and conversion of life in our daily lives, as we commit to family and community, as we listen and respond to God, and as we remain open to Christ's healing and transforming touch.

Stability

Stability is a call to remain where we are and to find grace in that relationship, place, or situation. For a nun or a monk under Benedictine Rule, it is a vow to remain in a particular community. Esther de Waal explains that the basic reality of life reflected in the call to stability is "the fact that you must learn to live with your fellow brethren [or sisters], those to whom you are committed."[2] The concept of stability means that we can find God right where we are and have God at the center of our lives.

The vow (or *value*) of stability can translate to any relationship such as family, marriage, friendship, or church community. Benedict says it's *here*, where we are right now, that a life of grace will unfold when we live in the present. We don't need a different family, a different friendship, or another church community. We stay *connected* with people and place, not fleeing or distancing ourselves physically or emotionally.

Obedience

The Benedictine practice of obedience involves *listening* to what God is saying in all aspects of life and *responding* to what we hear. We listen to Holy Scripture, to other people, to the world around us, to the circumstances of our lives, and to spiritual teachers or spiritual directors.[3] We listen to figure out what God is asking us to do in a certain situation or even with our lives. Then, in love, we respond to God's call.

Conversion of Life: *Conversatio*

Conversatio is a difficult term to translate into English. Its meaning is much debated. For a monk or nun, it can mean fervently living the monastic life as outlined in the Rule of Benedict, being open to conversion or transformation. Those of us outside a monastery or convent can also follow the Rule, living fervently as Christians.

Conversion of life is a balance to the concept of stability. While stability calls us to remain, conversion of life calls us to change and to grow, to be transformed by the Spirit. Conversion of life is made possible by a quality of *openness* that enables God to change our hearts.

We'll look at each vow in detail over the next three chapters.

CHAPTER 3

Stability
Staying Power

*The vow of Stability affirms sameness, a willing-
ness to attend to the present moment, to the reality of this place, these people, as God's gift to me
and the setting where I live out my discipleship.
We are discouraged from fantasizing some ideal
situation in which we will finally be able to pray
and live as we should. Instead Benedict says, "Be
here; find Christ in the restless teenager, demanding parent, insensitive employer, dull preacher,
lukewarm congregation."*

—ELIZABETH J. CANHAM[1]

When I was living in a small town in Indiana and looking for a job, my
father gave me some advice. "Get a job with the utilities," he offered.
"They're stable." Seeing wisdom in his suggestion, I applied to Indiana
Bell Telephone Company, where I went to work as a service representative
in the local business office. Little did I know that within ten years, divesti-
ture would break apart Ma Bell and years of instability would begin!

As a new employee I was amazed when I read the anniversary or
retirement announcements in the company newspaper: technicians with
thirty-five years of service, operators with forty-eight years, a forty-year
anniversary here and a forty-five-year retirement there. Multiple genera-
tions within one family would follow one another into the community
that was Ma Bell. A great example was a coworker whose father, grandfa-
ther, and two brothers all worked at the phone company. This wasn't at
all uncommon. Individuals and families were faithful to Ma Bell.

Why such loyalty and faithfulness to a company? I believe it was
because employees felt like part of a big family. Friendships and cama-
raderie flourished. And Ma Bell took care of you. The benefits were excellent. There were many and diverse opportunities within the company for

job changes, even career changes, and raises were pretty much assured. The company was faithful to the employees and the employees were, in turn, faithful to the company, most often remaining until retirement.

The Scriptural Roots of Benedictine Stability

Faithfulness to place and community, like employees had with the old Ma Bell, is the main ingredient in the Benedictine vow of stability. It's a faithfulness expressed through action and it's biblical in its derivation. All stability, the Bible tells us, is possible because God is faithful. In the Hebrew Scriptures, *hesed* is the word given for God's faithfulness: we turn from God but God does not turn from us. We run after other gods, yet God reaches out to us to draw us back again. The Divine Presence is constantly with us even when we choose to ignore this Presence. Sin separates us from God through our own actions, yet our actions don't determine God's actions. In spite of everything, God stays with us.

God's faithfulness to us is the model for Benedictine stability. Benedict says that we can be faithful because God is faithful.

> The one thing that we can hold onto is the certainty of God. Our stability is a response to that promise which reassures us that he is faithful and steadfast and that we should "never lose hope in God's mercy" (RB 4.74).[2]

God in Christ is our Rock and, as Christians, we want to put on Christ and become a rock, too. We want to have a firm and solid center at the core of our being so that we can withstand the unpredictability and transience of our world. What makes us steady is having a heart that rests in God. The psalmist expresses this idea beautifully: "My heart is firmly fixed, O God, my heart is fixed (Ps 57:7, The Book of Common Prayer, 664)." The New Revised Standard Version of the Bible has this translation: "My heart is steadfast, O God, my heart is steadfast." In his first letter to the Corinthians, Paul urges Christians to "be steadfast, immovable" (15:58). *Stability* also means to remain, abide, be united to, live in, dwell in, or stay with.

What Is Benedictine Stability?

Stabilis is derived from the Latin word *stare*, meaning to stand, to stand up, or to be still. From this comes the figurative meaning to be firm, to stand fast, to endure, to persevere, to be rooted. The essential feature is resting on a solid foundation, fixed by strong and unshakable roots.[3] In a nutshell, stability is the action of staying put, remaining steadfast and faithful to the situation in which God has placed us. It is persistently sticking with a situation, with people, and with God.

Monastic stability, as described by Benedict and as practiced by Benedictine women and men, is first and foremost a commitment to a place and a group of people in the belief that it is *this place* and *these people* who will help them find God. The English Benedictine Basil Cardinal Hume wrote this of stability:

> We give ourselves to God in a particular way of life, in a particular place, with particular companions. This is our way: in *this* Community, with *this* work, with *these* problems, with *these* shortcomings. The inner meaning of stability is that we embrace life as we find it, knowing that *this*, and not any other, is our way to God.[4]

Several years ago the Rule of Benedict was introduced to my parish in a seven-week program. One of the wonderful things that came out of this project was how it impacted Sr. Shane Margaret Phelan, a novice sister from the nearby Episcopal Convent of St. John Baptist. Purely as a matter of scheduling, I had arranged for Sister Shane to preach on the second Sunday of the program, when the topic was to be Benedictine stability. Unknown to me, Sister Shane was at the point in her novitiate when she needed to decide if she would take her first vows at this community. As she later explained to me, "I thought God had a great sense of humor asking me to talk about stability when I wasn't at all sure that I even wanted to remain in this community." But it was that call to preach about stability that moved Sister Shane to remain and take her first vows.

Stability is saying "Yes" to God's will for me in the place where I believe God has placed me and with the task that I believe God has given me to do. In this we follow Jesus, who embraced the task that God gave to him.

Benedictine stability is as countercultural in our day as it was in Benedict's. Our culture says, "Don't get tied down. Keep your options open. Be free. If it doesn't work (whatever "it" is), bag it. Go on to something or someone else." Stability takes a different approach.

Stability is a promise to *stay put* with the people with whom God has placed us. Stability is staying put right there, knowing that Christ is at our side to help us. Stability recognizes that there are times when God may place us in a situation not so much for what we can personally get out of it, but for what we can give to others.

Esther de Waal writes that a life guided by stability has both an exterior and an interior dimension. The purpose of the exterior dimension—staying in a place, relationship, or situation—is to establish what she calls "stability of the heart."[5] That means being content where we are because we believe that God placed us there and is with us in every part of our life. Where I am is important and counts because it is where God wants me. Stability of the heart is important in our mobile culture. Our physical homes may change, our jobs may change, or the circumstances of our lives may change, yet we can carry with us a core that is constant—our rootedness in Christ. From that center we draw strength.

Stability and Living in the Present Moment

Henri Nouwen, priest and writer, went through a period of time when his life felt disjointed. The piece-parts of lecturing, traveling, counseling, and his spiritual life did not feel unified, and for him, this was exhausting. You and I face a similar situation. Our lives have many parts and responsibilities that can make us feel like we're in an old movie with the action sped up, as we chase from one disjointed activity or responsibility to another.

Nouwen discovered that what he needed was an *inner stability* that would be constant even though he was on the go. The key was to find this inner stability:

> Now I see that I was all mixed up, that I had fragmented my life into many sections that did not really form a unity. The question is not, "Do I have time to prepare?" but, "Do I live in a state of preparedness?" When God is my only concern, when God is the center of my interest, when all my prayers, my reading, my studying, my speaking, and writing serve only to know God better and to make him known better, then there is no basis for anxiety.[6]

Nouwen then described how this inner stability brought him acceptance and peace with wherever he was or whatever he was doing.

> Wherever I am, at home or in a hotel, in a train, plane or airport, I would not feel irritated, restless, and desirous of being somewhere else or doing something else. I would know that here and now is what counts and is important because it is God himself who wants me at this time in this place.[7]

This is an expression of living in the present moment and of finding God in daily life, two important themes of stability and of Benedictine spirituality. Stability asks us to live in the present moment and to accept and respond in love to whomever and whatever God has given to us. Stability is not just saying, "Oh well. I can't do anything about this so I might as well accept it." Stability is actually wanting the situation we are in because we know that we can find God in it regardless of how difficult it might be. This isn't easy! But stability asks us to take off our boxing gloves, physically and mentally, and instead, hold out our hands to one another, as Jesus reached out his hand to heal.

Underlying all external and internal stability is living with Christ at the center. The entire Rule points to Christ. Benedict says, "Prefer nothing to the love of Christ" (RB 72.11). With our eyes on the Lord, we can stay put and respond in love.

The Value of Stability

I had a plant that was slowly dying. I hadn't overwatered it and the light was sufficient, yet its leaves were becoming dry and brittle. What to do?

As a person with a "black thumb," I just couldn't figure out what I was inflicting on this innocent victim in my house. One day I picked up the plant and noticed that the roots were hanging out of the bottom of the plastic pot. I'd placed the plant in a slightly larger decorative pot than it needed, so its poor little roots were just wafting about in midair, thirsty and dry. When I did the not-so-simple thing for me—proper repotting—the endangered plant recovered and is thriving to this day.

Roots are important and need tending. Too many people have roots that are just hanging out, not firmly planted in soil. The mistaken impression is that life will be better if we can just pick up easily and move. We think that we are free when we keep our options open. What can happen, however, is that we become chained to restlessness. We jump from relationship to relationship, from job to job, from purchase to purchase or from mood to mood and still feel at a loss. We find ourselves in constant search of something that will root us. The Benedictine concept of stability is essentially realistic because it acknowledges the human desire to be rooted. "Everyone needs to feel at home, to feel earthed.... Without roots we can neither discover where we belong, nor can we grow."[8] Being rooted helps in making decisions and choices. Being rooted and grounded in Christ and the Gospels, as Benedict suggests, gives us a center that is holy. We can tap into the power of the Spirit in every aspect of our lives. We can stay the course.

Author Phyllis Thompson uses the image of a tree to describe stability.

> [A tree] stands firm because its root system is set deep in the earth providing the tree not only with nourishment, but also with the suppleness that allows it to bend and sway, but not snap. For individuals, then, an interior depth and stability are vital to their survival and give them an exterior flexibility.[9]

A tree that is moved from place to place can't take firm root. It will ultimately wither and die. If we move from place to place in our hearts or choose not to remain connected to our communities, we will wither for lack of growth. St. Anselm, eleventh-century Benedictine monk, writer, and archbishop of Canterbury, wrote that to pursue a holy life, one must "set down roots of love" in one place.[10]

What Stability Does

Stability calls us to work out our problems with the people who are a part of our lives. When we flee physically or emotionally, we only bring our old problems with us into the new situation or relationship. The truth is, if I don't work out my problem with *this* person, I'll end up working out the same problem with the *next* person. Best to stay put and work things out!

Stability prevents us from running away from necessary development. Progress is not possible without growth pangs. We think it is, however, and respond by projecting our inner dissatisfactions on the community. We blame others for the negativity we experience in ourselves. Stability keeps us from being buffeted about by our moods or doubts. We surrender them to God and seek God in the situation before us. We can recognize that our passing moods don't necessarily represent the true desires of our hearts. Such thinking can help us stay put until balance returns.

Stability encourages the skill of looking for the best in the other person. Negative thoughts and judgments are easy, and negative pronouncements may make us feel better or even superior for a while. But in the end, all it does is separate us in hurtful ways. Stability, on the other hand, enables us to look for the good in each person.

Stability also brings a call for forgiveness. When we choose to be in a community—whatever that community is—there are bound to be differences and often little quirks about other people that annoy or anger us. There can also be major disagreements. Living in a community puts before us the opportunity to practice forgiveness.

Our commitment to stay put helps us move beyond those temporary blips on the screen of life to embrace the bigger picture. A vowed sister explained to me that when she wants to flee a place, a situation, or a person, she recalls her vow of stability. Remembering her vow is a way that puts momentary frustrations in perspective. Those of us outside the vowed life can do the same once we commit to the value of stability.

Stability and Our Communities

Stability and community are closely interwoven, for community is the workshop for stability. I don't think our lives are so far removed from our cloistered sisters and brothers. You and I live in community, too; our communities are family, marriage, friendships, church, social organizations, and so forth.

Stability is an important ingredient in relationships, especially with family members. Yet we can find it hard to fully commit to these or to any relationship. Instead we live with "one foot out the door," physically or mentally. Episcopal priest Brian Taylor cautions that "as long as we keep even one opening in the back of our mind, we cannot reap the benefits of a fully committed love relationship. We will always be only partly 'there.'"[11] Our goal is to be fully there, sharing both good times or bad, times of harmony or disagreement, fully embracing the relationship in faith. Stability also discourages us from deferring love until we find a community or relationship "worthy" of it. The barriers to love are within us and until we dismantle them, no community, marriage, or friendship will meet our standards.[12]

Benedict writes that the workshop where those who follow the Rule are to practice the spiritual craft is "the enclosure of the monastery and stability in the community" (RB 4.78). Like the monks and nuns who have taken vows and follow the Rule within a monastic community, we toil faithfully within our various relationships and communities, following the Christ of the Gospels as best we can. For us, family is most often the primary community for learning and practicing stability. The responsibility for establishing a stable family life rests with the parent/s. Undoubtedly there are times when parents want to flee home and children. Yet, they stay and persist through the challenges before them. Families must find stability primarily in persons rather than places. The relationship between husband and wife or between partners must grow and deepen. Whether a single-parent or a two-parent home, parents can create a sense of belonging and security so that the family is able to reach out to face the unknown. They can help family members feel comfortable because they know where they are, where they've come from, and where they're going. This fosters a sense of inner stability that leads further to a secure sense of identity and self-worth

While the goal of stability is to stay put and work things out, stability does not mean we remain in unhealthy or abusive relationships. Stability does not force us to stay where we are not safe. Stability does not ask us to remain in a place where we cannot grow and flourish. Our primary stability is in God. We can trust that God will guide us to make changes in our life and relationships necessary for our physical and emotional well being.

Attaining Stability

How can you and I practice and live Benedictine stability of place and heart? It seems to me that *persistence* is the most important way to a life of stability. In chapter 58 of the Rule, Benedict describes the process by which an individual is received into the community—a process that requires persistence.

> Stability is achieved through perseverance, through holding on even under great strain, without weakening or trying to escape. It involves endurance, a virtue we do not often talk about today . . . stability means persevering with patience, and St. Benedict understands patience in its original sense of a readiness to accept suffering, even to death.[13]

The old adage is "When the going gets tough, the tough get going." Benedict might change this to "When the going gets tough, the tough hang on." We hang on where we are, in the situation we are in, and with the folks who are there with us. As we stay put, we find God's presence and grace.

This very stability brings a *staying power* that enables us to persist. We persist in situations. We persist in relationships. We persist in community. We remain connected to the other person even when we'd rather "bag it" and run away, physically and/or emotionally. This takes an attitude of humility where we remain open to the person or this situation, seeking not our own way but what God is trying to teach us through that person or situation. We recognize that fleeing will not allow us to grow, so we root in and stay connected, exploring what God wants us to learn. We stand at the foot of the cross as we continue to hold on against all odds.[14] It's a way that we die to Christ and for Christ.

Yet, our staying power is often compromised by the mood of the moment. We might intend to stay connected, but a mood takes over and we flee. Br. Cyprian Smith sees two ways to reach the place where we're not buffeted by our moods and can remain in stability.

> First—we stay put and not run away from the situation we are in, whatever our present feelings about it may be.
>
> Second—we pray for the acceptance of God's will as it appears in the present moment.[15]

Prayer is important. In prayer "we relax into [the] circumstances, we go loose, we let go of worry, and trust in God who is leading us and carrying us."[16] If we can do this in prayer, we can grow to do the same in the difficult situations we face.

When I'm faced with a situation from which I'd rather flee on the wings of a dove (Ps 55:6), I turn to Scripture. Using the prayer of *lectio divina* I seek God's help through the words of Scripture. So often this has helped me to persist, to stay connected to the persons involved, and, with the grace of stability, to work out the problem. I describe such an experience in the interlude for this chapter on pages 58–60.

Brother Cyprian also makes two suggestions that we can use to grow in stability. First, *not to run away from our present situation or try to change it, unless it is clearly bad and needs to be changed.*[17] We are inclined to change too quickly.

> We blame circumstances for our unhappiness and restlessness, when the true problem is with ourselves. It is more often we who need to change, rather than the external situation. All the major spiritual teachers of the world have been telling us this for centuries, but we are very reluctant to believe it. We shall make no progress spiritually unless we do believe it, stop running away, and open ourselves up generously to God in the actual situation which is ours at this present moment.
>
> The grass is not really greener on the other side of the fence; the kingdom of Heaven is not far away in some remote place; it is here and now, and we are more likely to find it by staying put in our monastery, in our family, in our present work, than by running off somewhere else.[18]

Second, Brother Cyprian advises us *not to run away from ourselves.* Stability is standing in my own center and not trying to run away from the person I really am. We need to accept who we really are with all our graces and faults. Stability is living in the present moment, turning from the voice in our heads that says "If only" about what happened yesterday or what might happen tomorrow. Instead, we remind ourselves that God is present right where we are now with these people and in this place. We don't need to look somewhere else where we think God might be.

The challenge for us is to remain constant in our steadfastness. In Matthew's Gospel, when Peter sees Jesus walking on the water in the midst of a violent and dangerous storm, he leaves the boat and begins walking toward Jesus. Peter was firmly fixed until he looked around and saw the waves and felt the wind tearing at him. Then he lost faith and began to sink into the sea (Matt 14:28–31).

There are times when we are like Peter, dealing with the swirl of life around us, distracted by worries, frustrated with people, and ready to run from it all. Literally we begin to sink. But, like Peter, we, too, can reach for the outstretched hand of the Lord. Christ will catch us and restore us to steadfastness.

Stability, Community, and Our Baptismal Covenant

In the Episcopal Baptismal Covenant, five questions frame our promise to lead a life that follows Jesus Christ. Four of these relate to community and relationships.

- Will you continue in the apostles' teaching and fellowship, in the breaking of the bread, and in the prayers?
- Will you proclaim by word and example the Good News of God in Christ?
- Will you seek and serve Christ in all Persons, loving your neighbor as yourself?
- Will you strive for justice and peace among all people, and respect the dignity of every human being? (See The Book of Common Prayer, 304–5.)

To fulfill each one, we need to stay connected to others and to commit to these relationships fully. It's only in this way that we can love enough to take the action that our Covenant requires. Stability will bring us to this love and to this action, for the purpose of the vow is to attain "stability in love—a stability which corresponds to living the Word of God and the love of Christ."[19]

If you belong to another denomination, review your Baptismal Covenant or catechism and find connections with stability. I'm sure that you will find that Benedictine stability will help you fulfill your baptismal promises.

Stability: A Home in Christ

The telephone company is certainly no longer a model of stability. In fact, there is little in this contemporary world that is stable. Change is the byword. But we have a home and that is Christ. When we are firmly fixed to Christ, we can negotiate even the most difficult change. He is the source of the *staying power* that helps us to stay put and remain connected and in the present moment, seeking to do whatever God sets before us.

 TOOLBOX
Practicing Stability

Benedictine stability is the rock on which the practice of the Rule rests. Unless we "stay put" we cannot hear what God is asking us to do. Unless we resist the temptation to flee physically, emotionally, or mentally, we won't catch the transforming power of God. These tools will help you reflect on and practice stability in your daily life.

Tool #1: Stability and Community

Purpose of the Tool. To reflect on Benedictine stability within the communities you belong to.

Background on the Tool. We don't often step back and look at ourselves within the different relationships of our lives. Doing so can help us to take steps toward stability. We can stay put so that we can find God in these relationships and do the healing work that's often needed.

The Tool

Use these questions to think about your stability within the communities of which you are a part.

- Take a moment to name all the communities you belong to, including family, friends, church, civic groups, work, school, and so on.
- What is your level of comfort and involvement within each? Do you feel more rooted and stable in some than in others? What might cause the differences?
- Do you ever find yourself wanting to flee from certain people, or conversations about certain subjects? If so, what are these?
- What might God be asking you to learn about yourself in difficult conversations and situations?

Tool #2: Inner Stability

Purpose of the Tool. To help you assess and develop inner stability.

Background on the Tool. Life can often become fragmented as we jump from one task to another, one place to another, or one mood to another. Henri Nouwen observed the need for an *inner stability* to remain calm and to be focused on whatever he was doing.

The Tool

First reread the section about Henri Nouwen on page 48 of this chapter. Nouwen was concerned about having enough time to do the many tasks that crowded into his life. Sound familiar? It does to me! Here are a few questions and suggestions.

- What are the various piece-parts of your life?
- When do you feel fragmented? When do you feel the *most* fragmented? When do you find it especially hard to focus on tasks at hand?
- What are the times when, like Father Nouwen, you'd rather be somewhere else doing something else?
- Thinking about your answers to these questions, can you identify why you feel fragmented or desirous of being elsewhere?

If you're anything like me, the reason I often feel fragmented or want to be somewhere else is that I feel I don't seem to have time to do all that needs to be done—a common complaint in twenty-first-century America. Sometimes, too, we can feel that what we're doing is "just a pain." The key is to be able to live in the present moment. Living right where we are and not in the past or the future will help us to develop inner stability. There are ways that we can help ourselves do just that.

- Tell yourself there's enough time to complete everything you need to do. This will give you an immediate sense of calm and help you focus on where you are.
- Envision God as your center, where God is already, and see that, no matter where you are or what you're doing, God is with you. God is the unity in your life whose presence holds you like gravity to the earth.
- Accept that God has placed you where you are to do God's work: in this place, with these people, and at this task. Conscious acceptance connects us with God and brings inner stability.

Here's one last question to think about: How might you come to know God more deeply through the various and diverse things that you do each day?

Tool #3: Stability and Change

Purpose of the Tool. To reflect on Benedictine stability as we are considering making a change.

Background on the Tool. Benedictine stability gives us a touchstone for change where we can assess whether or not the change is valid for us or just an attempt to flee from a person or situation.

The Tool

- Are you thinking about making a change in a job, a relationship, or in a particular situation? What is that relationship or situation?
- Ask yourself honestly, "Am I running from something here?" If you're not, great. But if you feel you are, what might it be?
- What might you do to be able to stay put? For example, are there adjustments you could make in the situation or relationship?
- Bring the situation to God in prayer.

Staying in situations that damage us is *not* stability. Stability asks us to remain in situations that may be difficult but not destructive.

- Is there a situation that you are in now that is not life-giving or is destructive?
- What steps can you take to help you deal with this situation or enable you to make a needed change? Ask God to help you.

Tool #4: Stability and Faith

Purpose of the Tool. To reflect on Benedictine stability as it relates to your faith and your relationship with God.

Background on the Tool. To stay put in our daily lives, meeting challenges and working on our relationships with others, we need to rest firmly in our relationship with God.

The Tool

The following questions can help you think about stability in your life of faith. I invite you to take a few moments to read and reflect on them. Begin with a prayer asking God to help you be honest and to be open to the guidance of the Spirit.

- Does my commitment to God change depending on the circumstances of my life?
- When do I feel closest to God? When do I feel farthest from God? What might cause the latter?
- Do I trust in God's presence and help in my life?

- Do I strive to follow Jesus where I am, or am I more inclined to be on the lookout for ways to escape from people or situations?
- Is Christ at the center of my life, my decisions, and my relationships, or have I replaced him with idols of my own making?
- Am I faithful in my practice of prayer, however I choose to pray?

Tool #5: Stability and Perseverance

Purpose of the Tool. To help you reflect on the important connection between perseverance and stability.

Background on the Tool. Perseverance is a tool to help us practice stability in our lives. Perseverance gives us the "grit" to hang on, to stay connected with other people, and to work through the barriers that keep us from healthy relationships.

The Tool

Here are some questions to help you identify areas in your life that call for perseverance and some ways to find that perseverance.

- Determine a circumstance in your life that calls for perseverance. What is an obstacle that you would rather escape? Is it inside you or outside you?
- Now, what would it look like if you were able to persevere? In other words, if you pictured yourself staying put in this situation or relationship, what do you see yourself doing or saying or thinking?
- What steps can you take to put these ideas into action?
- Now think about other obstacles in your life and ask yourself the same questions.

All of us have had situations in our past that called for perseverance. Often we've been able to persevere in spite of great obstacles. Recall such a time.

- What was the situation? What did you do to persevere?
- Did persevering help you stay put and work things out?
- What resources did you draw on in order to persevere?
- How might you call on these resources to help you stay put in a situation you face today?

Often, lightening up can help us with perseverance. We can fixate on situations or relationships that cause us heartache or difficulty. A way to persevere can often be to turn our attention elsewhere for a while. With God's help we can choose to focus on something that will bring joy and satisfaction into our lives.

∼ *Interlude* ∼
A Lesson in Persistence

The action of staying put—stability—is often made possible by the ability to persist. Persistence in a situation, with people, and around issues of relationship can reap the fruits not only of growth for oneself but also growth for others. We need reminders to persist when our minds and feelings are telling us to flee. Perhaps you've had challenging or frustrating experiences from which you wanted to fly away on the wings of a dove (Ps 55:6), but you hung in there and learned more than you would have imagined? I had an experience like that last year and for me the learning was all about Benedictine stability.

I'd been dealing with a challenging situation at the church where I was rector. The difficulties were a frequent topic of conversation with God in my daily prayer. Scripture from the Daily Lectionary of The Book of Common Prayer was part of my prayer routine. Reading back through my prayer journal, I can see that ongoing discouragement and frustration were rampant. Yet now and then, God managed to break through my distractions.

One morning as prayer began I thought, "How am I going to keep at this?" It was clearly an issue of stability in Benedict's terms. In truth, I wanted to "bag it"! But during prayer that day, I turned to the daily reading from 1 Timothy and found these words:

> I solemnly urge you: proclaim the message; be persistent whether the time is favorable or unfavorable; convince, rebuke, encourage, with the utmost patience in teaching. As for you . . . carry out your ministry fully. (4:1–2, 5)

I wrote in my journal:

> This is what stopped me. Persist whether I think it is worth it or not, whether I see any results or not. God had this message for me! You do not have the authority to evaluate what you are doing. God will do it. It goes on—"Convince, rebuke, encourage, with the utmost patience in teaching." Wow! What an example of God getting the message to me!! Thank you God!

I was renewed and ready to go on. It was only later that day that I discovered that I had turned not to *1* Timothy, the reading for the day, but to *2* Timothy. Wrong book, right message! I was stunned and grateful. I got the message. Persist whether I see any results or not. Persist in spite of the response of others. It's not my place to evaluate what I'm doing. God will do this. These words carried me through difficult days.

All was not resolved, however, and my struggles continued. On another day I journaled, "Help me, Lord! Help me stay the course. Help me to learn what I'm supposed to learn. Help me go on. Help me find meaning." Several days after this the Scripture for the day provided encouragement: "For we have become partners of Christ, if only we hold our first confidence firm to the end" (Heb 3:14). Once again this drew me back to a place where I found hope. I realized that I was not alone and that I had a fabulous partner—the Lord! Throughout this difficult time Scripture sustained me and helped me go on with renewed energy and focus to work through the issues with the folks involved.

I also would turn to the Rule again and again for inspiration and guidance. Themes of the Rule began to weave in and out of my work and my life in the Spirit: living in the present moment, balance among all areas of life, charity and love for others, living a Gospel-centered life, and, not the least, following the values of stability, obedience, and conversion of life. These values helped me to stay the course, to listen to what was happening, and to be open to learning from these experiences. When I wanted to flee, physically or emotionally, because of my own difficulty in coping with the situation, Benedict's stability provided an image of what I needed to do: stay put, listen, and learn.

Benedictine stability calls us to remain where we are and stay connected to the situations and people around us. Through Scripture and the encouragement of friends to "stay the course," God was telling me to "hang in." And like the cellarer in Benedict's monastery who was charged with distributing the goods of the monastery to the monks, remaining charitable in the face of negative reactions to what they distributed (Rule, chapter 31), I was to follow suit and keep my own reactions separate from those of others. If someone was negative, I could be understanding; if someone was angry, I could remain calm.

Benedict called the Rule "a school for the Lord's service" (RB Prologue 45). The Latin word *schola* could have many meanings in Benedict's time—a specific place or group of people, a time of preparation or learning.[20] Our challenges can become the *schola* or school where we uncover our issues on a deeper level and take steps toward becoming a stronger and more mature person. These situations become our learning ground when we realize we're not to avoid them, but rather to meet them head-on with love, understanding, and faith.

Putting the Ideas into Practice

Maybe you've had a similar experience where you hung in there and learned. This is one of the great benefits of practicing stability. When we stay put, we learn about each other and about ourselves. We have an opportunity to grow not only in our maturity but also in faith.

Take some time to answer these questions. If you've chosen to use a journal, record your answers there.

- Recall a time when you faced a difficult situation. What resources helped you "stay the course"?
- What did you learn about yourself? About others?
- How did the experience impact your faith? What was the role of your faith and your relationship to God and God in Christ in the experience?
- You made it through that experience in good order. What situation are you facing today that can be helped by knowing that you made it through a similarly difficult experience before? What steps can you take to stay the course? Who can give you guidance and support?

Remember always to pour out your heart before God (Ps 62:8).

CHAPTER 4

Obedience
We Listen to Respond

Our ultimate goal is this: to forget ourselves.
To be satisfied in life
We must transcend the desire for satisfaction.
We must cast off our own appetites.
We must free ourselves from our own self-centeredness.
In order to accomplish this,
We must practice obedience.

—JOHN MCQUISTON[1]

This may very well be the least popular chapter in the book. Who wants to obey?

As twenty-first-century Americans, we're independently minded people. Obedience hits us in the most sensitive part of our personality—the desire to do what we want. That's why obedience is hard. To be obedient is often equated with being incapable of making decisions or with a lack of individual initiative or creativity. We have images of oppressive institutions where individual dignity suffers, or of wimpy people who can't "get it together." And if obedience *is* in our vocabulary at all, it probably describes what we feel that others owe to us! But is this what Benedict meant by obedience? In this chapter we'll decipher the meaning of Benedictine obedience and explore its relevance to our lives.

Benedictine Obedience

In chapter 3, we looked at stability as a staying power centered in God. Obedience is the next step. Obedience is the action we take when we exercise both physical and emotional stability.

The Latin root for *obedience* is *obaudire*, "to listen thoroughly." As we learned earlier, the very first word of the Rule is "Listen." Benedict says to listen to his instructions with the ear of the heart. Listen not just with the mind in an intellectual exercise, but with the heart, which is the root of love. Follow the instructions willingly with the utmost energy and determination (Prologue 1). This kind of listening, and specifically listening to God, is the main task of a monastic.

> For a lifetime, the monk's first obligation is always "to listen." He will listen—and listen to God—in the reading of the Scriptures, in the liturgy, in the *Rule*, in the tradition, in his abbot, in his reading, in his quiet prayer, in his fellow monks, and in his own heart.[2]

Another way to describe obedience is putting on the mind of Christ. We are to think and act as Jesus would. Paul describes this in the beautiful hymn found in Philippians.

> Let the same mind be in you that was in Christ Jesus,
> who, though he was in the form of God,
> did not regard equality with God
> as something to be exploited,
> but emptied himself,
> taking the form of a slave,
> being born in human likeness.
> And being found in human form,
> he humbled himself
> and became obedient to the point of death—
> even death on a cross (Philippians 2:5–8).

In a beautiful expression of faith and love, Benedict says that "unhesitating obedience . . . comes naturally to those who cherish Christ above all" (RB 5.1, 2). When we love Christ, obedience follows.

In the Rule, the abbot or abbess, as the head of the monastery or convent, holds the place of Christ, and monks and nuns offer them unhesitating obedience. Benedict describes *obedience* in the Rule as both *listening* and *responding*. Those who practice obedience set aside their own concerns, plans, and tasks, even going so far as to leaving a work unfinished (eeek!) in order to quickly respond to the request. The requested action would be completed without hesitation, almost at the same moment the request was made (5.7–9).

Obedience is listening to God, to another person, and to our lives and responding to what we hear because of love. We surrender our self-will as we choose to be obedient to God. Our obedience to others is the way that we live out our obedience to God.

The model for this obedience is Christ. Following in Jesus' footsteps, the monk is obedient to God by showing loving obedience to his superior, by listening to the voice of authority, and by responding with the requested action.

Benedict's abbot or abbess is far from being a dictator. The "job description" offers wisdom for anyone in authority today, whether they are a business manager, a club president, or a parent. The abbot or abbess is to have the character and the integrity of leadership that a good parent would have. Think about how the instructions below apply to your own roles and responsibilities. The abbot is to do the following:

- lead a life that would teach what was good and holy not only by what he said but by what he did—the old quip "Do as I say and not as I do" was not in Benedict's vocabulary (2.12);
- never teach or ask for anything that would be incompatible with Christ's instructions (2.4);
- avoid favoring one person over another (2.16);
- hate the sins but love the brothers (64.11); let mercy triumph over judgment (2.13 and 64.10);
- show foresight and consideration in the orders that he would give (64.15) and strive to be loved rather than feared (64:17);
- not be easily agitated or anxious, or demand too much of others or be a perfectionist or be filled with suspicion of others (64.16);
- follow in the footsteps of Jacob who said "If I drive my flocks too hard, they will all die in a single day" (Gen 33:13 RB and RB 64.18).

To be obedient to the abbot or abbess as Benedict describes is not a slavish response to a despot!

It is also important to know that the community played a role in understanding obedience to God's will. In chapter 3 of the Rule Benedict instructs that if anything important is to be done in the monastery, the entire community is called together to give advice to the abbot concerning the issue at hand. All are to be heard. In fact, Benedict says that special care should be taken to listen to the younger members of the community, because God, he explains, often reveals what is better to the youngest (3.3).

Obedience and Community

In a chapter devoted to "Mutual Obedience," we read in the Rule that not only are the brothers to obey their superiors, they are to obey one another (71.1). Obedience is accountability in community and in relationships. We are accountable to God and to others. Obedience is an expression of love and the acting out of mutual responsibility. We put others before ourselves.

If obedience is characterized by listening and responding in love, then obedience needs to be a part of any healthy, caring relationship or community where we strive to be honest and open and can even disagree with one another.

When St. Benedict wrote his Rule he was trying to build up a spiritual family. He wanted his monks to be content and find fulfillment. But these are everybody's goals: what St. Benedict said holds good for all family life, for parents, for children, for society as a whole. Obedience is our response and we can often be clearer about its nature if we think of it as acceptance.[3]

Too many of us opt for what Scott Peck, in his book *The Different Drum,* calls "pseudo community," which is rooted in conflict avoidance, ignores individual differences, and speaks about others in generalizations.[4] That's why Benedict's Rule can be of such value for us in the Christian community. Of all communities, we in the church need to practice and model healthy, supportive, Christ-centered living together that deals with conflict in a healthy way, celebrates diversity, and looks at each person as a beloved child of God. To achieve this high standard, we obey one another (71.1), we listen and respond to one another in love, patiently understand one another's weaknesses—of the body or of the character (72.5)—and even try to *outdo* one another in our obedience to each other (72.6), showing sincere love toward others (72.8). Finally, we are not to act in our own best interests but in what we see is best for others (72.7).

Obedience is appropriate in every relationship, not just one of subordinate to superior. For example, a mother obeys her child by getting up in the middle of the night to provide comfort or food. Coworkers obey one another by sharing tasks. Friends obey one another by taking the time to listen. In the Benedictine sense, obedience is not what we expect *from* others. Obedience is what we do ourselves *for* others. Our concern is not with "the other" but with ourselves.

The call to obedience often comes in the interruptions to our plans and our days, as we exercise the muscles of stability.

Stability says: Stay put physically and emotionally.
Obedience says: Set aside what you are doing. Focus your attention on the person before you to discern what God is asking you to do.

I read somewhere a long time ago that life happens in the interruptions. Interruptions are opportunities to practice obedience.

Basil Cardinal Hume offers this explanation of obedience:

In everyday life we encounter all kinds of situations which are a constraint upon our initiative and our freedom in carrying out our tasks. Other people's plans, other people's arrangements, other people's ideas or, quite simply, other people, frustrate us in one way or another. We are prevented from pursuing our ends, from carrying out our ideas as we would wish, because there are others who have plans and ideas—or simply because there are others!

This, I think, is what St. Benedict had in mind when he talked about being obedient to each other. He did not mean just taking orders from others: he meant, rather, accepting the limitations which others impose upon us by the very fact that they are "others."[5]

Obedience and Listening

Obedience in the Christian tradition means "learning to tune in and to listen to God's word."[6] God speaks to us all the time in the circumstances of life. Benedictine monk Cyprian Smith explains that "our part is to be perpetually alert and attentive, so as to hear and digest what is being said, to catch the flashes of light as the veil is momentarily lifted."[7]

To listen to all of life, we must first listen to where God speaks with particular clarity and force: in prayer and through Scripture.[8] That's why the prayer of *lectio divina* is so important. In *lectio* we hold before God the circumstances of our lives and let God speak to us about them through Scripture. Experiencing the prayer of *lectio divina* will help us begin to find God in all aspects of our lives. (See chapter 2 for information on this form of prayer.) We must also keep in mind that God's Word comes to us not only in Scripture but also in the circumstances of life.

It's a challenge to listen and to really hear. David Steindl-Rast cautions us that there's plenty of "background static" that prevents us from hearing this eternal and personal Word. When we try to tune in to the distant station that is God's voice, we hear the near-by station: the loud voice of our self and its desires, wishes, hopes, and fears. To get rid of this static, Steindl-Rast says that we should hand over our self-will to someone in whom we trust.[9] For the monastic, that means the Rule, the liturgy, the abbot, the traditions, and the community and the people in it. For us, it means God and those in our own communities of family, church, work, and so forth. Obedience becomes a means to an end.

This is where stability comes in. Staying put and doing the best we can to live in the present moment and being attentive to whatever is before us at *this* moment is what makes listening and responding possible. I can't offer God's love and care to the person before me if my mind is on yesterday, tomorrow, or on what I'm fixing for dinner tonight. I cannot be Christ's hands if I'm not fully there to discern what his hands would do. In this passage from the Prologue, Benedict describes obedience as a kind of waking up.

> Let us open our eyes to the divine light that comes from God, and our ears to the voice from heaven that every day calls out this charge: "*If you hear his voice today, do not harden your hearts*" (Ps 95:8 RB and RB Prologue 9–10).

Obedience, then, is being alert to what's happening around us and responding to this voice from heaven as Christ would. When we hear God's voice, we respond in obedience with hearts filled with love. Obedience is laying aside my plans, my desires, my life, for God and for others. Benedict, however, recognizes the necessity of meeting individual needs. Obedience isn't denying ourselves in a spirit of martyrdom. True obedience, healthy obedience, comes when we place God in the center of our lives to help us balance our needs with those of others.

Grumbling in the Heart

The response of obedience must be spontaneous and joyful. Obedience must be given gladly. What matters isn't the deed itself but the *motivation* behind the deed. Benedict hopes that we listen and respond wholeheartedly.

While he can be most understanding and charitable towards the frailty and weaknesses of human nature, Benedict does not tolerate grumbling or, put another way, murmuring. Whether audible or in the heart, Benedict sees grumbling as not only injurious to one's soul and spiritual journey, but also injurious to community. In fact, other than the Scriptures, murmuring is mentioned more times in the Rule than any other single item!

In chapter 34 of the Rule, "Distribution of Goods according to Need," Benedict is aware that resentment and jealousy could accompany the allotment of goods within the community and cautions his monks against what he sees as the evil of grumbling. A grumbler, he says, will undergo a heavy penalty (34.6–7). Another reference comes in chapter 40, where Benedict suggests the proper amount of drink (wine). Benedict would have had no wine but explains in a humorous passage that it was impossible to convince the monks of his day of this. Let us agree, he reasons, to at least be moderate in the consumption of wine. And so he allotted a half bottle for each monk per day, but recognized that even that could cause complaints and followed this up with a caution against grumbling.

Why is Benedict so adamant against grumbling? Grumbling is detrimental to both the spiritual life and to the community as a whole. A resistant or whiny attitude creates black holes of negativity.[10] While it may make us temporarily feel better to complain about a situation or a person, it won't help us accomplish anything good. Grumbling about someone else or gossiping is probably the most dangerous thing we can do in a community or even a family. Even silent grumbling spills over to our communities, for it affects the way we interact with others. Grumbling adds a destructive negativity and permeates a community so that the whole becomes unwell.

> To the people who sign up but then complain, we ask them not to sign up; give us the gift of not murmuring about it.[11]

One of the beauties of the Rule and Benedict's wisdom is his flexibility, guided by a desire to respond to the varying needs of those in his community. He is willing to make adjustment in the "regulations" that will minimize grumbling. For example, in chapter 41 he details the times for daily meals, regulating fasts, and specifying when the monks will eat their main meal. During the summer the main meal was taken in the midafternoon. Two days a week the monks would fast until then. He explains, however, for those working in the fields, or if the heat was oppressive, the abbot could stay the fast and allow the noon meal every day. The abbot was free to adjust the schedule so that souls would be saved and the brothers might do their tasks without justified grumbling (41.2–5).

Throughout the Rule, Benedict made similar adjustments in regulations for the tasks, ages, and physical conditions of the monks. Such flexibility acknowledges differences in individual needs and circumstances that can support growth without imposing demands that would lead to what Benedict saw as the evil of grumbling.

Obedience and Humility: The Twelve Steps of Humility

As we can see, obedience is definitely not for the faint-hearted! We might ask ourselves why we even want to obey. I think we strive to be obedient because we love God and others as ourselves. When we consider the needs of others first, we replace competitiveness and aggression with generosity and mutual consideration.[12] But we must have great faith and courage to leave our own desires behind and respond in love to others. How can we do this?

Benedict writes that the first step of humility is ready obedience(5.1). Humility is the basis for Benedictine spirituality. Humility is *not* humiliation. The humility that Benedict advocates is the state of mind that subordinates my will to God's in the realization that, lo and behold, I am not the center of the universe.

Episcopal priest and author Brian Taylor explains the primacy of God's will over self-will that is at the heart of obedience and humility.

> We like to think of ourselves as independent people, able to think for ourselves and decide what is best for us. Indeed, God gives us intelligence and judgment to use. But there come times when our own stubbornness and desire are challenged by circumstances and we are left with a choice; we can either go on willfully following what we had set out to do, or we can open ourselves to what has been presented in God's wisdom. If we are to be faithful, we must be humble enough in these circumstances to stand aside and accept the will of God. This is obedience.[13]

In a nutshell, humility is placing God first. Humility is the opposite of narcissism. Narcissism is a concentration on self. Humility admits that our life and our gifts are given to us by God and therefore to be used as God sees best. We must continually surrender to God's power in our life and in the lives of those around us.[14] The reason that humility and obedience are linked is that we cannot listen or respond if we believe that we're the center of life. We cannot listen or respond if we believe that our way is the only way.

Benedict describes the task of achieving humility as climbing a ladder with twelve steps, embracing the action required on each rung. He explains this ladder in great detail in chapter 7 of the Rule. The ladder is our life on earth. Our soul and body are the two sides of the ladder; between these are the twelve steps of humility. Volumes have been written about each step. Here I offer a simple "translation" of the twelve steps along with a comment. Benedict used Scripture in his description of the ladder. I've included selections of these quotes as well using the New Revised Standard Version of the Bible.

The Twelve Steps of Humility

1. To accept that God is present in my life and to live from that awareness. This step is the foundation on which all the others rest. God always sees us and knows what we're about. We, then, need to be vigilant over our behavior, striving to turn from evil and to do good. I like to use the following prayer by David Adam each day to remind myself of God's presence.

> Make me aware, O Lord,
>
> of the eye that beholds me
>   the hand that holds me
>   the heart that loves me
>   the Presence that enfolds me.[15]

Benedict quotes Scripture extensively in this step. Here are just a few examples:

> The Lord knows our thoughts. (Ps 94:11)
> O Lord, all my longing is known to you;
> my sighing is not hidden from you. (Ps 38:9)

2. To make doing God's will my prime directive. In the enduring cult television series *Star Trek*, the crew members of the starship *Enterprise* had a prime directive to help others but not to interfere with another planet's culture. Likewise, our prime directive is to do God's will in our lives and not to interfere by letting our own wills take over. In this we follow Jesus who said,

> I have come down from heaven, not to do my own will, but the will of him who sent me (John 6:38).

3. To recognize that I cannot always be in control, and to listen and respond to those who are—to be obedient. Letting someone else direct us can be very difficult. We need to be flexible enough to step aside and follow another's lead. Benedict says that we are to imitate Jesus.

> He became obedient to the point of death (Phil 2:8b).

4. To be patient and steadfast when our obedience places us in a difficult or unfair situation. We need to hold fast when things don't go our way or when our obedience places us in an unjust situation. We stay centered on God and remember that

> the one who endures to the end will be saved (Matt 10:22).

5. To practice self-disclosure with someone I trust. Benedict recognized the importance of knowing oneself and declaring our faults or misdeeds as a form of healing and growth. We can search out a person with whom we can share our thoughts. Once these are shared we can forgive ourselves and others, we can practice new behaviors, we can let the past go.

Some denominations have practices and/or liturgies that may be used to frame this disclosure within the context of the church. The Book of Common Prayer of the Episcopal Church contains two forms for a liturgy entitled "The Reconciliation of a Penitent."[16] Absolutions may be pronounced only by a priest but any Christian may be asked to hear a confession.

> Then I acknowledged my sin to you, and I did not hide my iniquity; I said, "I will confess my transgressions to the Lord," and you forgave the guilt of my sin (Ps 32:5).

6. To be willing to do the most menial tasks and be at peace with them. Benedict encourages us to accept the circumstances of life as they come to us. We mustn't think we're too good to do certain things. And we are to be content with who we are and what we have. Benedict says that we're to recognize that we are no better than "a brute beast" toward God (Ps 73:22).

7. To truly believe in my heart that others are better than I am. Now this is getting tough! But the truth is, if we believe—even a little—that others are better than we are, we'll be able to learn from them. A beginning to doing this step is to be honest about who we are and to recognize that we don't always have the best answer or the best intentions in every situation. In *Humble Pie: St. Benedict's Ladder of Humility*, Benedictine oblate Carol Bonomo describes this step as admitting our *littleness*. "Littleness in itself isn't the virtue," she writes. "Admitting it, owning it, and being cheerful in it is."[17]

> It is good for me that I was humbled, so that I might learn your statutes (Ps 119:71).

8. To take no action except those endorsed by people who show wisdom and understanding. In this step Benedict advises the reader to take no action unless it is in line with the Rule or the elders of the monastery. For us, this means that in addition to checking in the Rule, we can seek out mentors and guides who will show us the actions to take that have value and the paths that are worthy to walk.

9. To listen more than to talk. Another challenge! One of the most difficult things to do is to listen. Benedict says that silence is preferred over talking and adds this quote from Scripture:

> When words are many, transgression is not lacking (Prov 10:19).

10. To not laugh excessively. I like laughter for it lightens my heart and not only makes me feel better, but it has physical benefits, too. But sometimes laughter can be harmful: we can laugh at another's expense or indulge in sarcastic laughter or giddy laughter. With this step we let go of unnecessary or hurtful laughter.

> A fool raises his voice when he laughs (Sir 21:20).

11. To speak quietly and briefly with humility and restraint. This step is the third to address issues of communication. Again Benedict stresses the importance of generosity in conversation where we speak gently and briefly.

12. To know myself and my sinfulness and therefore to be humble inwardly and outwardly. Should we ever reach this step, our demeanor would be calm and centered. Our humility would be apparent to all our companions, shining forth regardless of whether we are working or praying or helping others. Like the tax collector in a story that Jesus told, the person who reaches the top rung says this prayer of the heart:

> God, be merciful to me, a sinner (Luke 18:13)!

This list may seem overwhelming. Yet it all starts with the first step, acknowledging the presence of God in our lives, which makes the other steps possible. Benedict writes the greatest amount on this first step. He admonishes us to guard ourselves at every moment from sins and vices that appear in our thoughts, in what we say, in things we do, in pushing our self-will, and in our physical desires (7.12). He asks us to always remember God's commandments to us (7.11) and that God is a loving parent who faithfully wants and waits for our repentance and amendment of life (7.30). He reminds us that God always sees us (7.13).

Sr. Joan Chittister writes that this awareness of God always present will bring a "wholesome fear that comes from the ethical responsibilities of being a creature of God." She offers this question to ask ourselves to determine how humble we are: "How aware am I that anything I do in any way is a part of working out the will of God?" With that question, she explains, "you consciously place all you are before God and He becomes the norm of your existence rather than your projects."[18] And so, we walk with our eyes on God. God is the reason and the motivation for all our actions. We do everything for God.

Cultivating Obedience

How can we cultivate obedience? *Cultivating* is a good word to use when considering a desire to become more obedient. Obedience takes much weeding to root out parts of ourselves that rebel against the very idea of obedience.

A way to begin is to practice loving God and to love our neighbors as ourselves, Jesus' great commandment. This will become for us a touchstone and a guide. When we're stymied by circumstance and unsure of what to do, we can recall this commandment. This act of selflessness alone will help us to be open to where God is calling us in a certain situation. This is obedience!

Several years ago those of us who were working at the church with the homeless families from the Interfaith Hospitality Network each received a wristband with "WWJD" imprinted on it. "WWJD" stands for "What Would Jesus Do?" Perhaps this is another good reminder for Benedictine obedience. We not only observe and hear. We act on what we observe and hear, in deep consideration of and for others.

Taking us out of ourselves, obedience brings us into a world that is far greater and more freeing. I think we rarely can see just how limiting our own wills are. It has been described that our own freedom is an illusion. In obedience we accept the limits that life has placed on us and live out those limits in love. We will always have responsibilities. We can embrace these, accepting them in our heart, or we can fulfill them with "grumbling in the heart," as Benedict would say. The latter way leads to misery, the former way to freedom.

> If we conform our intention to the will of God we are set free from the limitations of our own self-will. . . . [A]t the root of obedience is a free, personal, humble, loving surrender to the will of God, a bending of our whole person to the infinite will of God.[19]

The problem is that we'll never achieve this freedom if we live intent upon our own autonomy and independence. Following our own desires without consideration for others will lead to alienation and strife and separate us from God and from others. We will continually be in conflict, as our desires bump up against those of others.

Instead we need to find God's will by letting go of our desires, substituting a desire to genuinely serve God and others. "We do what we are given to do, accepting that it is the Will of God."[20] Regardless of the kind of work that you and I do—and whether or not we like it or find it rewarding—we can "simply do it as an act of service."[21] We can view our daily tasks and responsibilities as God's will for us and do them in love. The most holy responsibility is to love one another and to let this love guide our choices and our actions. This is obedience.

Giving Our Life to God

Benedict gathered ordinary people around him, giving them a new way of looking at the world that put God at the center of their lives. This is key, for once this starts to happen we see and experience life differently.

> The work which was boring and tedious takes on a new resonance and significance. Deeds which are performed, not out of love of self, but out of love for God, have an infinite depth of meaning and value out of proportion to the value of the deeds in themselves, which may be quite small.[22]

But be careful. It's much easier to *talk about* obedience than to *live* it. So to do more than talk, we need to place our lives in the hands of God. When we choose to give away our lives to God, we begin to realize that we're co-collaborators with God and are *not responsible* for *everything*. We use what's been given to us creatively, attentive to our lives and to God's presence. Through obedience we grow. Listening and responding in love, we take our part in furthering Christ's kingdom in the world.

> This grounding in love remains the vital element. Ultimately obedience will come from the heart, and it will be the expression of what we most deeply and truly desire. At the root of obedience is the free, humble, loving surrender to the will of God; the willing obedience which says "Yes" with our whole person to the infinite love of God, so that outward observance springs from inward assent, a bending of our free will toward the will of Christ, which will finally make us collaborators with him.[23]

Obedience and Our Baptismal Covenant

It's clear that there's a deep relationship between obedience and our Baptismal Covenant. The following three questions seem to relate most closely:

- Will you persevere in resisting evil, and, whenever you fall into sin, repent and return to the Lord?
- Will you seek and serve Christ in all Persons, loving your neighbor as yourself?
- Will you strive for justice and peace among all people, and respect the dignity of every human being (Book of Common Prayer, 304–5)?

In obedience we turn away from the evil of placing ourselves at the center of the universe. As we listen to God present in Scripture and in all of life around us, we find opportunities to serve Christ in all persons and in all situations. We're free enough to respond to life with "the mind of Christ," setting our own agendas aside and following instead our Lord's way of justice and peace in whatever challenge or need is before us. Because we have opened our hearts in love, through obedience we can share God's love with those around us.

TOOLBOX
Listening and Responding: Benedictine Obedience

Benedict gives us a new way to look at obedience, a way that considers more what we can give to others than what others owe to us. Benedictine obedience asks us to live with our eyes on God and our wills given to God. We're to be both steadfast in our responsibilities and open to unexpected opportunities.

Here are a few tools to help you bring Benedictine obedience into your life. There are also suggestions about how to become aware of and curb "grumbling in the heart," as well as a tool to help you practice humility.

Tool #1: The Steps to Obedience

Purpose of the Tool. To recognize that the essence of obedience is to be alert to God's presence in our lives and to respond to God's direction, however it comes, with love and compassion.

Background on the Tool. Obedience is simply listening to God and responding to God's call to be a loving person in the relationships and in the situations we encounter daily. These words from the Prologue to the Rule give us a wonderful picture of how we can practice obedience:

> Let us open our eyes to the light that comes from God, and our ears to the voice from heaven that every day calls out this charge: *If you hear his voice today, do not harden your hearts* (Ps 95:8 RB and RB Prologue 9–10).

The Tool

Benedictine obedience is a two-step process.

1. *Open your eyes to the light of God's presence.* This light will both guide and encourage. The light is always there. Open your eyes, ears, and heart and answer this question: what is God asking me to do or be in this situation?
2. *Let Christ guide you in the way of love.* His voice calls out, "Do not harden your hearts." With a gentle heart, love, seek peace in conflict, practice forgiveness, and be patient. When you feel your heart hardening against a person or situation, it's a warning to set aside your ego and let Christ be your guide.

Conscientiously practice the above two steps.

Tool #2: Remembering a Time of Obedience: A Guided Meditation

Purpose of the Tool. To provide an opportunity to recall and reflect on a prior experience of obedience.

Background on the Tool. Obedience isn't just doing what we need to do; it's seeing what needs to be done and then doing it with a heart of love. It's listening and responding to what God is placing before us.

The Tool

This tool is a guided meditation that will put you in touch with a time when you've already practiced obedience. Ask someone to read this passage to you slowly, so you can concentrate on the visual images that come to your mind.

Get ready by placing both feet on the floor and sitting comfortably with hands on your lap, back straight. Relax. For a minute or two, breathe in and out slowly, consciously relaxing your muscles. Then say a brief prayer asking for the presence of the Spirit. Then continue slowly, pausing between the questions.

You are a young girl or boy, as you were many years ago. You are remembering a situation that moves your young heart to compassion. There is a situation or person before you that seems to draw you into becoming involved, into showing your concern or taking action. What is the situation? Picture it in your mind. Who is present? Envision them and yourself in the situation. What do you feel as you observe and listen? What action do you feel that you should take?

Now, visualize yourself taking this action, as you did years ago. What do you feel like now as you take this action in your imagination? What was the result of the action?

When you are ready, return to the present.

Reflecting on the Exercise

- What did you experience? How was it positive? How was it negative?
- What plans and needs did you have to set aside to take this action?
- In the experience you recalled, how did you embody the qualities of obedience by listening and responding?

(Note: This exercise may also be done recollecting an experience as an adult.)

Tool #3: Tools for Practicing Obedience

Purpose of the Tool. To provide several ways that obedience can be put into practice.

Background on the Tool. Benedict asks us to listen for God in all circumstances of life. We need reminders for how to do this. It all begins with the desire to be obedient—to listen and respond.

The Tool

1. Pray for the will and the desire to listen to God and respond to what you hear. The truth is we must *want* to be obedient to God and to one another, so pray for a willing heart.

2. Listen to God in every way you can. Be attentive to God in Scripture, in prayer, in books, through others, and in the various situations of life. Listen for God's voice making suggestions and giving hints about what you should do. Self-will speaks in a loud and demanding voice, insisting on rights and well-laid plans. God speaks softly, so softly that it's easy for the voices of desires and needs to cover God's quiet call.

As you move through the day become aware of the difference between the loud voice of your desires and the quiet voice of God. Try to follow that quiet voice.

3. Use interruptions to practice obedience. Today when your boss, coworker, spouse, partner, or child comes to you at an inconvenient time, set aside your agenda and be fully present to them. Listen and respond.

4. Remember the teachings of Jesus. Jesus taught us how to love. In *Living with Contradiction*, Anglican author Esther de Waal writes, "The giving and receiving of love is at the heart of God's plan and purpose for each of us."[24]

Ask yourself, "What is the loving thing that I can do, or say, or be in this situation?"

5. At the end of each day, review the day and your actions. Where did you hear God calling you to take a loving action? Did you respond? If not, what was the obstacle in your way? Forgive yourself and pray for the grace to try again.

Tool #4: Grumbling: Recognizing and Stopping That Voice

Purpose of the Tool. To help you reflect on "The Art of Grumbling" in your life.

Background on the Tool. Benedict cautions us against the practice of grumbling, which destroys us as well as the communities of which we're a part. We can grumble to ourselves. We can grumble out loud to others. Either way, damage results.

The Tool

RECOGNIZING GRUMBLING

Grumbling is a natural pastime so it may be hard to recognize. However, there are signs.

- Negative thoughts about a person or situation
- Obsessive thoughts about a person or situation

- Comparisons between ourselves and others that place us in a superior role
- Expressions of envy, jealousy, inferiority
- Expressions, either to self or out loud, that justify our behavior
- Talking negatively about certain people
- Persistent negative feelings about life
- Absence of a sense of humor

Add your own thoughts to the list above. What are other signs of grumbling?

"SURELY NOT I, RABBI?"

When Jesus told the disciples that one among them would betray him, Judas responded, "Surely, not I, Rabbi?" to which Jesus responded, "You have said so" (Matt 26:25). Are we aware at all of how much grumbling we really do? Our response might be the same: "Surely not I, Lord?" Yet, we think our thoughts at lightning speed. Grumbling happens before we're even aware of it. Grumbling is undoubtedly a part of our normal speech.

Over the next few days or weeks, listen to your thoughts.

- Do you hear grumbling in your heart?
- What kinds of situations bring about your grumbling?
- Who do you grumble about and why?

FREEDOM IN CHRIST

There are probably millions of antidotes to grumbling, but here are some suggestions:

- Ask yourself: what is God asking me to learn from this person or this situation? Obedience asks us to listen to our life.
- Consider that you might not have the only answer. Remember that there are usually many ways to accomplish a task.
- Each of us has been given gifts. Your gifts are not the same as another person's. Perhaps you have a gift that can help the person you're grumbling about.
- Whenever you catch yourself grumbling, pray for the person and for yourself.
- When you catch yourself grumbling, repeat a favorite Bible verse or give your hurt to the Lord, who can heal the hurt so that you won't even need to grumble.
- Consider that the other person may be dealing with a difficult issue or situation. Be understanding. Be gentle.
- What is so important to you may not be as important to the other person. Lighten up.

- Talk to the person. Maybe there is something that needs to be resolved. Practice the fine art of forgiveness.
- Consider the vastness of the universe. Is grumbling worth the effort? Why not love instead?
- Remember this: Jesus had much to grumble about: disciples who rarely understood him, a huge workload, religious leaders who criticized him and/or sought his death, and people who flocked to him for self-serving reasons. Although he may have spoken strongly from his frustration with others ("You brood of vipers!" (Matt 12:34), we have no record that Jesus ever grumbled!!

Tool #5: The Practice of Humility

Purpose of the Tool. To encourage you to practice the twelve steps of humility.

Background on the Tool. Climbing the ladder of humility is a life-long process. Just as with a real ladder, we can't leap from the ground to the top rung but must carefully move up one step at a time. It is hard to climb a ladder when we are carrying something heavy. If Benedict's ladder is our life, what we haul onto it is our ego. We must let our ego fall to the ground so that we're free to climb more easily and quickly.

As you work with this tool, keep in mind that it's essentially a process that helps us to loosen the grasp on our cherished selves!

The Tool

True humility comes from the inside through a change of heart and through growth into maturity. Yet, I've always felt that it can't hurt to "get the feet moving." This tool is designed to do just that: get our feet moving on the path of humility.

The twelve steps are listed below. Review the explanation of the steps beginning on page 67.

Try taking a step every week, or every other week, to consciously and conscientiously reflect on and practice. You may wish to enter some dates as you work through the list.

1. To accept that God is present in my life and to live from that awareness.
2. To make doing God's will my prime directive.
3. To recognize that I cannot always be in control, and to listen and respond to those who are—to be obedient.
4. To be patient and steadfast when obedience places me in a difficult or unfair situation.
5. To practice self-disclosure with someone I trust.
6. To be willing to do the most menial tasks and be at peace with them.

7. To truly believe in my heart that others are better than I am.
8. To take no action except those endorsed by people who show wisdom and understanding.
9. To listen more than to talk.
10. To not laugh excessively.
11. To speak quietly and briefly with humility and restraint.
12. To know myself and my sinfulness and therefore be humble inwardly and outwardly.

⌒ *Interlude* ⌒
Sitting Still

One of the most difficult challenges that we have in our daily life is to listen: to really be present so we can listen carefully to others, to ourselves, and to what the flow of life around us is saying. We can be so distracted by what's on our plate or by what happened yesterday or last year, or by what we think will happen later today or tomorrow or next year. But if you and I don't listen, how can we know if the voice we hear telling us to do something is our voice or God's voice?

Listening is critical to Benedictine spirituality. Listening is what the vow of obedience is all about. It's easier, I think, to reflect on the practice of listening than that of obedience. Obedience doesn't get high marks today as a sought-after quality.

Yet Benedictine obedience isn't a mindless following of orders given and received. Benedictine obedience is making a choice about how we live into our relationship with God. Obedience is about how you and I take our part in cocreating a loving world with God in Christ as baptized Christians.

The Benedictine practice of obedience involves *listening* to what God is saying in all aspects of life and *responding* to what we hear. We listen to Holy Scripture, our liturgy, other people, the world around us, the circumstances of our lives, and spiritual teachers. We listen to figure out what God is asking us to do in a given situation and even with our lives. Then, in love, we respond to God's call.

This, then, is Benedictine obedience.

A Story of Listening and Responding

One Sunday a year or so ago, my friend Mary Beth attended a special choral concert in a local church. Knowing that it would be a great musical experience she arrived early and carefully chose her seat—a place in a particular row right on the center aisle. In satisfaction she settled in to wait for the music to begin, eager to have the music spill over her mind and heart, washing away the tension that she'd been feeling over the past several days.

Right after the performance started an usher appeared next to her with a young girl about nine years old. With a gesture he indicated that she was to sit in my friend's row. Mary Beth pulled in her knees expecting the young girl to step in and take a seat beyond her. However, the girl made no move to go around, so Mary Beth grudgingly moved over. What was going to be a wonderful, peace-filled and inspiring concert became a battleground between frustration and obedience.

"The first thing that offended me," Mary Beth confessed, "was that when she sat down she smelled so bad—like stale cigarettes. She probably lived with people who smoked. I thought to myself, 'I'll just move over in the row to get away from the sickening odor.' But suddenly I heard a very quiet voice inside my head. 'Sit still. Just be quiet and sit still. You can sit there for an hour.'" Mary Beth didn't move.

Other annoyances followed. The girl had a cardboard box of jujubes, which she proceeded to consume noisily during the concert. As each morsel was extracted from the box, the remaining candies rattled loudly. And that wasn't all: at one point the girl spilled her candies. When they tumbled onto the floor and under the pews, the girl sprang from her seat and crawled around to retrieve them. My friend's frustration burned hot, but the voice in her head continued to speak. "Be quiet. Just sit still. Let it go. Be quiet."

"Then," my friend related, "all during the music she tapped her foot on the floor. As a mother and teacher, I've spent a lot of time helping children learn how to behave. I wanted to turn to her and say, 'In a concert we don't tap feet to the music,' but I heard that very quiet voice within me saying, 'Don't say anything. You can just sit here for this hour and give up your well-planned concert. Let it be.'"

With each new choral piece the foot tapping would begin again and Mary Beth would think, "I'll just tap her knee," but the voice continued. "Just sit still and be quiet." It was a continuing dialogue between the loud voice of her frustration saying, "I need this," and the quiet voice of God saying, "Just sit still and be quiet. That's the kind thing to do. You can do that for an hour. Just sit still."

"During the concert we sang several hymns with the choirs," my friend said. "I noticed that the young girl had a lovely voice."

When the concert was over Mary Beth spoke with a woman who had been sitting in front of her. "While I spoke with this woman," my friend said, "I noticed that the girl stood next to me as if she was waiting. After I finished talking to the woman I knew, I turned to the girl and smiled. We shook hands and I asked her name."

"You have a beautiful voice," the girl said to my friend.

"Thank you," Mary Beth answered. "You do, too. Do you sing in a choir?"

"Yes," the girl responded. "Just at church."

Then Mary Beth said something that came to her unexpectedly. It was a gift from God to this young girl who smelled of stale cigarettes and tapped her foot annoyingly to the music. "Your voice is a gift from God," my friend said, "and he wants you to use it to glorify him all your life." Then the young girl left my friend.

The woman who had been speaking with Mary Beth turned to her and said, "I'm so glad you spoke to her because she comes from a terrible family. She has so many problems. Everyone here at the church tries to look out for her."

Hearing this, Mary Beth thought she might just sit down and weep. "I thought, 'Why did I hear that voice?' It was insistent throughout the whole concert. It was a voice that ran counter to a natural part of me, the part that had planned the perfect concert experience and that wanted to have it. But I could feel what the little girl would have felt had I said anything: 'Here's one more adult telling me to be quiet.' I thanked God for helping me to hear the voice and to be obedient to a kinder part of myself."

Later in the week Mary Beth's Bible study group was reading Psalm 39 and Philippians 2:1–11. When she read the psalm, Mary Beth thought, "It sounds to me like God wants to make sure the learning of the previous Sunday at the concert was understood."

> I said, "I will guard my ways
> that I may not sin with my tongue;
> I will keep a muzzle on my mouth
> as long as the wicked are in my presence."
> I was silent and still;
> I held my peace to no avail;
> my distress grew worse,
> my heart became hot within me (Ps 39:1–3).

In a true manner of *lectio divina*, listening to God in Scripture, my friend said, "Suddenly I had a new thought. I realized that the wicked the psalm spoke of were not outside me but that part of me that had burned hot within me when I wanted to react to the girl. But God helped me hold my tongue. God answered my unsaid need and her need as well. The voice just came."

Benedictine Obedience

My friend's experience was a model of Benedictine obedience: listening to the voice of God, however and whenever it comes, and following the lead of that voice. God's voice is quiet and we must be still in order to hear it.

Mary Beth had been reading a book that a women's group at my church was using at the same time, Joan Chittister's *Wisdom Distilled from the Daily*, which is about applying Benedict's Rule to our lives today. "If I hadn't read that book and been made aware that I needed to be quiet in order to hear God's voice, I don't think that I would have ever heard it that day in the concert," she explained. That's why it's so important for us to talk about these things and to explore the different ways we can make ourselves available to God. When we set aside our own desires and needs to act in love toward others, we're following what Paul said in his Letter to the Philippians: "Do nothing from selfish ambition or conceit, but in humility regard others as better than yourselves. Let each of you look not to your own interests, but to the interests of others. Let the same mind be in you that was in Christ Jesus (Phil 2:3–5)."

In the Rule, Benedict explains it this way: no one should pursue what they deem best for themselves but what they determine is best for another (72.7); each person should be patient with the physical and character weaknesses of others (72.5); and finally, people should compete with one another in the practice of obedience (72.5).

"Be quiet. Sit still. That's the kind thing to do. You can do that for an hour. Just sit still."

Let us step forward into life with joy and encouragement, knowing that God will help us—as God helped Mary Beth—to be obedient. Let's listen, as Benedict says, "with the ear of our heart" and be ready to share the love that God has given to us.

Putting the Ideas into Practice

This story illustrates two important things: the practice of Benedictine obedience in daily life and the importance of mindfulness in our spiritual life. If my friend hadn't been on a mindful journey in her spiritual life, she may not have responded to—or even heard—the voice calling her to be obedient. Or she might have heard the voice and not responded to the call to love-in-action. We need to continually learn from our spiritual teachers: people, worship, Scripture and other books, or even reflecting on our own experience. As we learn we become more aware of life around us and more attuned to the endless opportunities that God places before us to be loving, caring human beings.

Here are a few questions for reflection.

- Have you had an experience similar to Mary Beth's, when you released your well-laid plans or desires to serve another person? What were the circumstances?
- How did you respond? How did you feel about the experience then? How do you feel about this experience now?

If you can't think of such an experience, remember that the calls to listen and respond come to us constantly. Opportunities abound: during a busy time at work when a coworker interrupts you to talk, or when a child shows you a newly drawn picture, or a friend calls on the phone. That's when I try to remember what I read somewhere: life happens in the interruptions!

Since you're reading this book you're interested in spiritual growth. Are there other channels of learning that you could explore: for example, writings from our great spiritual teachers, past and present? A spiritual director can provide guidance for your spiritual journey. Consider talking to your priest or pastor about this and find someone who can journey with you.

Pray for help and be patient.

CHAPTER **5**

Conversion of Life
Openness and Transformation

*Stability does not imply a static response to life. . . .
The vow [of] Conversion of Life makes it clear
that dealing with change is also essential. By this
vow the monk recognizes that he is not yet fully
the person God created him to be, that he is on
the way to knowing himself as one loved and
created in the divine image whose call is to be as
Christ in the world but who has not yet arrived.*

—ELIZABETH CANHAM[1]

Ma Bell was a good employer. During my first year as a service rep, I was delighted to find that we had a number of free days, including Christmas Eve. A week after that, I was lounging in bed around 8:30 a.m. on New Year's Eve day, happy that the company was so generous with days off, when the phone rang. I reluctantly rolled over and picked it up, only to hear the voice of my exasperated supervisor on the other end of the line. "Where are you, Jane?" she asked, sounding exasperated. "Don't we have New Year's Eve day off?" I queried in shocked surprise. "What?" she barked. ""No, we *don't* have the day off! How soon can you get in here?" Not recognizing that a certain action would have been appropriate, I said that I wasn't feeling well anyway and wouldn't be coming in. Two days later I found myself in the manager's office listening to an ultimatum.

During this first year I'd been ill a number of times, missing multiple days of work—too many, according to my supervisor. If I wanted to keep my job, I'd better show some commitment, or I'd be free to look elsewhere for employment.

This was a turning point in my behavior. I sat there listening carefully to what my manager and supervisor were saying, painful as it was.

I took their words to heart. I became a model employee, following to a tee what was called, tongue-in-cheek, the "Bell System ethic." The next time I was ill, I came in to work in spite of a temperature of 102! Transformed in action and in commitment, I was promoted to management the following year.

Although I hadn't a clue at the time, this experience was an example of what the process of Benedictine conversion of life is all about. I hadn't embraced the community work ethic and was told that if I wanted to remain in that community (*stability*) I needed to follow the expected rules. I *listened* to what my supervisor and manager were saying and *responded* with the appropriate action (*obedience*). This led to a change not only in my behavior and commitment to my job but also to who I was at work (*conversion of life*).

A parallel example in Benedict's time might have been a monk who frequently opted for a toasty, warm bed instead of rising in the chill hours of the early morning for Vigils. In a chapter on being late to chapel or to meals, Benedict encourages the brothers to be on time and to take their proper place because nothing is preferable to *Opus Dei*, the Work of God (43.3). With a heart full of understanding and charity, in the next verse Benedict explains that the opening psalm of Vigils is to be chanted very slowly in order that the brothers can get to their seats before the "Glory to the Father" is finished so as to not be tardy. As abbot, however, Benedict would ultimately confront this less-than-committed brother to give him every chance to do what is required and needed, just as my manager and supervisor did for me. For Benedict, I believe, the motivation for promptness isn't so much an issue of following the rules, although that's important. The issue is that tardiness of any kind prevents a person from experiencing something fully and completely. Benedict is ultimately concerned with the individual's soul.

Neither the sleepy monk—nor the naïve service rep—were living their vocations deeply enough to embrace the transformation that would lead to positive change and growth. I was missing becoming a skilled worker. The monk was missing total immersion in the monastic life that would bring him to a deeper relationship with God.

The Meaning of Conversion of Life

With the addition of the vow of conversion of life (*conversatio morum*), we complete the three vows every monastic takes when formally entering a Benedictine community. For those of us outside monastic life, these vows are the values that can guide our lives. Conversion of life is a balance to stability. While stability calls us to remain, conversion of life calls us to change and to grow, to be transformed by the Spirit. It has an outward dimension and an inward dimension. Outward behavior or attitudes change as well as the inner self. God works with both dimensions.

Conversion of life is made possible by a quality of openness that enables God to bring about a change of heart. For monks or nuns, conversion of life means embracing their vocation fervently, remaining open to the possibilities of conversion and transformation. For us, conversion of life is being a Christian fervently and remaining open to transformation by God, as we strive to live by the Gospels and our Baptismal Covenant. We follow the Rule that is Christ. Writer Sheila Garcia explains conversion of life as "being constantly asked to turn to God" by submitting to the Rule where purity of heart is the goal.[2] For Benedict, it is a "vow to live as a true monk, in renunciation of the world, in perfect obedience to the voice of Christ."[3]

Benedict believed that transformation could best happen in a chosen community where the monk would vow to stay (stability). Benedict's monks were called cenobites. They resided in a monastery, where they would live under a rule and an abbot (1:2), so that true transformation could happen. There were other monks who did not live in community: hermits who lived alone, sarabaites who made their own rules, and gyrovagues who, as Benedict explained, wandered about from place to place making up their own rules based their desires and the enticing lure of gluttony (1.10–11). True to Benedict's stance on grumbling, he follows the short descriptions of these wayward monks by observing that it's best to leave unsaid any further comment on the sad life these monks have chosen (1.12).

Our Conversion of Life

Do you and I have wandering, gyrovague tendencies? Absolutely. When things get rough or when we get frustrated, we want to move on and miss the opportunity for transforming growth. We move on, carrying on our shoulders the burden of our immaturity or, at the very least, the kinks in our personality, and find the same problems in the next job or the next relationship. Instead, we need to make a vow of stability, to stay put physically and emotionally, so that we can change as God would have us change and reap the grace of conversion of life.

God is always working on ways in which we can be transformed. We are imperfect and sinful people, and no one could deny that we need to grow in the grace of Christ. We need to be open to change and transformation to become who Christ calls us to be.

> It means that we have to live provisionally, ready to respond to the new whenever and however that might appear. There is no security here, no clinging to past certainties. Rather we must expect to see our chosen idols successively broken. It means a constant letting go.[4]

Letting go, especially of our egos, isn't easy, but Benedict gives us some encouragement. In the Prologue to the Rule, he says not to be overwhelmed with fear and flee the path to salvation. It is narrow at the beginning, he says (Prologue 48); it will be difficult and will bring about many small deaths. But as we allow our egos to die to Christ, his beauty will fill our whole being.

Like obedience, conversion of life and the transformation it brings doesn't happen in a vacuum but in community: family, friendships, work group, or church community, for example. The faults we find in others rub against us and call us to emotional and spiritual maturity. We ask God to help us transform annoyance into understanding and frustration into patience. Over time these step-by-step conversions bring us to a different place. We become a different person. Conversion of life is "being committed to [our] own adulthood."[5]

> If you are not committed to your own adulthood, if you are just coming in and going out, letting others take care of all the ragged edges of our life together, then you will forever see the problem in someone else. If you want to know if you are committed to your own adulthood ask yourself, "In the last three things that bothered me in this community, whom did I blame?"[6]

Episcopal priest and author Elizabeth Canham talks about the value of the vow of *conversatio* to all communities, including the family.

> We live our lives in the world, in families, and churches where we discover only too often that we hurt others, judge them, let them down. Sometimes we try to manipulate or coerce people to satisfy our own needs instead of freeing them to be themselves. Sometimes, like the prodigal [son] in the gospel story, we take what we can get and use our resources wastefully until we discover our own poverty and the love we have despised. Then it is time to return. It is time for conversion of life, for asking forgiveness and starting over. The vow of Conversion of Life is not about "saving face" but about accepting ourselves and accepting one another in all our humanness. This is how God accepts us and this is the essence of healthy community, one in which there is an atmosphere of openness and hospitality where change is possible.[7]

Conversion of life is a process where, again and again, we recognize that we've turned from God, we listen to how God is calling us back, and we take action to return to living a gospel life. It's a process whose goal is not the self-focused goal of self-fulfillment. Our goal is Christ, a goal reached only by continual struggle.[8] One monk described the process of living in a monastery simply as: "We fall down and get up again. We fall down and we get up again." This can describe our own journey into Christ. We fall down and we get up again each day of our lives. Our goal is Christ: union with him and more faithful following of him. We are to respond with totality to his call, "Come, follow me!" When you and I fail in our attempts, instead of getting called into the manager's office for an ultimatum, Christ reaches out to us in mercy and in love, and we can begin once again.

Conversion of Life as Change

Conversion of life is a process that involves change, but there is a delicate balance between stability and change, between acceptance of a situation and working to change a situation.

> As in monastic life, Christian lay living must balance stability and change. Conversion means that all of one's life must be open to the possibility of change in order to respond to the challenges God gives us. . . . Change is not the result of our own desire for excitement. It should not be an attempt to escape from difficult or monotonous circumstances. Rather, change is the result of genuinely listening to God and trying to discern his plan for my life.[9]

It's often helpful to talk with a wise friend or a spiritual guide to discern whether the desire for change is an "escape from" or a "path to." This help in discerning God's direction is critical. Knowing the value of community, Benedict advises his abbots to always seek the input of others in the community when making important decisions (3.12). He quotes from the Book of Sirach: "*Do everything with counsel and you will not be sorry afterward* (RB 3.13 and Sir 32:24 RB)."

On the other hand, to live is to face constant change. Changes in job, changes in residence, changes in family members, births, deaths, separation, and divorce—to name only a few—can wear us down and make us resistant to change. We can add to this list the endless changes that happen between parents and children as the children grow physically and emotionally, spread their wings, and fly from the nest. How can the practice of conversion of life help us negotiate these changes?

First and foremost, conversion of life means that we are to live fervently as a Christian. When we seek to follow Christ, we have a touchstone for all our thoughts, actions, and decisions. So it's critical that we have ways to establish a constant connection with him. We do this through prayer, reading Scripture, and corporate worship, and by practicing an awareness of the presence of God.

Second, conversion of life encourages a positive and constructive response to change. Conversion of life asks us to remain open to the grace that can be found in change. Instead of fighting change, we look to see what we can learn from it. We're willing to evaluate each situation to discern where God is calling us now, rather than just following our old patterns.

Finally, we also need to be aware that other people can call us to conversion of life. Our interactions with others expose who we are, often calling us to change.[10] Conversion of life brings an openness to growth and change, a willingness to look at ourselves and to be challenged by God and by others.

Three Practices That Support Conversion of Life

Whether we live inside or outside a Benedictine monastery or convent, conversion of life means to vow to live as best we can as Christians and to be open to God's transformation. Three practices can support this process. One is to live in the present moment. Another is to always be aware of our impending death. A third is taking action that will enrich our relationships with God, neighbor, and self. We will look at each of these now.

Practice #1: Practicing the Presence of God

To be open to God's transforming power through conversion of life, we need to practice both stability and obedience. We stay put and stay present to those around us. We listen to what God is calling us to do and respond to this call. A key to following this process is to be aware that God is always present. In various places in the Rule, Benedict speaks of this awareness as always watching our actions and thoughts. He admonishes us to guard ourselves at every moment from sins and vices in our thoughts and words, for God sees all that we do (7.12–13). Quoting from the Psalms, he reminds us that God knows our thoughts as well:

Indeed, there is not a word on my lips,
But you, O LORD, know it altogether (Ps 139:3).[11]

Why is the awareness of God so important? Is it just for fear of a watchful God? No, it's much more than this. As we become more and more aware of God in our daily life, our own importance recedes and God's importance increases. We become more in tune with God's will for the moment, for the day, and for our lives. Yet there are obstacles:

The chief thing that separates us from God is the thought that we are separated from Him. . . . We fail to believe that we are always with God and that He is part of every reality. The present moment, every object we see, our inmost nature are all rooted in Him. But we hesitate to believe this until personal experience gives us the confidence to believe in it.[12]

How do we become more aware of God's presence?

The first step is to trust that God is indeed present in all of life around us. As we can't see the wind but can feel it touch our face, so, too, we can't see God, but can see God's touch in life around us. Second, we need to accept the fact that we can find this presence in everyday life. While powerful spiritual experiences and ecstasies come to some, most of us will find God in the ordinary stuff of life. The key is to be present, right where we are. Then we can see God however God is being revealed at that moment: in the beauty of the day, in the voice of a family member, or in an opportunity that beckons us. Third, we need to also accept that an intimacy with God develops gradually over time. We need to be patient as we walk on our spiritual journeys.

Life in a monastery or convent is geared to finding God in the present moment. The bells of the monastery or convent call those in religious life to experience that moment. They stop whatever they're doing and move to prayer because that's the task of the moment. This focus on the Divine Office ultimately helps them find God in all of life and helps them to live in the moment regardless of what they are doing.

David Steindl-Rast explains that when people first come to the monastery they expect to be taught "some kind of spirituality." Instead, he says, people are taught that when you take off your shoes you put them parallel to each other. They are taught the proper way to walk and to eat. "This is the real thing," he explains. "Those little acts all help make us mindful. Everything is arranged in a particular way, so that we will be present where we are."[13] We are to be present to "that word that comes out of the silence." It is an unconditional listening, not only to Scripture but in every situation, with our hearts.[14] We seek what it is that God would have us do every moment. "The purpose of Benedictine spirituality is to make life significant and sacred and full of meaning."[15]

You and I need to live in the moment, too. It's not easy, for our minds jump from thoughts of yesterday to concerns about tomorrow. We can, however, find creative ways to not only remain present to what is happening now but also to recall God's presence throughout the day. One suggestion I have heard is setting our watch alarm to chime each hour. Each ring of the alarm calls us to the moment, as the bells call the monastic to the moment. With each ring we can pause briefly and pray. The Toolbox at the end of the chapter will give you some additional ideas about practicing the presence of God.

Practice #2: Keeping Death Always before Your Eyes

An important teaching in the Rule is that we must always keep our own deaths mindfully in our awareness. Benedict says, "Day by day remind yourself that you are going to die" (RB 4.47). To remember our death each day helps us live more fully and be more present to life around us. Benedict wants us to focus on the important things in life, living with integrity, in response to the Gospels.

Hour by hour keep careful watch over all you do, aware that God's gaze is upon you, wherever you may be. As soon as wrongful thoughts come into your heart, dash them against Christ and disclose them to your spiritual father (RB 4.48–50).

To remember that we will die is a way Benedict is helping us remember to live.

Many sundials in the old monasteries bear the inscription *memento mori*: remember that you will die. But there are also some that say *memento vivere*: remember to live. And there is really no difference between these two admonitions.[16]

Keeping death before our eyes can motivate us to live life fully and deeply as Christians. The by-product of this deep living is positive change and growth. Benedict expresses urgency.

Run while you have the light of life, that the darkness of death may not overtake you (John 12:35 RB, RB Prologue 13).

Run, Benedict says. Run "toward the goal for the prize of the heavenly call of God in Christ Jesus" (Phil 3:14).

Some suggestions for positive ways to live mindful of our own death may be found in the Toolbox.

Practice #3: The Tools for Good Works

Following the Rule, obeying the abbot, praying as an individual, participating in corporate worship, and doing good works are all ways that lead the monk to a life of conversion. In chapter 4 of the Rule, Benedict describes good works in detail.

Benedict lists seventy-three actions he calls "tools of the spiritual craft" (4.75). Each one is a pithy reminder of how we are to relate to God and to one another. They include actions toward others, actions that lead to psychological maturity, and actions that lead to spiritual maturity. They are "disciplines that guard the heart and open the soul to the Holy."[17]

In laying out the tools, Benedict weaves passages of Scripture in and among his own ideas. Here are just some of the ideas in the chapter, with the scriptural quotes in italics.

- First, *love the Lord God with your whole heart, your whole soul and all your strength, and love your neighbor as yourself* (Matt 22:37–39 RB; Mark 12:30–31 RB; Luke 10:27 RB; Rule 4.1–2).
- *Deny yourself so that you can follow Christ* (Matt 16:24 RB; Luke 9:23 RB; Rule 4.10).
- Relieve the condition of the poor, *give clothing to the naked and visit the sick.* (Matt 25:36 RB) . . . Help the troubled. Console those who sorrow (Rule 4.14–16, 18, 19).

- Do not act from your anger. Let go of a resentment (Rule 4.22, 23).
- Do not repay *evil for evil* (1 Thess 5:15; 1 Pet 3:9; Rule 4.29).
- Do not grumble (Rule 4.39).
- Place your hope only in God (Rule 4.41).
- Listen willingly to holy reading, and pray often (Rule 4.55, 56).
- Do not love to quarrel (Rule 4.68).
- Flee from haughtiness (Rule 4.69).
- Pray for your enemies because you love Christ (Rule 4.72).

So that none of us despair at the length of the list, he closes it with these words: "And finally, never lose hope in God's mercy" (RB 4.74).

Embedded in these tools is a statement that seems to me to be the bottom line in expressing where conversion of life is leading us.

> Your way of acting should be different from the world's way; the love of Christ must come before all else (RB 4.20–21).

Christ is to come first in our lives. The Toolbox at the end of the chapter will help you apply this practice of good works to your daily life.

Resurrection with Christ

Easter is at the heart of the monastic experience and of the Christian experience. When we allow our lives to be transformed by God we experience a resurrection. We die and we rise with Christ.

> You were dead through the trespasses and sins in which you once lived, following the course of this world. . . . But God, who is rich in mercy, out of the great love with which he loved us even when we were dead through our trespasses, made us alive together with Christ . . . and raised us up with him (Eph 2:1, 4–6).

If we are to be transformed and experience this resurrection with Christ we may experience suffering. We may need to leave behind once cherished parts of ourselves. We may need to face resistance from those we love. We may need to make major changes in our lives. Yet our goal is Christ and, with Paul, we can echo these words: "this one thing I do: forgetting what lies behind and straining forward to what lies ahead, I press on toward the goal for the prize of the heavenly call of God in Christ Jesus" (Phil 3:13–14).

Conversion of Life and Our Baptismal Covenant

Conversion of life is part of our Baptismal Covenant. The second of the five questions addresses the need and the process of conversion of life:

> Will you persevere in resisting evil, and, whenever you fall into sin, repent and return to the Lord?

Resisting evil and coming to repentance are only possible because of the beliefs that form the first three questions of our Covenant:

> Do you believe in God the Father? Do you believe in Jesus Christ, the Son of God? Do you believe in God the Holy Spirit?

Christians are called to "transcend themselves and put their faith in God. Letting go of what we cling to, we are free to respond to the Lord."[18] This is what conversion of life is all about. Like the newly gathered community described in the Acts 4, we prepare our hearts for continual conversion. Through conversion of life we not only change outward behavior but experience an inner transformation: we become holy. The core of conversion of life is that from now on God, and not the self, will be the center of life. We become new creations in Christ. "So if anyone is in Christ, there is a new creation: everything old has passed away; see, everything has become new (2 Cor 5:17)!"

 TOOLBOX
Conversion of Life

While stability asks us to remain where we are and obedience to listen to God, conversion of life calls us to change and to grow, to be transformed by the Spirit. This is made possible by a quality of openness that enables God to bring about a change of heart in us. We become new creations as we live into Jesus' Great Commandment to love God and neighbor as self.

Although the grace to live a godly life and to be continually transformed into the heart and mind of Christ is God's action, you and I can practice ways to remain open to the grace that continually pours out upon each of us. This section of the Toolbox gives you ways both to follow in Jesus' steps and to remain open to God, ready for transformation and growth. I've also included another method of prayer called "Centering Prayer."

> Do not be daunted immediately by fear and run away from the road that leads to salvation. It is bound to be narrow at the outset. But as we progress in this way of life and in faith, we shall run on the path of God's commandments, our hearts overflowing with the inexpressible delight of love (RB Prologue 48–49).

Tool #1: What Kind of Follower Am I? Hermit, Sarabaite, Gyrovague, or Cenobite?

Purpose of the Tool. To help you be aware of basic ways to practice being a Christian.

Background on the Tool. In chapter 1 of the Rule, Benedict describes four kinds of monks. Sarabaites were loyal to the world, had no abbot or superior, and made up their own rules. Gyrovagues wandered about from place to place and were bound to their own desires and wills. Cenobites lived in a monastery under a rule and an abbot. Hermits lived alone and had passed through monastic life to achieve a self-reliant status where they were able to fight the devil and their vices without the help of others.

The Tool

This is a bit of a tongue-in-cheek tool. Yet I believe that the definitions for the four different kinds of monks that Benedict detailed in the Rule can be a useful tool for exploring how we live our life and our faith practice. We may discover that we need to root ourselves in one place or to consider the wisdom of others or that we need more time to be alone, and so on.

Read each category that follows. For each action, decide which of the four types you're most like: sarabaite, gyrovague, cenobite, or hermit. Write your "monk-type" on the line given for each.

Making decisions _____

Dealing with conflict in a relationship _____

Deciding what is right and what is wrong _____

Making purchases _____

Spending free time _____

Seeking direction from self or others _____

Prayer _____

Now, see which type is dominant. Benedict encourages us to be cenobites. Are you?

There may be times we lean to one, then another depending on the circumstances: it might be fun, for example, to be a gryrovague when you are out on the town for an evening. But if you and I are always on the move, making our own rules without consulting the wisdom of others, we will (a) probably make a fair number of mistakes and (b) most likely not be in the right place at the right time to experience transformation.

Tool #2: Practicing the Presence of God

Purpose of the Tool. To provide ways to stay aware of God's presence.

Background on the Tool. In the chapter we discussed the importance of being aware of God's presence in our lives. Some of the best suggestions I've encountered for living in the presence of God come from a seventeenth-century monk named Brother Lawrence. The tradition is that Brother Lawrence found God while working in the kitchen of his monastery. Maybe this is why I feel that his thoughts are so relevant! He truly listened for God in the ordinary stuff of life—a key to Benedictine spirituality.

The Tool

By taking intentional action to recall God's presence throughout the day, we can become more open to God. Here are several suggestions made by Brother Lawrence that we can bring into our own lives. Try taking them one at a time.

   1. Stop and turn to God throughout the day. Brother Lawrence says that whatever we're doing, we should periodically stop and turn our hearts to God in love and praise. We can thank God, praise God, say that we love God—whatever. He suggests saying a few words such as "My God, I am wholly yours" or "God of love, I love you with all my heart" or "Lord, fashion me according to your heart—or such other words as love may suggest at the moment."[19] It doesn't matter what we say but that we turn our hearts to God. Use words that help you best to show your love of God.

   2. Talk to God at all times. Brother Lawrence also says that we should "converse lovingly with God at all times, and especially when we are tempted or are in distress or are in a time when we feel distant to God."[20] And so, as we do our work, instead of mumbling to ourselves we can talk to God. As Paul said, "Do not worry about anything, but in everything by prayer and supplication with thanksgiving let your requests be made known to God" (Phil 4:6).

   3. Give our work to God. He encourages us to dedicate our work each day to God. This can be done as we get up in the morning, by saying something like "I give you this day" or "This one is for you!" Another great way is to ask God for help before we begin each task.

To use this tool, start by choosing one of the above three actions to practice. Ask God to help you and be patient with yourself. It took even Brother Lawrence a long time to become expert at practicing the presence of God. Over time you'll find yourself growing more and more aware of God's presence with you. You'll become better able to listen for God each day and to be open to the transforming touch of your Loving Creator.

Tool #3: **Keeping Death before Our Eyes**

Purpose of the Tool. To provide positive and life-giving ways to stay aware of our death.

Background on the Tool. Benedict says that to live well we need to remind ourselves daily that we will die.

The Tool

Just a few suggestions:

- When you wake up in the morning, give thanks for the gift of the new day.
- Always remember that you see for God. This was brought home to me several years ago when I saw for the first time a starry sky unobstructed by human lighting. I looked up and, in joy, laughed at the sheer beauty of the sight. Then it came to me: God doesn't see the heavens in this way unless I stop, look up, and really notice the wonder.

     In what situations have you "seen for God?" When have you been Christ to others?
- Write your obituary notice. Include such things as what you enjoy, what is important to you, for what you wish to be remembered, the gifts of heart, mind, and spirit that you've given to others, and whatever else expresses your life.
- Lastly, in Benedict's words, "Day by day remind yourself that you are going to die" (RB 4.47) and seek the joy in life.

Tool #4: **The Tools for Good Works: A Job Aid for Christian Living**

Purpose of the Tool. To give hands-on, intentional practice of actions that support Christ-centered living.

Background on the Tool. In chapter 4 of the Rule, Benedict identifies the dimensions of Benedictine life that we can practice each day to get our feet, hands, mouths, minds, and hearts moving in the right direction of Christ-centered living. Benedict lists seventy-three actions that he named as "The Tools of Good Works." Each tool is an action that supports growth of Christ's Spirit within us and calls us to conversion of life.

The Tool

Read through the partial list of the Tools of Good Works. I have included half of the tools from chapter 4 of the Rule, "The Tools for Good Works" and have used the verse number from the Rule. Should you wish to see the remaining tools, check a copy of the Rule. You'll find that some apply more readily to your situation than others. In prayer, choose one or two tools to focus on and intentionally practice for the coming week. After that, choose others.

The Biblical Imperative 1–2
[1]*Love the Lord God with your whole heart, your whole soul and all your strength,*
[2]*love your neighbor as yourself* (Matt 22:37–39 RB; Mark 12:30–31 RB; Luke 10:27 RB).

Other Imperatives 3–21
[6]*Do not covet* (Rom 13:9).
[8]*Honor everyone* (1 Pet 2:17 RB).
[9]*Never do to others as you would not want done to yourself* (Matt 7:12 RB; Luke 6:31 RB).
[10]*Deny yourself so that you can follow Christ* (Matt 16:24 RB; Luke 9:23 RB).
[12]Do not seek personal comforts.
[14]Relieve the condition of the poor.
[18]Help the troubled.
[20]Do not let your actions model worldly behavior.
[21]The love of Christ must come first.

Relationship with Others: Part I, 22–33
[22]Do not act from your anger.
[23]Let go of a resentment.
[26]Never turn from someone who needs your love.
[29]Do not repay *evil for evil* (1 Thess 5:15; 1 Pet 3:9).
[31]*Love your enemies* (Matt 5:44; Luke 6:27).

Relationship to Self 34–40
[34]Do not be *arrogant* (Titus 1:7).
[39]Do not grumble.
[40]Do not say negative things about others.

Relationship to God 41–50
[41]Hope only in God.
[42]Acknowledge God and not yourself for your goodness and talents.
[43]Own up to the bad things you might do, take responsibility for them and admit them.
[47]Every day face the reality that you are going to die.
[48]Every hour be aware of what you are doing.
[49]Acknowledge that God sees you at all times and in all places.
[50]When evil thoughts enter your heart, fling them immediately onto Christ and share them with your spiritual director.

Act with Humility 51–62
[51]Watch your lips and guard against evil or vicious talk.
[52]Do not talk excessively.
[55]Listen willingly to holy reading.

[56]Pray often.
[57]Every day admit your wrongs to God in prayer with tears and sighs.
[58]Turn away from doing wrong things.

Relationship to Others: Part II, 63–73
Reaching Out to Others
[63]Live God's commandments in all your actions.
[65]Do not hate anyone.
[66]Do not be jealous of anyone.
[68]Do not love to quarrel.

Hope in God 74
[74]And finally, never lose hope in God's mercy (RB 4.74).

Tool #5:   Being Quiet with God through Centering Prayer

Purpose of the Tool. To introduce the prayer technique of Centering Prayer as a way to be quiet with God.

Background on the Tool. One of the ways that we can become more aware of God in our daily lives is to spend some quiet time with God. Taking time with God is like taking time to notice the natural beauty around us. When we take the time to purposefully stop what we're doing and enjoy for a moment the beauty of tree, sky, cloud, flower, and sunset, we find ourselves noticing the beauty of the world more and more as we move through our tasks each day. A relationship with God is similar. If we take the time to be with God, we'll begin to be more aware of God's presence.

Quiet time with God is also life-changing. We let God into our souls where God can work in secret, smoothing out our rough edges and helping us to grow in our ability to love. We become gentler yet stronger as God touches to heal and encourage.

The challenge is this: how can we be quiet before God? We're people of action and sitting still isn't something we can readily do. Plus, our radiowave minds are always picking up this channel or that: what am I going to fix for dinner? What will I say to "X" today? I wish I hadn't said that to "Y." We find ourselves thinking about yesterday, today, and tomorrow.

The Tool

BACKGROUND ON CENTERING PRAYER

If we wish to be quiet with God we need ways to calm our restlessness and move beyond the chatter that clutters our minds. One very effective way is that of Centering Prayer. This form of prayer was developed by three men of St. Joseph's Abbey in Spencer, Massachusetts. Thomas Keating, M. Basil Pennington, and William Menninger based their interpretation on the prayer form practiced by the author of *The Cloud of the*

Unknowing, written in the early days of the English language. In the fifth century a monastic named John Cassian also wrote about this form of prayer. Later, when Benedict wrote his Rule, he advised his monks to go to the writings of St. John for instructions on prayer.[21] So, when we pray this way we are in the company of many, many faith-filled people, including Benedict. Some of the many books on Centering Prayer are listed in "Suggested Reading" on page 203. Centering Prayer is sitting quietly with God who is in the depths of your being. You gently rest in God, "not thinking, or feeling, or imagining, or speaking, or promising. . . . Just being with the One we love. And who loves us."[22]

THE SACRED WORD

The key to being open to and remaining in God's presence in Centering Prayer is through a sacred word. In his book *Open Mind, Open Hearts,* Fr. Keating explains that this word is sacred not because of its meaning but because it "expresses your intention to open yourself to God."[23] The word or phrase is not an end in itself—it is a sign or arrow pointing in the direction you want to take and a way to draw you to God. This sacred word should be one that expresses your love for God. Here are a few examples but feel free to choose whatever works for you.

> God
> Love
> Joy
> Come Lord Jesus
> Hope (or Trust or Faith)
> You are my shepherd
> My peace
> Maranatha (ma-ra-na'-tha) (This means "Come Lord Jesus" in Aramaic.)

THE TECHNIQUE OF CENTERING PRAYER

Begin prayer by sitting quietly. Then, bring the sacred word into your mind "as gently as if you were laying a feather on a piece of absorbent cotton."[24] You do not repeat it audibly or even in your mind. It's not meant to be a mantra; it is just *there.* As you continue your prayer, thoughts will undoubtedly stream through your head. Let them pass by without particular notice and without grabbing them. If you find yourself pausing to look at one of these thoughts, taking it up, examining it, fretting over it, then gently recall the sacred word and return to God. I like to think of my word as a way to let go of thoughts, to focus again on my love and desire to be with God, and to remind myself that God is directing my prayer, not me!

Here is a brief summary of this form of prayer. Decide on your sacred word before you begin.

1. *Find a time when you can be undisturbed for a given time.* Five or ten minutes to start is fine. Start small. Father Keating recommends twenty minutes twice a day.
2. *Get comfortable in a chair with your eyes closed and feet flat on the floor.* If you feel restless take a minute to breathe slowly to calm yourself.
3. *Gently place your sacred word into your mind and heart.*
4. *When thoughts enter your mind let them pass by. If you find yourself noticing them or looking at them, simply return to the sacred word.*
5. *Close prayer with a prayer of thanksgiving or the Lord's Prayer.*

SOME HELPFUL THOUGHTS

The editor of *The Cloud of the Unknowing* offers some words of advice: [25]

- Before prayer, "simply raise your heart to God with a gentle stirring of love" (chapter 5).
- Center all your attention and desire on him and let this be the sole concern of your heart (chapter 3).
- Distractions will come as you recall a person or a situation or a struggle. It's okay. Just ask God to bless the person or situation and gently return to your word or phrase (chapter 4).

I offer two other points to remember: (1) Expect distractions. When the distractions come, don't beat yourself. It's okay and part of being human. Relax. Just return to your word.

(2) Accept the fact that nothing may happen on a conscious level. Centering prayer allows God to work deep within us. We may not consciously experience anything. That's also okay. Centering Prayer allows us to access God dwelling in our depths. We can trust that God *is* working inside us. The fruits of this prayer come as God gradually transforms us into a new creation. Spending time with God in Centering Prayer helps in our ongoing transformation, as we open ourselves and our hearts to God in trust. Our part is to show up and make ourselves available. God will do the rest.

Finally, I close with some words from M. Basil Pennington about the goal of Centering Prayer (or any prayer, for that matter).

> In prayer we seek God. We do not seek peace, quiet, tranquility, enlightenment; we do not seek anything for ourselves. We seek to give ourselves, or, rather, we do simply give ourselves, even without attending to ourselves, so whole is our intent upon the one to whom we give: God. He is the all of our prayer. [26]

∼ Interlude ∼
Daily Transformations

Grrrrr . . . Ruff, ruff, rrrrrrrruffff!

Ever have one of those days when all you want to do is bark at the world? Days when insignificant events like a dropped glass or misplaced car keys foreshadow the frustration of things yet to come? Days, or maybe even weeks, when you're in an all out battle to remain patient, present, and understanding of others. Days when you long to trade in family or job for shiny new and perfect ones? Days when bark becomes bite as we nip away at our family, our coworkers, our friends? Nip, nip . . . *chomp!* These are the days when we sit defiantly on the principles of conversion of life, forget remaining open to God, forget practicing the presence of God. The Tools for Good Works? Not a chance! Arms crossed tight to our bodies, we sit defiantly on top of the mandates to love one another as Christ has loved us (John 13:34) and to serve the Lord with gladness (Ps 100:2). We glare at anyone who dares come too close.

Benedictine conversion of life asks us to remain open and accepting of life around us so that the Spirit of Christ can work its transforming power. Conversion of Life says to live as a follower of Jesus Christ. Put on his heart, his mind, his hands, and his eyes. Be present so that God can become more and more present in you. This is pretty hard to do when we're growling. The problem is that we can get stuck in growl-mode and can find it nearly impossible to break free.

I recall one growl-mode I fell into recently. The reason for it escapes me, yet I can clearly recall my mood. I was discouraged, frustrated, angry, tired, and barking. The sad thing is that while I was being discouraged, frustrated, angry, tired, and barking, I missed lots of wonderful things: enjoying the beauty of the day, having hope for the future, looking forward to conversations, taking pleasure in small tasks completed. And living fervently as a Christian, which the vow (or value) of conversion of life asks me to do.

When I get into these down-moods, I sometimes find my car taking me to a particular store. It's a place that sells sporting goods, skiing in the winter and hiking and golf in the summer. I try on shorts, pants, and tops that are light and wick away the moisture from your skin when you are on a vigorous hike. I could get these anywhere, but I go to this particular store because that is where Monica works. When I enter the store, Monica greets me with a big smile and warm hug. Seriously, has this happened to you in one of the megastores that dot the landscape? Not in my experience. After I spend time in the store—sometimes even finding a thing or two for my next hiking trip—I leave refreshed and ready to tackle the issues that don't seem so bad anymore after all.

My car also takes me visiting, sometimes to a homebound parishioner, like Marie. The most frequent word I heard Marie utter was "thanks." Gratitude permeated her whole outlook on life. I found this to be restorative. She also had the gift of helping people around her get another view of themselves. She saw people in a positive light, so people were able to see the positive in themselves. I'd leave Marie's with renewed hope in situations and in myself. Her death saddened me, yet I'm profoundly grateful that we shared time together.

When I think about Monica and Marie and so many other people in my life who hold out their hands to guide me through the darkness, I can clearly see the wisdom in Benedict's insistence on community. He realizes the value of people ministering to one another. We're healed by God through others. We're encouraged to keep trying. We can do this because we are helped by others. We can do this also because others are living examples for us.

Problems don't go away. What changes is our view of them. In Greek this is termed *metanoia*, or a turning around. We turn away from the dark to the light. Transformation happens—a mini-conversion of life.

Putting the Ideas into Practice

Benedictine conversion of life brings about a continual transformation within us. Every day we should let go of what is inside us that blocks our vision. I know that once I have left growl-mode, I can look back on what disturbed me and ask some questions.

- What bothered me and why?
- How might my growl-mode have been a call from God to change in some way?

Here are a few questions for your own reflection.

- What makes you growl?
- How does it impact your day? Your life?
- Have you had a similar experience with being in growl-mode and then being released? What was the situation and how was it resolved?
- What do you do to break the mood? Does this involve other people or are you by yourself?
- How might growling be related to fear?
- What are some of the ways that you might more fully trust God?

PART III

More Tools for Daily Life

W hile the Benedictine vows form the core of the Rule, St. Benedict also provides direction and inspiration for a Christ-centered life that touches on many other areas of day-to-day living. In this part of *St. Benedict's Toolbox*, we'll explore some of these teachings found in the Rule.

We'll first learn about the Divine Office, the corporate prayer services of Benedictine communities, and consider how this spiritual discipline might become part of our lives. Then we'll look at the Benedictine view of hospitality, work, and service, and explore how Benedict's ideas might help us. This part also includes chapters on how to keep a holy Benedictine Lent and how to develop our own rule of life.

Remember to use the exercises in the Toolboxes to help you put Benedict's teachings into practice. The appendix on pages 188–90 gives a complete list of all the tools.

CHAPTER 6

Walking through the Day with God
Praying the Divine Office

We believe that the divine presence is everywhere . . .
but beyond the least doubt we should believe this to
be especially true when we celebrate the divine office.
—FROM *THE RULE OF BENEDICT*, RB 19.1

The cornerstone of the Rule of Benedict is the Divine Office, also called *Opus Dei*, "the Work of God." Other names used are "the Daily Office" or "the Hours." *Office* is made up of two Latin words: *opus*, or "work," and *facere*, or "to do." *Officium* was used to mean "duty," as in moral or ethical behavior, or "what you're supposed to do."[1]

Praying the Divine Office is still the main work of each monk or nun under the Rule of Benedict. Beginning in the middle of the night, long before dawn, and running through to the evening, the community meets eight times to praise God and to ask for guidance and help. Benedictine spirituality puts great emphasis on this form of corporate prayer. To pray the Benedictine way, you and I need to establish some form of daily discipline of the Divine Office, in addition to our personal daily prayer and the constant recollection of God's presence in our lives.

The Divine Office first appeared in written format in the fourth century as a fully developed form. It showed strong influences from the Jewish synagogue and from private devotions. Like the synagogue service, it combined prayer, psalms, and readings.[2] The liturgy of the Divine Office consists primarily of psalms. In Benedict's day, Christians believed that Christ was present in Scripture in the same way that Christ was present in the Eucharist. Reading Scripture, whether the Old Testament or the New Testament, was an intimate communion with the Lord.

In the Rule, Benedict prescribes corporate prayer eight times in a twenty-four-hour period. The services, with their approximate times, are as follows.

Vigils: Middle of the night
Lauds: Predawn
Prime: "First" hour, 6 a.m.
Terce: "Third" hour, 9 a.m.
Sext: "Sixth" hour, noon
None: "Ninth" hour, 3 p.m.
Vespers: "Evening" hour, 6 p.m.
Compline: Before bed

Each hour is associated with a particular spiritual need such as praise, gratitude, obedience, blessings for us and for the world, commitment, forgiveness, vigilance, and so forth. Benedict carefully details the psalms to be used at these services, including canticles, responses, and hymns. Most of the service was chanted, a practice followed by many religious communities today. Let's take a look at one of these "hours" to see how they're structured, using the service of Lauds as found in chapters 12 and 13 of the Rule.

Benedictine Lauds

Introduction

Psalm 67 without refrain (said slowly so all can be present for the next psalm!)
Psalm 51 with refrain ("alleluia" refrain on Sundays)

Psalmody

Two variable psalms (selected psalms for specific days of the week) with refrain

Sunday:	Psalms 118	Psalm 63
Monday:	Psalm 5	Psalm 36
Tuesday:	Psalm 43	Psalm 57
Wednesday:	Psalm 64	Psalm 65
Thursday:	Psalm 88	Psalm 90
Friday:	Psalm 76	Psalm 92
Saturday:	Psalm 143	First part of Saturday Canticle

Canticles (poetic Scripture) and praises

Includes the *Benedicite*, the "Canticle of Three Young Men" on Sundays with refrain
Psalms 148/149/150 under a single refrain

Reading and concluding prayers

Lesson from the Epistles (Revelation on Sundays)
A responsory (text that moves between leader and congregation)
Ambrosian Hymns
Versicle (a verse usually coupled with a response by congregation)
Gospel Canticle—*Benedictus Dominus Deus Israel*
("The Song of Zechariah")

Litany (prayers)

Conclusion

The Lord's prayer recited aloud by the abbot.
Keep in mind that in Benedict's day everything would be recited by heart.

The importance of the Divine Office cannot be overstated. In chapter 19 Benedict states that God is everywhere, quoting from Proverbs: "The eyes of the Lord are in every place, watching on the evil and the good" (Prov 15.3 RB and Rule 19.1). But without any doubt, Benedict concludes, this is especially true when the Divine Office is said (Rule 19.2).

The remaining chapters on the Divine Office explain the liturgy to be used for the remaining offices. Benedict insists that the full 150 psalms be said each week. He considers these efforts tepid in comparison to the Holy Fathers, zealous and influential monks who lived before Benedict in the early time of monasticism, who completed these readings in a day (18.23–25).

Early in the sixteenth century, Thomas Cranmer condensed the Divine Office into two services of Scripture and prayer: Morning Prayer and Evening Prayer. He felt that the morning and evening services of lauds and vespers, popularly known as *matins* and evensong, were the principal offices for daily worship[3] and envisioned these services to be led by clergy in church. Today's Episcopal prayer book also contains a noonday prayer service, as well as a late evening service called Compline, which may be considered "descendents" of the early Divine Office.

The Gifts of the Divine Office

Perhaps the most important gift of the monastic life is that of imposing a framework of prayer on the pattern of daily life.[4]

Habitual Recollection of God's Presence

Whether or not we live in a religious community, the ideal toward which we strive is to be in continual prayer as we do all the activities of daily life. The Divine Office is a corporate expression of this continual prayer. In the midst of a busy day, it's a way to turn our thoughts intentionally to God. The Divine Office helps us establish the constant recollection of God by setting aside time to focus specifically on God throughout the day. Through the Office, God becomes the touchstone to all our work, rest, and play.

Yet the Divine Office is more than a remembrance of the moment. This "something more" is Holy Scripture. As we return to Scripture day after day in the Divine Office, we return to our source of truth. God speaks to us through Scripture, which keeps us from straying totally into our own moral and spiritual world. Scripture is a balance to our free-form and personal prayer.

Beginning, Focusing, Quitting

Another gift of the Divine Office is that it teaches us to begin, to be fully present, and to finish any task. These concepts of beginning, focusing, and ending are addressed in *The Rule of Benedict for Beginners* by Will Derkse. He explains that the art of beginning is both external and internal. "A true *beginning*," he says, "is difficult."[5] Prayer is to begin when the bell rings, even if the heart and mind are far from prayer . I can truly relate to this, not only in my prayer life but with other things as well. I sit down to pray and somehow a gong goes off in my head that calls my mind to wander. Before I know it, my thoughts have strayed from one subject to another. Although my body is at the appointed place of prayer, my mind is already at my desk at work. Or I'm at my desk studiously writing down things to do, when in actuality I'm inventing busywork that postpones a difficult phone call. Ever find yourself just staring out into space?

To let go of one thing and move into another can be a challenge. Yet the structure of Divine Office can help us hone the skill of beginning. When it's time for prayer we leave our task unfinished (horrors!) and turn to God.

Derkse also reminds us that while beginning is difficult, so, too, is quitting. I have a great tendency to just keep on working, forgoing breaks, striving to finish something in an unrealistic time frame, or, when a task is enjoyable, keeping at it much too long. Or, have you ever left a meeting but grumbled about it all the way home? The meeting may have been over but you definitely hadn't quit it.[6] I can relate to this, too.

Quitting means that we *live in the present moment* and *direct our thoughts to something positive* to help us do just that. The goal is to lay down whatever needs to be set aside with a good feeling. Let the meeting go! "The most important reason to quit something in the right manner is to begin something else with the right attitude."[7] We begin a task with our hearts, minds, and bodies; we end a task again with our hearts, minds, and bodies. What's in between—the task, the prayer, the Divine Office—we do with full attention.

In his chapter on the discipline of doing the psalms in the Divine Office, Benedict instructs that the psalms be sung standing, with mind in harmony with voice (Rule 19.7). In other words, be attentive. Our minds are to be in the present where we can find God. But being present can be just as challenging as beginning or quitting. One distraction can be the urge to finish. Have you ever been to a concert where, one by one, you've mentally checked off the pieces on the program as they were performed? Have you ever hurried to finish something to get on to the next thing? The problem is that if you and I focus our attention on finishing, then whatever we're doing doesn't get our complete attention, be it work or prayer or even recreation. Instead, give to whatever you do your "quiet and dignified" attention.[8]

The Divine Office gives us a gift of the repetition of a pattern—of first beginning the prayer, then focusing on it, and finally finishing it— that is part of the rhythm of doing the Office throughout the day. With the repeated call to prayer, we learn:

- to begin immediately what needs to be done
- to give the task our complete attention
- to let that attention be focused, quiet, and dignified
- to quit when we're finished[9]

A Blurring of Boundaries

Another gift of the Divine Office, or Hours, is that, over time, this way of praying begins to blur the boundaries between prayer and activity[10] as all become one with God. This unity with God is perhaps the greatest benefit to our life of frantic activity.

> We move from activity to rest to activity again, all in a consciousness that God is over us, alongside us, and in us. Our praying is cyclical and rhythmic. Rather than experiencing our existence as disjointed and unconnected, we feel a continuous flow as one hour is followed by the next.[11]

Immersing ourselves in the psalms of this liturgy will enable the very words of these psalms be with us in all circumstances of life. Frequently I find that a verse of a psalm will pop into my mind during the day as a response of praise or as a petition to God for help. This recollection of the psalms not only reconnects my thoughts to God, it also reminds me once again that all life can be prayer. An aim of monastic life is to "let the psalms become so much a part of one's consciousness that they surface unexpectedly, in response to the circumstances of daily life."[12]

The Holiness of All Things

In Benedictine spirituality everything is holy. When we pray the Divine Hours by using a form of morning or evening prayer or by recalling God intentionally at specific times throughout the day, we reinforce this idea of the holiness of all things. Our work and our prayer meld together so that work becomes prayer and prayer becomes less work. We'll discuss this more in chapter 9, when we explore the holiness of Benedictine work. As we pray throughout the day, we strengthen our relationship with God, learning to better hear and see God in all the circumstances of our lives.

An Invitation to a Deeper Relationship with God

The hours aren't magic; they won't prevent illness or tragedy or difficulties. They're not an escape from life's pressures but a way to gain strength to meet those pressures. The hours aren't an achievement but a way to gently hold us in the remembrance of God's presence. Through them, we turn attention from ourselves to God and open ourselves to a deeper relationship with God.[13] This deeper relationship will sustain us through life's challenges.

In *The Cloister Walk*, Kathleen Norris writes of the impact of saying the psalms three times a day with a Benedictine community during several prolonged stays as an oblate. She speaks of the way immersion in the psalms works a conversion from self-focus to God-focus.

> What the psalms offer us is the possibility of transformation, of converting a potentially deadly force such as vengeance into something better. What becomes clear when one begins to engage the psalms in a profound way—and the Benedictines insist that praying them communally, every day, is a good place to start—is that it can come to seem as if the psalms are reading and writing *us*. . . . I did begin to sense that a rhythm of listening and response was being established between me and the world of the psalms. I felt as if I were becoming part of a living, lived-in poem, a relationship with God that revealed the holy not only in ordinary words but in the mundane events of life, good and bad.[14]

Can We Pray the Divine Office Today?

There was a man in the fourth century named Arsenius who would raise his arms in prayer at sunset and wouldn't lower them until sunrise the next day, when he would prostrate himself before the "Risen Son."[15] Arsenius was indeed a spiritual athlete. My view, however, is this: for a twenty-first-century mother to pray the Divine Office would be a feat even greater than that of Arsenius!

Most of us are unable to find a community close by with whom we can pray the Office, let alone break away from busy schedules seven times a day to pray with devotion and intensity. Can we do a form of the Divine Office and reap the benefits it can bring to our lives?

It may seem that the demands are too great. Yet an important characteristic of the Rule can help us say, "Yes": there's no absolute model in Benedict's Rule. After going through the order of psalms for the Divine Hours in meticulous detail, Benedict closes by saying that whoever has a different idea of how to distribute the psalms should go ahead and do what he deems better (18.22). With this last point in mind, each of us should be moved to dip ever so slightly into the world of the Office. It's possible to adapt these prayers to our busy lives. See the Toolbox at the end of this chapter for some suggestions.

Keep in mind that it's best to start small. For example, if you're Episcopalian, you might begin by using one or more "hours" from the Daily Devotions in The Book of Common Prayer, which I've included as tool #2 in the Toolbox for this chapter. Or use a similar liturgy from your own denomination. The Episcopal Book of Common Prayer also has Morning Prayer, Noonday Prayer, Evening Prayer, and Compline. Any may be used. The Toolbox gives other alternatives. You can even use the Internet and pray on-line.

As you step into a practice of the Divine Office, be gentle with yourself. To be faithful to the Rule, I've started a practice of saying the hours using either The Book of Common Prayer, a series of books by Phyllis Tickle entitled *The Divine Hours: A Manual for Prayer*, or Judith Sutera's *Work of God: Benedictine Prayer*. I'd love to report rousing success, but, in chapter 4 of the Rule, "The Tools for Good Works," Benedict writes, "Do not be deceitful" (4.24). There are days when I forget to quit a task in order to say the Office. Sometimes I don't remember until evening. Sometimes I'm reading the Office with my mind elsewhere or I focus on finishing so I can get back to what I was doing.

Take heart. In the Rule, Benedict gives us two directives that indicate flexibility: Christians should pray daily and participate in corporate prayer. So, at the very least, if we don't have any form of regular prayer today, we can establish private prayer as a new and ongoing priority. And we can meet with our church community on Sundays or on other days to take part in corporate prayer.

One final thought: whether or not you and I can participate in communal prayer such as the Office, we *can* make it a priority to find moments throughout our day to conscientiously and lovingly recall our Creator.

> There is nothing more important in our own list of important things to do in life than to stop at regular times, in regular ways to remember what life is really about, where it came from, why we have it, what we are to do with it, and for whom we are to live it. No matter how tired we are or how

busy we are or how impossible we think it is to do it, Benedictine spirituality says, Stop. Now. A spiritual life without a regular prayer life and an integrated community consciousness is pure illusion.[16]

The Divine Office and Our Baptismal Covenant

As a part of the Episcopal Baptismal Covenant, we promise to continue in the apostles' teaching and fellowship, in the breaking of the bread, and in the prayers.[17] The efforts and discipline we exercise to meet with our community for corporate worship help us keep this promise. Even reading Morning Prayer or Evening Prayer or one of the smaller offices brings us into communion with the countless people throughout the world who are doing the same or a similar form of corporate prayer—an awesome thought. When we pray Noonday Prayers, we join not only Anglicans in this country and around the world, we also join with our sisters and brothers of other denominations and churches, lay and monastic, who are stopping other work of the day to pray as One Body in Christ.

As the Divine Office, in total or in part, becomes part of our daily routine, the time we spend with God, with one another, and in reflection shapes us and gives us the will and understanding to live the remaining questions of our Covenant with God.

TOOLBOX
Ways for Busy People to Pray the Divine Office

One of the most meaningful ways we can listen for God in our daily life is to spend some time with God in the ancient tradition of praying the Divine Office. While those in religious life return to the chapel for prayer throughout the day, those of us outside this life can still return to God throughout our day in an intentional way. How we choose to do this will depend on our life style, our style of spirituality, and even our technical savvy.

Various ways that the Office might be incorporated into your life are explained here. *The amount of time you spend each day is less important than your faithfulness in prayer.* Start with one thing that seems doable, given your willingness and your time. Once that's become part of your daily routine, consider adding another time for prayers. What I have found is that when I begin such a practice, God gives me strength to continue and even grow the practice.

The following suggestions are given in no particular order. One is not more worthy than the other. Look them over; then choose one that suits you.

Whatever forms you choose, praying the Office is life-changing because, more and more, your whole day will become prayer. Stopping regularly to praise God and to give thanks, even for a brief moment, will help you listen for and hear God in the daily life.

So what is next? Well, what time of day is it now, as you read? The next canonical hour is waiting. This framework of prayer pauses invites you to enter the stream of continuous remembrance of what is real: God's being with you and in you. The word "enjoy" comes to mind and suggests what can happen. You will enter a companionship that causes you to be in joy. This commonest of days is a sacrament of God, the visible form of invisible grace.[18]

Tool #1: Stop to Give Thanks

A simple way to begin a contemporary and abbreviated Daily Office is to stop what you're doing and give thanks at specific times during the day. How you organize this is up to you.

One way is to intentionally give thanks at these general times during the day: upon waking up, before breakfast, midmorning, noon, mid-afternoon, before dinner, and at the close of day. Another way might be to set a wristwatch alarm for the times between breakfast and dinner. When the alarm sounds, you stop what you're doing and offer a prayer of thanksgiving. Or pray in the car as you wait for your children or drive to work or to various appointments. Experiment with different plans and see what works for you.

In addition to spontaneous prayers of thanksgiving, you could also try reading using a psalm that expresses thanksgiving or praise. Here are a few that you could use:

Psalm 9	I will give thanks to the LORD with my whole heart …
Psalm 33	Rejoice in the LORD, O you righteous …
Psalm 34	I will bless the LORD at all times …
Psalm 47	Clap your hands, all you peoples …
Psalm 67	May God be gracious to us and bless us …
Psalms 96–98	Good psalms of praise …
Psalm 100	Make a joyful noise …
Psalm 138	I give you thanks, O LORD, with my whole heart …
Psalms 145–150	All great praise psalms!

Tool #2: Daily Devotions

The Book of Common Prayer is a wonderful resource for praying the Daily Office. Consider using "Daily Devotions for Families and Individuals" that begins on page 136. Offices are given for morning, noon, early evening, and the close of day. Do each small office or choose one or two.

For each of the mini-offices, read as shown. Or you may replace the Psalm and Reading with that found in the Daily Lectionary that begins on page 934, "Concerning the Daily Office Lectionary." Here you'll find a psalm and readings from Hebrew Scriptures, the Epistles, and the Gospels for each day of the year. There are two versions of the Daily Office Lectionary, Year One and Year Two. The Daily Office Year One is used when Easter is in an odd-numbered year. For example, in 2005 we use Year One Scripture. At Advent 2005, we move to Year Two.

If you don't have the Book of Common Prayer, you can use the liturgies for "Daily Devotions" that follow (pp. 137–40).

In the Morning

From Psalm 51

> Open my lips, O Lord, *
> and my mouth shall proclaim your praise.
> Create in me a clean heart, O God, *
> and renew a right spirit within me.
> Cast me not away from your presence *
> and take not your holy Spirit from me.
> Give me the joy of your saving help again *
> and sustain me with your bountiful Spirit.
>
> Glory to the Father, and to the Son, and to the Holy Spirit: *
> as it was in the beginning, is now, and will be forever. Amen.

A Reading

Blessed be the God and Father of our Lord Jesus Christ! By his great mercy we have been born anew to a living hope through the resurrection of Jesus Christ from the dead. *1 Peter 1:3*

A period of silence may follow.
A hymn or canticle may be used; the Apostles' Creed may be said.
Prayers may be offered for ourselves and others.

The Lord's Prayer

The Collect

Lord God, almighty and everlasting Father, you have brought us in safety to this new day: Preserve us with your mighty power, that we may not fall into sin, nor be overcome by adversity; and in all we do, direct us to the fulfilling of your purpose; through Jesus Christ our Lord. *Amen.*

At Noon

From Psalm 113

> Give praise, you servants of the LORD; *
> praise the Name of the LORD.

Let the Name of the Lord be blessed, *
from this time forth for evermore.
From the rising of the sun to its going down*
let the Name of the Lord be praised.

The Lord is high above all nations, *
and his glory above the heavens.

A Reading

O God, you will keep in perfect peace those whose minds are fixed on you; for in returning and rest we shall be saved; in quietness and trust shall be our strength. *Isaiah 26:3; 30:15*

Prayers may be offered for ourselves and others.

The Lord's Prayer

The Collect

Blessed Savior, at this hour you hung upon the cross, stretching out your loving arms: Grant that all the peoples of the earth may look to you and be saved; for your mercies' sake. Amen.

(or use this)

Lord Jesus Christ, you said to your apostles, "Peace I give to you; my own peace I leave with you:" Regard not our sins, but the faith of your Church, and give to us the peace and unity of that heavenly City, where with the Father and the Holy Spirit you live and reign, now and for ever. *Amen.*

In the Early Evening

This devotion may be used before or after the evening meal.

O gracious Light,
pure brightness of the everliving Father in heaven,
O Jesus Christ, holy and blessed!

Now as we come to the setting of the sun,
and our eyes behold the vesper light,
we sing your praises O God: Father, Son, and Holy Spirit.

You are worthy at all times to be praised by happy voices,
O Son of God, O Giver of life,
and to be glorified through all the worlds.

A Reading

It is not ourselves that we proclaim; we proclaim Christ Jesus as Lord, and ourselves as your servants, for Jesus' sake. For the same God who said, "Out of darkness let light shine," has caused his light to shine within us, to give the light of revelation—the revelation of the glory of God in the face of Jesus Christ. *2 Corinthians 4:5–6*

Prayers may be offered for ourselves and others.

The Lord's Prayer

The Collect

> Lord Jesus, stay with us, for evening is at hand and the day is past; be our companion in the way, kindle our hearts, and awaken hope, that we may know you as you are revealed in Scripture and the breaking of bread. Grant this for the sake of your love. *Amen.*

At the Close of Day

Psalm 134

> Behold now, bless the LORD, all you servants of the LORD, *
>   you that stand by night in the house of the Lord.
> Lift up your hands in the holy place and bless the LORD; *
>   the LORD who made heaven and earth bless you out of Zion.

A Reading

> Lord, you are in the midst of us and we are called by your Name: Do not forsake us, O Lord our God. *Jeremiah 14:9, 22*

The following may be said

> Lord, you now have set your servant free *
>   to go in peace as you have promised;
> For these eyes of mine have seen the Savior, *
>   whom you have prepared for all the world to see:
> A Light to enlighten the nations, *
>   and the glory of your people Israel.

Prayers for ourselves and others may follow. It is appropriate that prayers of thanksgiving for the blessings of the day, and penitence for our sins, be included.

The Lord's Prayer

The Collect

> Visit this place, O Lord, and drive far from it all snares of the enemy; let your holy angels dwell with us to preserve us in peace; and let your blessing be upon us always; through Jesus Christ our Lord. *Amen.*

> The almighty and merciful Lord, Father, Son, and Holy Spirit, bless us and keep us. *Amen.*

> (From The Book of Common Prayer, 1979, Episcopal Church USA[19])

Tool #3: Use the Daily Office in The Book of Common Prayer

Using The Book of Common Prayer of the Episcopal Church and the Daily Lectionary for Scripture, read Morning Prayer and/or Evening Prayer. You might do the complete Office or only part of the Office. The Canticles may be changed according to the Church Year; because of the length, I haven't included them here. The prayer book also includes beautiful liturgies for Noonday and for Compline, the last office of the day.

If you're from another denomination or church, explore your worship book and other resources from your church to find similar services of prayer for morning and evening.

Tool #4: Pray on the World Wide Web!

Yes, St. Benedict is now on the Web! You can log into a website and pray with others around the nation and around the world. Here are a few available at the time of writing.

www.missionstclare.com   This Episcopal-based site leads you through Morning or Evening Prayer. On the home page, choose a calendar, either to read on-line or to print. Then, on the calendar, click either Morning or Evening Prayer for today. Hymns and sung responses are also included. When you pray on-line, you can sing hymns and other parts of the liturgy accompanied by an organ. Noonday Prayer and Compline are taken from "Daily Devotions for Families and Individuals."

www.universalis.com   This is Roman Catholic–based liturgical prayer, with the psalms and readings for each hour of every day. The site includes morning and evening prayer and readings for the other hours. It's a bit more complicated but is doable.

www.liturgyhours.org   This site presents Morning, Evening, and Night prayer via Adobe Acrobat format.

www.satucket.com   This website provides lectionary resources for the Daily Office.

www.oremus.org   This website provides resources for prayer on the Internet, with daily prayer and other worship aids including hymns and liturgical texts. The site accesses other sites such as the Mission of St. Clare listed above.

www.gratefulness.org   This website provides a link to resources to help nurture gratitude, including brief nonscriptural readings and music for each of the eight hours from predawn to before bed. RealPlayer is needed. The following is taken from the website:

> Even in the midst of our busy, agenda-driven lives, we pause now and then to drink in the day's rhythms: the startling radiance of a sunrise, the power and heat of high noon, the peace of the evening's ending. Meeting the Angel of the Hour allows us to deepen this grateful response to the real rhythms of the day. European cathedral bells, Gregorian chant, and Fra Angelico's magnificent images accompany us as we embrace an ancient understanding of the word "hour": not as clock time, but as a measure of soul.[20]

Tool #5:   Pray through Work

Corinne Ware's *Saint Benedict on the Freeway* helps readers incorporate the Rule of Benedict and the Daily Office into contemporary life. It provides a version of the Hours that might be used or adapted to fit a daily schedule at work.

Vigils. If you're are awake at night, this would be an appropriate prayer. Use the darkness simply to be with God, aware of the Holy Presence in your quiet hours. Prayers can be simple.

Lauds. Wake to thank and praise God. Spend some time in prayer and contemplation.

Prime. Look over your to-do list for the day and ask God to be in all you do that day.

Terce. Midmorning is break time. Deeply breathe in God's spirit before returning to your morning's tasks.

Sext. At noon it's time to consider the whole world and its needs.

None. As you leave work and return home, let go of the day's events. Forgive and ask for forgiveness.

Vespers / Compline. Close the day with prayer and bedtime reading. Entrust your life to God until you greet the morning again with thanksgiving.[21]

Tool #6:   Purchase a Book to Guide You

Many wonderful books are now available that can guide you through Morning Prayer, Evening Prayer, and other Hours. Here are just a few.

The Divine Hours: A Manual for Prayer (Doubleday): Phyllis Tickle, an Episcopal author, has written three books providing morning, midday, and vesper offices for the entire year. She includes all readings and responsories for each day.

Work of God: Benedictine Prayer (The Liturgical Press): Judith Sutera, O.S.B., provides morning and evening prayers in a two-week cycle. Psalms and Scriptures are included.

Pray without Ceasing: Prayer for Morning and Evening (The Liturgical Press): This is an expanded version of *Work of God*, with morning and evening prayers for the Church year with music.

Prayer at Night's Approaching (Morehouse Publishing): Episcopal author Jim Cotter provides evening prayer for a one-week cycle. Prayers, Scripture, and responses are included.

Tool #7: **The Art of Beginning, Being Present, and Quitting**

Purpose of the Tool. To help you focus on what work is before you.

Background on the Tool. In *The Rule of Benedict for Beginners*, Will Derkse explains the importance of beginning a task immediately, being fully present to the task with a relaxed dignity and calm, and finally quitting that task.[22] Although the Daily Office can teach these skills, we can also practice them as we do our daily activities.

The Tool

Here are a few suggestions to help you become aware of how you focus on tasks as well as to hone your ability to begin, to be present to, and to complete each thing you do calmly and mindfully.

- First, reread "Beginning—Focusing—Quitting" found under "The Gifts of the Divine Office" in this chapter on pages 108–9.
- As you begin tasks or activities during the day, be aware of boundaries. Awareness is the first step to being able to establish clear boundaries between tasks. Is it hard for you to begin a task? As you move to a new task do you think about what you'd been doing before or what you'll do afterward? Do other thoughts interfere with your ability to concentrate on the task before you? Do you find it hard to set aside what you were doing before?

  If you catch yourself thinking about what you just did instead of what is before you, gently set aside the past activity and focus on the present.
- Assess whether or not you are fully present to the task or are just rushing to finish it. Do you hurry through what you need to do or are you calm and able to focus on each part of the task before you? Are you in the present moment or are you driving to completion?

  If you find yourself focusing on finishing, just become attentive to whatever you need to do at that very moment: dial a phone number, fold a towel, pull a weed, talk to a coworker. Take a deep breath or two. Relax. Let the task itself be the important thing.
- Assess whether you can finish a task and let it go.

  As you move to another task or situation do you find yourself looking back, being unable to let go of what just happened or what you just completed? If so, the remedy is the same: concentrate on the present moment, what you are doing *right now*. Whatever happened, or didn't happen, let it go. The sun will still rise and set and you'll have another chance. Try this prayer:

  > I leave the past with you.
  > I live the present for you.
  > I entrust the future to you.[23]

CHAPTER 7

Benedictine Hospitality
Hearts Overflowing with Love

> *Hospitality isn't about anything as simple*
> *as the best china, lace napkins, and crystal*
> *wineglasses. It might include those, but the*
> *real meaning of hospitality has to do with*
> *what one friend called "making room inside*
> *yourself for another person."*[1]

My first experience working in a soup kitchen was at St. Peter's Church in Morristown, New Jersey. Many things caught my attention: the dedication of the volunteers, the quantity of food served, the many people who came, the young families, the sense of community. But what struck me the most was that the volunteers called the people who came to the soup kitchen "guests"—not patrons, or attendees, or the poor, or even just "people." They were guests: guests of the soup kitchen and guests of all of us who prepared and served the meal.

I was moved by the way volunteers interacted with their guests. Many greeted each person, sometimes by name and sometimes in a foreign language. Some inquired in a friendly and open way how the guests were doing that day or, if it were especially hot or cold, asked the how they were managing that challenge. Many asked each guest with great courtesy what they'd like to be served and wished them a good lunch. The food was both a symbol of that care and tangible evidence that needs were being met. I saw patience as some guests needed or wanted special attention. I saw care and concern.

Respect, care, absence of judgment, encouragement, welcome, friendliness, ministering to the needs of others in the spirit of Christ: all these were found in the soup kitchen and all are a part of Benedictine hospitality. In this chapter we'll explore St. Benedict's ideas of hospitality, love, and forgiveness. As we do, we will reflect on how his ideas can apply to our lives.

What *Is* Hospitality?

When we think about hospitality, what comes to mind? Perhaps it's having friends over for a special dinner that we've spent time planning and preparing. We may use our best china with the coordinating silver and elegant crystal wineglasses or offer a relaxed and fun barbeque or party. We might prepare favorite foods for the children and even have fun activities for them so they'll enjoy the time together while the grownups converse around the table. Certainly this is hospitality. Yet hospitality can be so much more.

The word *hospitality* derives from the Latin word *hospitalitas*, which comes from the word *hospes* or *guest*. We show hospitality to others when we receive them as guests. We can receive people in this way every day, every hour, and not just for a meal. I can even show my hospitality to you as a guest by receiving you warmly into this book. (Hello and welcome again!)

Benedictine Hospitality

Benedict believes in hospitality. In Benedictine monasteries and convents, visitors are to be received promptly, with respect and in love. To do this, Benedict requires that someone always be available to greet a visitor. Find a brother who has some sense, Benedict says, and knows how to receive a message and relay a response; someone who is older and not apt to wander away. Give him a room by the door (66.1–2). Instruct him to greet all visitors with words like, "Thanks be to God" and to attend quickly to their needs with gentleness and warmth (66.3–4).

The utmost humility is shown to all guests regardless of their station in life, and every effort is to be made to make them feel welcome. The key to Benedictine hospitality is the recognition of Christ in each visitor.

> All guests who present themselves are to be welcomed as Christ, for he himself will say: *I was a stranger and you welcomed me* (Matt 25:35; RB 53.1).

Benedict says that the poor and pilgrims are to receive a special welcome because in them Christ is especially received (53.15). Benedict asks us to live a life of love and service, reaching out to others because we see Christ in everyone. So when you and I receive a guest at home, in a soup kitchen or in the seat next to us on an airplane, we are receiving Christ.

The truth is, however, that we can be manipulative and self-serving. We disregard another person's viewpoint. We consider others as annoyances that must be dealt with. We fail to see need around us. We close our fists and hold in our love. In short, we become self-protective and, in the process, miserable. Episcopal priest and author Elizabeth Canham reminds us "that people do not enter our lives to be coerced or manipulated, but to enrich us by their differences, and to be graciously received in the name of Christ."[2] Looking for Christ in others keeps us living according to the Gospels. Think about it: if we really thought the other person was Christ, would we not lovingly serve her or him? In your own mind, imagine if Christ came to the door and you received him into your home. Once overcoming your awe and astonishment and seeing that he would immediately put you at ease, how would you treat him? What words would describe the qualities that you would convey to our Lord? Words like warmth, love, appreciation, adoration, respect, and joy might come to mind.

When we acknowledge Christ in others we acknowledge the part of them connected to God in Christ. I know people who, when they meet someone new, will silently greet the Christ in the person. We are to honor and adore the Christ within each person. This is what Benedict describes as hospitality. He instructs the superior and all the brothers to receive each guest with charity and humility. Acknowledging and adoring the Christ within the visitor, they are to bow their heads or even prostrate their bodies completely (53.2, 6–7). For Benedict, care for the guests of the monastery is a manifestation of a monk's willingness not only to be obedient but to also be open (*conversion of life*) to what each guest, as Christ, might teach him.

Not only are we to *receive* Christ in others as guest; we are to *be* Christ to others. Esther de Waal suggests two questions that we might ask ourselves to see if we are doing both.

> Endless people encountered, a mass of entertaining, constant coming and going, countless numbers of people and at the end of all this activity St. Benedict faces us with two very simple questions: Did we see Christ in them? Did they see Christ in us?[3]

At the end of a busy day, we can ask ourselves these same questions: Did I see Christ in the people I was with today? Were they able to see Christ in me?

Hospitality and Community

We generally think of hospitality as something we give to guests. Yet we can learn to extend the same courtesies to family, friends, church community, and workplace. Once again Benedict gives us a model for hospitality in community.

The monastery cellarer is responsible for dispensing goods to the members of the community. In charge of everything as directed by the abbot (31.3–4), Benedict's cellarer is a quintessential example of hospitality. He dispenses food to each brother without keeping them waiting (31.16). If he can't meet a brother's request, he replies kindly, reminded in the Rule that a kind *word is better than the best gift* (31.13–14; Sir 18:17 RB). He shows special compassion and care for the sick, children, guests, and the poor and is accountable to God for the way he treats them (31.9).

The Rule assigns a decisive place to the dignity of the person. Not only does Benedict explain how guests are to be treated, he also will not push the monks in his community beyond their capacity. At a time when denial of physical needs was considered a sign of holiness, Benedict wanted to make sure everyone had the food and clothing they needed.

The basis for Benedictine hospitality is love and respect. Drawing from Romans 12:10, Benedict tells his monks that "they should each try to be the first to show respect to the other" (RB 63.17). The NRSV version of the Bible translates this as "outdo one another in showing honor." We can apply this to families, to church communities, to the workplace, and to friendships. "All members of the family must be brothers and sisters in Christ, all on equal footing, all respecting and honoring one another. . . . Love in equality must begin at home, whether that home is a monastery or not."[4] The result will be harmony, which was something that Benedict cares for a great deal.

> Benedict cared nothing for status, he could let himself be overruled; he cared very much for harmony and reconciliation, that his monks should agree among themselves.[5]

The bulk of the Rule is instruction for living in community. Benedict asks us to see Christ in the face of those we see every day. We're to be Christ to those we meet, both stranger and family. As Christ welcomed all people and accepted them as they were, so, too, we can love each person as they are, not just if they measure up to what we expect them to be. In *The Benedictines* Dom (a title for a monk in certain orders) David Knowles explains the need to accept people as they are in community.

> As a member of a family the Benedictine comes to realize that charity is often better than zeal and sacrifice; that it is ill quarreling in a small boat on a long voyage; that he must accept from his brothers what they have and not demand from them what they lack.[6]

Rather than focusing on their faults, we can practice hospitality by seeing the good in other people, accepting them just as Christ has accepted us. St. Augustine said, "Have Christian eyes."

We can also do what Henri Nouwen, noted spiritual author and priest, details in *Reaching Out*. He describes hospitality as a space around us that we create for others in which they can come, be themselves, and discover who they are.[7] Whether stranger or friend, we can take the person before us into this friendly and encouraging space. We can look on the visitor with hospitality, not as an interruption, but as a call from God to love and serve another. We can follow what Paul wrote in his Letter to the Romans: "Welcome one another, therefore, just as Christ has welcomed you, for the glory of God" (Rom 15:7).

This space we envision around us, filled with love, care, and acceptance, will allow people to be free to see their God-given worth and gifts. It is truly a gift for others. Can you recall an individual in your own life who has created such a space for you? My experience is, in the presence of such a person, my self-worth and energy were rekindled even on the toughest of days.

I read *Reaching Out* when I was still working at AT&T. Just as in any workplace, there were people who I found frustrating, new people as well as long-time coworkers. I began to practice this discipline of imagining an empty space around myself. I started to mentally reach out to people in a welcoming and inviting way. I quieted my mind so that I could listen to *them* instead of wanting to make them listen to *me*. If there was a difference of opinion, I'd hear them out, doing my best to be fully present to them. The results of creating a welcoming space were amazing. My relationships with others, especially those with whom I contended, were better. I felt better. People felt accepted.

Isn't that what we all want—to be accepted, respected and loved?

Benedictine Balance: Hospitality and Solitude

An important part of Benedictine hospitality is that it balances the needs of the community with the needs of the individual. While monks are to show hospitality to guests and strangers, Benedict sets limits that respect the needs of the monks and life in the community (chapter 53). This reminds us that while we respect others and care for them, we also need to respect ourselves and care for our own needs. Too often immersing ourselves in the needs of others can lead to resentment. Benedict has us strike a balance; even Jesus went off by himself to pray and to refresh his spirit.

The balance of Benedictine hospitality and self-respect reveals that Benedict realized that human beings need time together and time alone. We need a balance of community and solitude. Esther de Waal writes that "the time for me to re-create myself is amongst the most urgent of all my needs. Only as I find time to live with myself and to love myself will I be able to live with others and love them as they need to be loved."[8]

Love and Hospitality

The teaching of Jesus could be summed up in one word: *love*. We are to love God and our neighbor as ourselves. The entire Rule of Benedict could also be summed up in this same word. Love is the underlying motivation for all the actions that Benedict describes for his monks and for us. Everything in the Rule points to Christ and to the Christlike love that we are to model in our lives. This indeed is as countercultural today as it was in Benedict's time. Benedict says,

Your way of acting should be different from the world's way; the love of Christ must come before all else. You are not to act in anger or nurse a grudge. Rid your heart of all deceit. Never give a hollow greeting of peace or turn away someone who needs your love (RB 4.20–26).

The Rule is "lived-out love,"[9] in the context of daily life and work. Benedict devotes a section of the Rule on mutual obedience as a way to show this love to others. The monks are to be obedient not only to the abbot but also to one another (71.1).

They should each try to be the first to show respect to the other (Rom 12:10 RB), supporting with the greatest patience one another's weaknesses of body or behavior, and earnestly competing in obedience to on another (RB 72.4–6).

They are to pursue what they judge better, not for themselves, but for others and to "show the pure love of brothers" (RB 72.7–8). "The Tools for Good Works," found in chapter 4 of the Rule and discussed in chapter 5 of this book, provide many other ways to show love by the way we treat one another.

One of the challenges is that the need for hospitality often comes when we're most occupied with other concerns. We're busy at home and a child runs to us with a picture scribbled in crayon, seeking our undivided attention and praise. We're at work frantically writing a report that's due today and a coworker hurries into our office, asking us to listen to some concern. What to do? Our choice to provide hospitality becomes a direct response to God's call to serve a person in need. It is an opportunity to practice Benedictine obedience, listening, and responding to God's call. When our hearts are "overflowing with the inexpressible delight of love" (RB Prologue 49), we will become more open to the situations in which God calls us to act. We'll set aside our plans and respond to one another with gracious hospitality and Christlike love.

When these interruptions happen to me, I often recall the story of Jesus after hearing of the death of John the Baptist. He'd gone alone by boat to a deserted place, but the crowd, hearing where he'd gone, followed him. We read in Matthew that when he came ashore and saw them "he had compassion for them" (Matt 14:13–14). This is the kind of compassion that you and I are to show. Esther de Waal writes, "The central message that I learn from St. Benedict is that Christ is the model for all our loving. It is in and through him that our loving must take place."[10]

Hospitality, Love, and Forgiveness

Forgiveness is key in Benedictine love and spirituality and critical to life in community. Benedict includes the Lord's Prayer in Lauds and Vespers, the prayer services that come at the beginning and at the end of the day, "because the thorns of contention are likely to spring up" (RB 13.12). His rationale is this: "Thus warned by the pledge they make to one another in the very words of this prayer: *Forgive us as we forgive* (Matt 6:12 RB), they may cleanse themselves of this kind of vice" (RB 13.13).

In the chapter "The Tools for Good Works," Benedict gives repeated instruction on forgiveness, often quoting verses from the New Testament:

Love your enemies (Matt 5:44 and Rule 4.31).

If you quarrel with someone, make peace with him before sunset (Rule 4.73).

Do not repay one bad turn with another (1 Thess 5:15 RB; 1 Pet 3:9 RB; and Rule 4.29).

The content of the Rule models forgiveness. For example, when explaining the disciplinary procedures for mistakes in the chapel, in the kitchen, in serving, or for failure to follow the Rule, Benedict insists that repentant brothers are to be readily forgiven (Rule chapters 44–46).

"Forgiveness is the greatest factor for growth in any human being."[11] When we chew over past resentments, past hurts, and past slights, lack of forgiveness hurts us more than the person we can't forgive. Our relationships with God and with others suffer, too. Lack of forgiveness saps energy, creates black holes of negativity, and takes up too much of our time. If we're to live, as Benedict says, with death before our eyes, we need to recognize that we must live fully *now*. Each day is precious and forgiveness is a path to whole and healthy living. Forgiveness builds up. Grumbling tears down. Forgiveness leads to freedom.

The truth is that sometimes all we can do is to pray for the *desire* to forgive. Yet, that is a beginning.

Discipline and Forgiveness

Although disciplinary measures are explained carefully, Benedict's underlying goal is forgiveness and reconciliation with any wayward brother. Yet for the protection of the monk and his soul as well as for the community as a whole, the Rule offers specific steps for each area to be disciplined. Even grumbling can be punished. From rebukes, to excommunication, from meals and prayers, to physical punishment, the abbot would determine the degree of the reproof to be employed. The abbot is to be especially concerned for brothers who have difficulty following the Rule. In a spirit of hospitality he is to recognize that he has care of souls that are sick (27.6) and to model the Good Shepherd who leaves the ninety-nine in the wilderness and goes after the one sheep that is lost (Luke 15:4 and Rule 27.8). Benedict cites a passage from Matthew's Gospel to explain the abbot's mindset as he makes decisions regarding punishment: "Those who are well have no need of a physician, but those who are sick" (Matt 9:12 and Rule 27.1). The abbot is to treat the wavering brother with the skill of a wise physician. Older and more mature brothers could be sent to unofficially talk to the wayward brother, to encourage him to humbly make amends and to comfort him so that he may not be "overwhelmed by excessive sorrow" (2 Cor 2:7 NRSV and Rule 27.2–3). Benedict instructs the other monks to pray for the errant monk, again emphasizing the desire not for punishment but for reconciliation.

If a monk refuses to make amends, the punishment increases in intensity to include, for example, beatings (28.1). Though this seems harsh to us, Benedict was concerned that such a sheep might "infect the whole flock" (RB 28.8). The last step is the surgeon's knife: the monk would be asked to leave. Benedict again draws on Scripture and says, "Drive out the wicked person from among you" (1 Cor 5:13 and Rule 28.6). The door may not be shut, however. According to the Rule, brothers who leave and want to come back can be readmitted up to three times (29.3). Benedict was willing to give his brothers repeated opportunities for forgiveness and reconciliation. You and I might pause for a moment and consider if we're willing to do the same.

Hospitality and Good Zeal

The word *zeal* derives from the Greek *zelos* or *zeal*. This word occurs in the New Testament as both a positive and a negative attribute. In its negative sense, *zeal* can mean jealousy, passion, fervor, or ambition. This is what Benedict would term as "wicked" or "evil zeal," which separates us from God (72.1). It's self-serving, lacking in moderation, and void of consideration for others. Benedict asks us to practice instead what he calls "good zeal," which draws us to God and to eternal life (72.2).

Good zeal is rooted in hospitality. It means supporting one another without murmuring or grumbling. It also means giving "oneself to others with joy, to seek what is agreeable to one's neighbor, to console [them], to cheer [them]—such is the true zeal of charity."[12] Benedict encourages his followers to practice this "good zeal" that is fostered by energetic love (72.3). He describes good zeal in action: showing mutual respect, being patient with one another's weaknesses, outdoing one another in showing obedience, pursuing the best for the other rather than for oneself, loving others, and fearing God (72.4–9).

The bottom line for hospitality is this: good zeal is marked by a deep consideration for others. But most importantly we must "prefer nothing whatever to Christ" (72.11).[13]

Hospitality and Justice

Benedictine hospitality is also concerned with issues of justice. Our hospitality is to extend beyond family, beyond neighborhood, beyond church, and beyond our local community. We're to seek Christ in far-reaching places of poverty and loneliness, extending hospitality in concrete ways. Hospitality says that the issues of the poor are *our* problem and that we must take steps for positive change in the lives of others. Hospitality is a call to action.

> Benedictine hospitality is more than simply thinking new thoughts or feeling new feelings about people we either thought harshly of before or, more likely, failed to think about at all. Benedictine hospitality demands the extra effort, the extra time, the extra care that stretches beyond and above the order of the day.
>
> Real hospitality for our time requires that, instead of flipping the channel or turning the page, we try to determine what it is about our own lives that is affecting these others. We have to wonder how we can help the poor at the doorstep who live thousands of miles away. Hospitality says that the problem is mine, not someone else's. It is my door and my heart upon which these people are knocking for attention.[14]

Benedictine hospitality must extend beyond family and friends to the world. We who have been given the resources of education, money, and freedom can use those gifts to help the impoverished and forgotten in this country and abroad. We can be the voice that calls for justice and equity.

Benedictine hospitality extends to the earth as well. The Benedictine tradition of agriculture and animal husbandry points to the care of creation. I would like to share a contemporary example. The Abbey of Regina Laudis, founded in 1947 in Bethlehem, Connecticut, is a community of contemplative Benedictine women dedicated to the praise of God through prayer and work. They chant the Eucharist and full Divine Office each day, while expressing the traditional Benedictine commitment to manual work and scholarship through contemporary media and professional disciplines. On about 400 acres of both wild and cultivated land, including a noncommercial working farm, professionally operated by the community, the nuns of the abbey raise dairy and beef cattle, swine, sheep, and oxen, with a developing specialty in breeds that need conservation. They're concerned with forest management, erosion control, recycling, waste management, and water quality. On their website they explain their focus on conservation and environment:

> The degree of reverence for creation mandated by St. Benedict sets a standard that has made Benedictines environmentally conscious from the beginning of their history. Some areas of the abbey land are especially designated "Environmental-Historical Preserve," which means they are reserved as part of the monastic enclosure, but also that they hold significant historical landmarks or contain fragile environments, such as wetlands or wildlife habitats that need to be protected.[15]

This community strives to consider all the aspects of the land as interdependent. Whatever they do with the land, they take into consideration both neighbors around them and in their region. Check their website at www.abbeyofreginalaudis.org.

The Benedictines of Regina Laudis know that we are guests in God's world, stewards of its resources, called upon to treat with reverence all that is given to enhance life. "Our commitment to reduce waste, recycle, and reuse where possible is evidence of our gratitude to the Creator and our respect for others."[16] We need to not only respect one another but respect the earth as well for all has been given to us as gifts from God.

Hospitality in the Twenty-first Century

The model of Benedictine hospitality outlined in the Rule provides a way to be Christ's welcoming servants today as both "receivers and givers of grace."[17] I'd like to share an example. Last summer, at the end of a hectic day, I was tired and anxious to get home. As I stepped out through the church door, I realized that the homeless family who was staying with us at the church must have arrived for the evening. (Each summer we housed families as a part of the Interfaith Hospitality Network in our county.) I thought, "I should go down and greet them and see how they're doing, but I really don't feel like it." Knowing that it was important that the family knew we cared, my sense of responsibility (obedience) won out. I wearily trudged down the steep stairs to the church basement, asking God to help me effervesce when I felt pretty uninspired. Walking into the room, I was greeted by the glad voices of mother and children. After hugs all around I sat down and spent fifteen or twenty minutes with them, inquiring about their day and talking about all sorts of things. When I got up to leave, I was a different person. I felt refreshed and energized. Had I just had a vacation and didn't know it? In truth my reluctant offer of hospitality was repaid tenfold. What small grace I felt that I gave poured back onto me as a wave of love.

All we need to do is to make that space of hospitality around us, as Henri Nouwen suggested, and to keep our eyes, ears, and hearts open to what God would have us do. When our center rests in God, we can empty ourselves as Christ did (Phil 2:7) and become free to replace hostility with hospitality. Then we can welcome friends or strangers as Christ at that moment and receive the surprising gifts that they bring.

We are often far from this today. We're often reluctant take time to be truly present to others, and we can find it difficult to accept people as they are. Yet, with our families, in our circle of friends, in the church, at work—and with Christ's help—we can set aside our agendas and our expectations about people. We can instead make room inside ourselves for others, one person at a time. We can provide a space of hospitality into which others may freely enter and feel safe because they know they're accepted. We can meet our families and friends, strangers and guests "with expanded hearts and unspeakable sweetness of love."[18]

Benedictine Hospitality and Our Baptismal Covenant

When we practice Benedictine hospitality we are putting into action the promises that we make in these three questions from our Baptismal Covenant:

- Will you seek and serve Christ in all Persons, loving your neighbor as yourself?
- Will you proclaim by word and example the Good News of God in Christ?
- Will you strive for justice and peace among all people, and respect the dignity of every human being?

Our Covenant reminds us that not only are we to *see* Christ in others, we are to *seek out* Christ in the lives and faces of those around us. Love makes this possible. We're reminded also of Benedict's instructions to be hospitable to ourselves, loving ourselves enough to take the time and effort to "replenish the well," and tend to our own physical, emotional, and spiritual needs. And as we seek Christ in others, so, too, are we to be Christ to others.

We're to be justice keepers and peacemakers, and to respect each human being as a child of God. Benedictine hospitality provides us a way to fulfill this promise.

Hospitality: The Gift of Presence

Hospitality is an incredible gift that we can give one another. It all begins when we can be truly present to another person. When we are present, focusing on the person before us or acknowledging the need of people who live far from us, we become channels for the Spirit of Christ. This is what I saw in soup kitchen volunteers as they served the both the physical and emotional needs of the guests. To be channels for the Spirit is what I pray for all of us.

TOOLBOX
Benedictine Hospitality

Benedict asks for a life of love and service, reaching out to others because we see Christ in everyone. Imagine if we began to treat each member of our family or religious community as if he or she were Christ? What if we did that at church? What if we looked at our coworker as if he or she were Christ? How would that change our relationships, our actions, our thoughts, and our hearts?

This section of the Toolbox gives some suggestions about how you can practice hospitality and develop the eyes that see others as Christ.

Tool #1: Becoming an Instrument of God's Peace

Purpose of the Tool. To provide a way of becoming an instrument of God's peace through prayer.

Background on the Tool. Benedict's Rule forms a way of life based on hospitality and love. This means that you and I are to be peacemakers in our relationships and in our communities.

The steps to becoming a peacemaker, like most anything else, begin with prayer. In prayer we declare before God our intention and desire to be a person who seeks harmony in our relationships. We pray for the ability to become Christ's channel and voice in our communities, home, friendships, church, and workplace. We open ourselves to God's transforming power.

The Tool

Perhaps there is no better prayer for expressing both our intention to be a peacemaker and the actions of peacemaking than the one attributed to St. Francis.

> Lord, make me an instrument of your peace.
> Where there is hatred, let me sow love;
> where there is injury, pardon;
> where there is discord, union;
> where there is doubt, faith;
> where there is despair, hope;
> where there is darkness, light;
> where there is sadness, joy.
>
> O Divine Master, grant that
> I may not so much seek to be consoled as to console;
> to be understood as to understand;
> to be loved as to love.

For it is in giving that we receive;
it is in pardoning that we are pardoned;
and it is in dying that we are born to eternal life. Amen.[19]

Pray this prayer every day. Watch for opportunities to sow the good seeds of peace! To practice sowing these seeds, take one element from the prayer—love, pardon, faith, hope, joy, and so on—and focus on this element for a day, a week, or another period of time. Then move to another seed.

Sow the seeds of peace, love, and pardon in your family. Sow the seeds of light and joy at work or at school. Sow the seeds of faith and hope at church, at the supermarket, or the gas station. Scatter these seeds of beauty every day wherever you are and the goodness you sow will grow in the hearts of those you touch.

Don't forget that you might need these seeds sown in your heart, too!

Tool #2—Tool #4: Putting Hospitality into Practice

Purpose of the Tools. To provide some ways to practice hospitality.

Background on the Tools. Every day there are opportunities for us to hear God's voice calling us to welcome others into our hearts by listening to others, by respecting them, by ministering to their needs, and by caring. When we practice hospitality, we become co-creators with God in making a more loving and equitable world.

The Tools

Here are suggestions for practicing and developing your hospitality skills. The ideas are organized into four areas covering hospitality to those who are near or far, to the earth, and within families.

We first need "a heart overflowing with love," so be sure to include the Prayer of St. Francis in your daily prayer. This prayer is included in Tool #1 above.

Tool #2: Hospitality to Those Who Are Near

- **Be present to others.** The greatest gift you can give others is your presence. This is an important way to practice hospitality. When you give others your full and complete attention you welcome them into your life. They know they're respected and cared about even if they're strangers or casual acquaintances.

   Being fully present often takes great patience and understanding. So, as Christ emptied himself to become human (Phil 2:7), you will need to empty yourself of whatever is pulling you away. These may be pressures such as responsibilities, a need to control, or to hurry another person along. Whatever distracts you, ask God to help you concentrate on the person before you right at that moment. Ask God to help you listen for who God needs you to be for that person.

- **Expect interruptions.** The opportunities for hospitality happen on God's timetable, not ours. Be flexible. The most important work we have to do each day is with the people Christ brings to us. Be open to interruptions for that is where life happens!

  We often encounter opportunities to make room in our schedules, in ourselves, for another person. Yet the moment can come and go quickly. Consciously be aware when someone needs a moment of kindness, a little attention, a gracious gesture. Do this both at home and at work.[20]

- **Receive the other as Christ.** When you meet someone, be it a friend or someone new, greet the Christ within that person. You can even imagine that you are talking to Christ. How does that change your interaction? Remember that seeing Christ and serving others as Christ is not about *them*, it is about *ourselves*. When you and I choose to look on a stranger, a family member, a member of our community, a church member, a coworker, or a person who serves us in a store as Christ, we don't change them; we change ourselves! We allow God to sanctify our own lives.

- **Create a free space for hospitality.** Instead of viewing the stranger with fear, ambivalence, or hostility, we can "create a free space where the stranger can enter and become a friend instead of an enemy."[21] Henri Nouwen says, "To convert hostility into hospitality requires the creation of a friendly empty space where we can reach out to our fellow human beings and invite them to a new relationship."[22]

  The challenge is that usually the space around us is occupied! Our busyness and activity, our concerns and desires, and our self-preoccupation take up this space. We need to be willing *to be silent* and to set these things aside so that we can both provide a free, open, and friendly space for others, and also be free to receive the gifts they bring to us.

  Creating this space requires an inner conversion that can't be manipulated. Yet even though this conversion must develop from within, we can still take some steps:

  1. Pray for God to create this empty space within you.
  2. When you meet a stranger, imagine a friendly, empty space around yourself. Look on the stranger with eyes of hospitality. Be open to them and even curious about the gift they may be ready to give you. Allow them to be themselves and to discover who they are in your presence.

3. Imagine this friendly open space with people you know well, such as family and friends. Carry this space into the workplace, the church, the supermarket, the roadways.

- **When you feel like escaping, remember stability and obedience.** There will be times when you'd rather run than practice hospitality. When this happens, remember the Benedictine vow of stability: *stay put!* Then move into the vow of obedience: *listen* and *respond.* Ask God to help you listen to how you are to be a co-creator through your hospitality.

   Recognize, too, that there may be times when you don't have the energy or wherewithal to be hospitable. But before fleeing physically or mentally, give it a try. Remember that when the Lord went off to rest, the crowds followed him. He must have been tired and wanted to be alone, yet he had compassion on the people who followed him and attended to their needs (see Mark 6:30–34).

- **Hospitality need not be a huge event.** If hospitality means making room for another person, even in small ways, what could you do differently to become a more hospitable person?[23]

- **Be hospitable to yourself, too.** Jesus said, "[L]ove your neighbor as yourself" (Mark 12:31). Take time to care for yourself in body, mind, and spirit.

Tool #3: Hospitality to Those Who Are Far

- **Read and think about the section entitled "Hospitality and Justice,"** found in this chapter on pages 128–29.

- **Participate in outreach programs that bring you face to face with the stranger.** Practice hospitality outside the circle of family and friends. Volunteer in a soup kitchen or shelter. Bring food to those in need. Help with projects that house the homeless. Share your skills by being a mentor. Work on a Habitat for Humanity site. All these and more are ways to extend our hospitality and co-create a better world with God.

- **At least once every three months participate in activities that address injustice.** Participate in activities such as the Bread for the World Offering of Letters. "Bread" advocates working through the government for the poor and impoverished of this country and worldwide, through the organization and through letter-writing campaigns done by citizens such as you and me. Their website is www.bread.org. For nontechies, they may be reached at 1-800-82B-READ (1-800-822-7323).

Another organization is Oxfam International. Oxfam is a confederation of twelve organizations working together in more than 100 countries to find lasting solutions to poverty, suffering, and injustice. Oxfam campaigns for policy and practice change on fair trade, conflict and humanitarian response, and on issues such as debt relief, arms trade, poverty reduction, and universal basic education. Their web address is www.oxfam.org and their phone number is 1-617-482-1211.

Amnesty International (AI) is a worldwide movement of people who campaign for internationally recognized human rights. Their mission is to do research and take action focused on preventing and ending grave abuses of human rights worldwide. In their work to promote human rights, they focus on the right to physical and mental integrity, freedom of conscience and expression, and freedom from discrimination. The site details ways to become involved. Their web address is www.amnesty.org and their phone number is 1-212-807-8400.

Many other sites can be found on the Internet. I typed "Advocacy Organizations" and did a Google search, which brought up *many* references. I found a helpful Google-sponsored site that listed major categories for advocacy organizations such as consumer activism, environment, human rights, seniors, women, and so on. Choosing a main category will bring a screen dedicated to that area, from which an even more detailed selection can be made. websites for specific organizations can be accessed from any of the screens. The initial list can be accessed through the following:

http://directory.google.com/Top/Society/Organizations/Advocacy/.

Remember to also explore organizations that are funded through your denomination or church.

- **Be aware of how your life connects with others. Are the consequences good or bad?** In *Wisdom Distilled from the Daily*, Sr. Joan Chittister writes that Benedictine spirituality asks us to recognize our connectedness with others and to be mindful of the impact of our decisions and habits on people we can't see. She provides the list below and asks us to consider how what you do in each area is connected to the world and other people.[24]

In the list that follows, underline those areas of your life in which it's easiest to see the consequences of your actions. Circle areas in which it's most difficult. This is not an evaluation of how you perform each of the following; instead, look at whether or not you're aware of the consequences to others of your decisions and actions.

my daily work
what I eat and how I prepare it
the clothes I wear
the way I spend my money
where I live
what I do with my free time
how I raise my children
the way I garden and care for my yard
the form of transportation I use
the way I exercise my political rights
where I shop
my involvement with my church or religious community
my volunteer activities
the way I invest my money[25]

For those areas in which you have trouble knowing the consequences, seek out information to help you understand the impact. A place to start is the organization Co-op America. Co-op America, a national nonprofit organization founded in 1982, provides the economic strategies, organizing power, and practical tools for businesses and individuals to address today's social and environmental problems. This organization can help us see the impact of where and how we spend our money. Information can be found at www.coopamerica.org or by contacting the organization directly at 202-331-8166.

• **Share!** Sister Joan writes that "hospitality is the act of giving what you have to everyone in sight. . . . It is an act of the recklessly generous heart."[26] So, empty your life of things that you don't need and share them with others. Clean out your closets and drawers. Bring things to a thrift shop where people who have less than you can purchase them for a small price. Share with those in need.

Tool #4: Hospitality to the Earth

• **Recycle, recycle, recycle.** If you're already recycling, think of ways that you can expand what you are doing. Help others to recycle.

• **Repair instead of purchase.** Conserve resources by checking if a broken item can be repaired.

• **Share instead of throwing away.** Instead of throwing things away, give them away. What you may no longer use may be just what another person has been needing.

• **Be respectful of the earth and its creatures.** Practice common courtesies toward the earth. Do not litter. Pick up litter when you find it. Do not disturb wildlife. Do not kill.

- **Conserve usage of resources.** Do not recklessly use resources like energy, water, and so on.

- **Buy only what you need.** Avoid frivolous buying. Conserve resources by buying only what you need. When you wish to make a purchase, ask yourself if the purchase comes from want or from need. Then make an informed decision.

- **Contact environmental organizations for information and ideas.** There are many organizations that are focused on providing ways to be hospitable to our beautiful planet. The Earthwatch Institute (www.earthwatch.org and 1-800-776-0188) engages people world-wide in scientific field research and education to promote the under-standing and action necessary for a sustainable environment. The National Resources Defense Council (www.nrdc.org and 1-212-727-2700) is a nonprofit organization that uses law, science, and the sup-port of members to protect the planet's wildlife and wild places and to ensure a safe, healthy environment for all living things. They can provide information on many environmental issues. Many other organizations may be located on the Internet through the Google site that is mentioned under Tool #3 in this Toolbox.

Tool #5: Hospitality in the Family

- **Talk to your children about hospitality.** Describe what hospitality looks like and why it is important. Help children find ways to prac-tice hospitality. Consider hospitality to pets, too.

- **Consciously practice hospitality.** Discover ways that you can prac-tice hospitality in your family. Be respectful of family members. Be ready to respond to their needs. Give them your undivided atten-tion. Be flexible. The most important work of the day is what you do and who you are in your relationships.

  Have a "Hospitality Day" where all members of the family prac-tice the fine art of hospitality.

- **Receive your family member as Christ.** Greet the Christ within each member of your family when they come home or when you come home. Imagine your child is Jesus as a child (Mary and Joseph probably had to discipline him, too, at least on some level!) Imagine that you're preparing dinner for Christ or taking care of yard work for Christ.

- **Extend hospitality to others as a family.** Welcome guests to your home. Bake cookies for a shut-in. Provide a small meal for someone who is ill or has just experienced a death in the family. Work together in a soup kitchen. Think of other ways your family could show hos-pitality to those outside your immediate circle of family.

- **Hospitality sometimes means letting someone be alone.** There are times when members of our family just need some time by themselves. This is true for children as well as for parents. Practice hospitality by allowing this solitude.

- **Be fully present to your family at mealtimes.** During meals, give your family the gift of your full presence. It's hard because you may be thinking about the day ahead or ruminating on what happened during the day. When you find yourself somewhere else, gently draw yourself back to your loved ones.

- **Be a recipient of hospitality.** Allow others to minister to you. Thank them.

Tool #6: Practicing Forgiveness

Purpose of the Tool. To establish a conscious practice of forgiveness.

Background of the Tool. In chapter 4 of the Rule, "The Tools of Good Works," Benedict again points toward reconciliation and the preservation of strong community made possible by selfless and loving interactions between people. We're all familiar with this truth: when we don't forgive, we hurt ourselves more than the other person. Even praying for the desire to forgive will be a step toward restoration of wholeness within ourselves and with others.

The Tool

There are two parts to this tool: (1) an ongoing practice tool and (2) a specific situation tool.

1. The Ongoing Practice of Forgiveness
There are two words to keep in mind for this tool: *let go.* Things happen every day that annoy us, hurt us, frustrate us, or make us angry. As they do, evaluate them and let go of the things that, in the end, really aren't critical. We can drive ourselves crazy by being "legalists" or by expecting too much of others. We can keep in mind, too, that our actions might just annoy, hurt, frustrate, or make someone else angry! So, practice forgiveness in the present moment. Each day be willing to let some things go.

2. A Specific Situation Needing Forgiveness
 . . . why keep a wound open when forgiveness can close it?"[27]
In our past or in our present, most of us have someone we can't forgive. We may not even be at the point where we even would consider forgiveness. For me these things are like large walls covered with tangled vines of thorns—impossible to climb over. These walls trap me in a dark,

moldy prison where I'm not at peace nor can I be myself. There's just no freedom. The way out is through letting go and forgiving.

Take a moment to name a person or situation that is like this for you. Now, when you think of this person or situation, how do you feel inside? Name this feeling or feelings.

No good, right? If you'd like to begin anew and gain some freedom, begin to open yourself to forgiveness.

- Pray for a forgiving heart.
- Pray The Lord's Prayer using that person's name.[28]
- Pray for the ability to separate the sin from the person.
- Begin a process of reconciliation through a letter, phone call, or visit.
- Keep your efforts focused on yourself. Place no expectations on the other person.
- Be willing to also forgive yourself.

Forgiveness can be a long process but a process where each step brings an increase of peace and freedom.

⤳ *Interlude* ⤳
Welcoming Christ

There's an ancient story about a monastery where all the monks were old, tired, and waiting to die. They'd long since lost their fire for the Lord and had long since ceased to really care about their fellow brothers. Although they shared the same living space, prayed together, ate together, and worked together, each monk lived in his own world with heart and mind turned inward.

No one came to the monastery. There were no visitors, no new brothers. The buildings were sadly in need of repair, but the monks didn't care. They felt it wasn't long until there'd be no monastery at all. Everything would return to the dust.

Then one day a holy man visited them. He was a monk himself. For a time he lived with the old brothers, prayed with them, talked with them, worked, ate, and slept with them. He was wise. The brothers turned their hearts and minds outward and listened to him.

When the time came for him to leave, this holy man stood before the brothers who were bidding him farewell and wished them God's peace. Some of the monks shook their heads sadly; there's nothing here for us now that you're going, they thought. But the visitor's last words to them were, "There is one among you who is Christ." And he walked away.

Well, the brothers were quite astonished. They looked at one another with surprise. Surely not Brother William, who never arrives at the chapel on time and never does his work either, for that matter. Surely not Brother Mark, who annoyingly slurps his soup. Surely not the abbot, who's always gruff with everyone. Christ wouldn't be late for chapel or neglect his work or slurp soup or be gruff. Yet their visitor was a holy and reliable man who had spoken the truth to them the whole time he was in their company. This too must be true. One among them *must* be Christ.

So each of the monks began to treat the other as if he *were* Christ, for they didn't know who it was. They looked for ways to serve one another and were kind to one another and shared with one another. Each did his work as a gift to the Christ who was among them. Each honored his fellow monk by listening with full attention and respect. They began to overlook little things that annoyed them about one another and began, instead, to see the good that was in very person.

Life began to flow back into the dying community. A vitality and joy was reborn that had been lost for many years. The people of the town nearby learned that something had changed at the monastery. In curiosity they came and in love they were received. Each was graciously welcomed and made to feel at home. Every effort was taken to care for their needs and each monk accepted visitors as they were. Men, women, and children came to be refreshed and renewed. The brotherhood grew as men came even from far away to join the community.

All the visitors and the new brothers were treated as if they were Christ, for the wise monk had said, "One among you is Christ."[29]

Putting the Ideas into Practice

The Rule tells us that we are to welcome others as Christ. Benedict asks for a life of love and service, encouraging us to reach out to others because we see Christ in everyone.

The important thing that I try to remember is this: hospitality, expressed in the Baptismal Covenant as seeking and serving Christ in others, isn't about *them*, it's about *me*. When I choose to look on another person as Christ, I don't change them, I change me. I can do nothing about who they are. But when I change my actions and *re*actions, everyone around me changes, too. The healing power of love flows out like concentric circles from a pebble dropped into a still pond. You and I can change so that God can bless and sanctify our lives and let us become gifts to others.

Even though becoming a person of true hospitality requires a change inside, we can take some steps to let God in to do this work of transformation (conversion of life). Like the monks in the story, we can choose to let our actions be motivated by simple, basic hospitality. There are countless ways to express hospitality as the result of life choices. Here are just a few. We can *choose*

- to be fully present to others
- to make room for others in our lives
- to set aside our own agendas and tend to the needs of others
- to look for the good in others instead of being consumed by their faults
- to forgive
- to see Christ in the faces of those we see every day

As you continue to journey with Benedict, take on one or two ways of hospitality, or choose your own way. Hospitality is a hallmark of Benedictine spirituality. Let's make it our hallmark, too.

CHAPTER 8

Keeping a Holy "Benedictine" Lent Anytime

I invite you, therefore, in the name of the Church, to
the observance of a holy Lent, by self-examination
and repentance; by prayer, fasting, and self-denial;
and by reading and meditating on God's holy Word.
—THE BOOK OF COMMON PRAYER,
ASH WEDNESDAY SERVICE[1]

You may be reading this book during Lent or it may be another season of the year. It doesn't matter what time of year it is. Benedict says we ought to live as if it were Lent all the time (49.1). If you'd like to take on that challenge—or if you're curious about the wisdom and experience that Benedict can bring to a future Lent—read on.

Benedict and Lent

In the Rule Benedict treats important subjects with meticulous detail, telling us how to live with others, cautioning us against grumbling, spelling out exactly how to pray the Divine Office, and writing a job description for the abbot. In chapter 49, he addresses how to keep a holy Lent.

Lent is the time to repent, to return to the Lord, and to once again make a right beginning. Benedict feels that a monk's whole life should be marked with the character and practice required in Lent. These are words for us, too. The life of *any* Christian ought to bear the characteristics of Lent. Why? In this season more than in any other we try to be realistic about who we are. We acknowledge our imperfections. We make a special effort to turn our lives around and let go of unhealthy behaviors. We take extra time to deepen our relationship with God through a spiritual discipline or through acts of charity. We become more serious about who we are as Christians: sinners in need of redemption. As difficult as it may be, practicing a daily Lenten-type discipline would hone our ability to follow the Lord and to take steps that would allow him to be the center of our life.

Benedict knows, however, that few people can handle Lent year round, so he encourages his monks (and us) to at least keep the season of Lent especially pure to make up for the failings of the rest of the year. He first prescribes several ways to accomplish this: "by refusing to indulge evil habits and by devoting ourselves to prayer with tears, to reading, to compunction of heart and self-denial" (RB 49.4). To look forward to Easter with joy and desire in our souls, Benedict suggests that during Lent we go above and beyond what we normally do for our spiritual disciplines by adding prayers to our normal routine and by denying ourselves some food, drink, sleep, and unnecessary talking or joking around. This becomes our offering to God to be done with joy (49.1–7).

You may find a certain familiarity in the Benedict's instructions for the observance of Lent. In The Book of Common Prayer of the Episcopal Church, the call to keep a Holy Lent found in the Ash Wednesday service bears a marked similarity to Benedict's. The prayers invite us to the observance of a Holy Lent "by self-examination and repentance; by prayer, fasting, and self-denial; and by reading and meditating on God's word."[2]

Holy Reading

In Lent Benedict includes an extra hour in the time for holy reading (48.14), making a total of three hours each morning. In chapter 48, "The Daily Manual Labor," Benedict prescribes specific time periods for manual labor and for *lectio divina*. Since the monks in his day needed to care for the fields, these times varied according to the season of the year. From October to the beginning of Lent, the brothers would read to the end of the second hour (48.19). Although the actual time for the second hour would vary depending on when the sun rose, we can think of the hours beginning at 6:00 a.m.

At the start of Lent, each brother was to receive a book from the library to read from beginning to end, straight through (48.15–16). What were these books? One scholar suggests that they were nine sections of the Bible,[3] which makes sense, given the importance that Benedict placed on Scriptures: "What page, what passage of the inspired books of the Old and New Testaments is not the truest of guides for human life (RB 73.3)?"

We know that Benedict's monastery library also contained other spiritual classics. He mentions several of these with praise in the last chapter of the Rule. The *Conferences* of the Fathers, their *Institutes* and their *Lives*, documents that describe the lives, other monastic rules, and beliefs of the early monastics, as well as the rule of Basil, are listed as important for cultivation of virtue. The Rule explains that these are to be read during meals to benefit the listeners (42.3). They most likely would also have been used by the monks during Lent.

Benedict is serious about this discipline of prayerful reading and study. He provides an outline of disciplinary steps that encourages the monks to keep at their reading not only during Lent, but at any time of the year. The Rule sends two senior monks to patrol the monastery during the times for reading to help the brothers focus on their task and to encourage them not to waste time or to interrupt their own reading or that of others with trivial conversation. Benedict hopes that monks will be obedient to their reading, but any monk found neglecting it would be rebuked twice, if necessary. On the third strike he'd be punished according to the Rule, not only to discipline him but also to discourage others from the same wayward behavior.

We might find this kind of policing a bit excessive. Keep in mind that Benedict lived in a violent and unstable time, when people may have entered religious life for reasons of security and safety. In spite of this possibility, Benedict was sincerely concerned about the souls of his brothers and wanted to see that everything was done to help them take time with the Lord to benefit this life and the next.

Benedict hopes the disciplinary measures he outlines would not be needed anytime, but especially so in Lent when he encourages the monks and us to "keep a manner of life most pure and to wash away in this holy season the negligences of other times" (RB 49.2–3).

Fasting

Besides adding prayers and holy reading of Scripture or another book, Benedict instructs that fasting is an appropriate Lenten discipline. This involves denying oneself some food, drink, sleep, or unnecessary talking or joking around (49.7). While we may have tried the first two, fasting from a particular food (chocolate?) or drink (coffee?), most of us probably haven't considered fasting from one of the other items on Benedict's list—sleep, unnecessary talking or joking around(49.7). Yet, these bear consideration. For example, we could forgo a half hour of sleep in the morning and use the time for prayer or to prepare a special breakfast for our family. We might even give ourselves that extra time so we can begin our day more calmly. We could also reflect on our habits of speech or on our actions to determine if there is something from which we could fast during Lent: for example, talking negatively about others, interrupting others, or that Benedictine favorite—grumbling.

What is the point of such a fast? First, Benedict says that giving up something for Lent will help us look forward to Easter with joy and spiritual longing (49.7). Second, our physical discipline becomes a spiritual offering. Fasting is a gift to God, a free-will offering over and above what we normally do (49.6). It's also a way to share in the sufferings of Christ. Third, by denying ourselves something we'd normally want or do, we exercise the muscles of patience and forbearance as well as hone our spiritual stamina. All this will help us be strong enough spiritually to work through whatever life deals us. Fourth, fasting can be a time to identify with those in the world whose life is a constant, and unchosen fast. Our hunger or abstinence from certain behaviors can remind us of the needs of so many in our world.

Fasting can become a yearlong practice on certain days of the week or in certain weeks of the month. We might consider fasting when God seems distant or when we're facing a particular challenge.

Keep in mind that not everyone can fast physically. For some, denying food or drink can be a physical danger. Challenge yourself, but be prudent.

Resisting Evil the Benedictine Way

While the Lenten disciplines described in the Rule are a special practice in response to our sinfulness, the Rule also offers other ways to live a holy life resisting evil. The vows of stability, obedience, and conversion of life, the Tools for Good Works, the Benedictine practice of hospitality, and the focus on living well in community are all tools we can use in our ongoing battle to resist evil. Benedictine spirituality doesn't shut us off from the world and its many temptations and distractions. Instead it helps us meet these while we retain a spiritual center in Christ. Prayer—our own and that of others—can help us keep our center.

Closing Thoughts and a Look at the Baptismal Covenant

The practices for Lent as described in the Rule are tools for living into the promise that we make in this question from our Baptismal Covenant:

> Will you persevere in resisting evil, and, whenever you fall into sin, repent and return to the Lord?

This question applies particularly to the season of Lent. The Rule reminds us that in Lent we resolve to take active steps to resist evil and gives us ways to work toward this end. The Rule presents tools for spiritual discipline of repentance. Through these we again make a right beginning as we return to the Lord.

TOOLBOX
Keeping a Holy Benedictine Lent Anytime

In his Rule Benedict says, "The life of a monk ought to be a continuous Lent," but he recognizes that "few, however, have this strength for this" (RB 49:1–2). Yet in the season of Lent or at times when we wish to make a special offering to God, we can willingly make a holy offering in some form of spiritual and personal discipline. I encourage you to talk to your priest, minister, spiritual director, or spiritual friend as you make your decision.

This section of the Toolbox gives you some suggestions from Benedict's Rule on keeping a holy Lent at any time of year. Godspeed!

Tool #1: Read a Gospel

Purpose of the Tool. To form a practice of spiritual reading using the Gospels.

Background on the Tool. During Lent the Rule instructs each person to have additional time for reading (48:14) and prayer (49.5). As we walk with Jesus to the cross, we can enter more deeply into his life by reading one of the Gospels. As you read and pray with Scripture, you are formed and transformed on both a conscious and an unconscious level. The words reach up to your mind and affect your thoughts and actions. The words reach down into your soul and permeate your very being in hidden ways that will transform your heart.

The Tool
- **Choose one of the Gospels**—Matthew, Mark, Luke, or John.
  Set aside ten minutes or more each day to slowly read the book you've chosen, using *lectio divina*. For a refresher on *lectio*, see Tool #1 in the Toolbox for chapter 2 on pages 36–37 and the tools on *lectio divina*.
- **Pay attention.** This can be a real challenge! Let your reading be mindful.
- **Let go of the "I must accomplish this" mindset.** This is not a project to be completed and checked off. This is time with God and time to listen to God. Whatever amount you read, that's what you read.
- **Just read slowly and let what happens, happen.** Sometimes you will receive insights, sometimes not. Be patient and open to God.
- **If you don't read the whole Gospel during Lent,** that's okay. The point is to read deeply, listening for God's voice.

God *will* reach out to you through this reading. Keep listening and you will hear. Blessed holy reading!

Tool #2: Read a Spiritual Book

Purpose of the Tool. To form a practice of spiritual reading of nonscriptural material.

Background on the Tool. In chapter 48 of the Rule, we read that each monk or nun is to be given a book from the library to read during Lent (48.15). From chapter 73 of the Rule, we know that Benedict encourages reading of the church fathers—mentioning the *Conferences*, the *Institutes*, and the *Lives* of the Fathers—as a way to strengthen one's relationship with God.

The Tool

There are many wonderful and inspiring books on spirituality, the Christian life, and prayer. "Suggested Reading" and the bibliography to this book list books related to Benedict and the Rule. Talk to your priest or pastor, check the bookstores or libraries, or ask friends in faith and find a book to settle in with during Lent—or any other time.

Use a slow reflective reading of the text for *lectio divina* as found in Tool #1 of chapter 2. Journal your thoughts and favorite passages. Make notes of other books that you'd like to read.

Tool #3: Replace Grumbling with Prayer

Purpose of the Tool. To help ourselves become aware of the pervasiveness of grumbling and to offer an alternative.

Background of the Tool. One of the most damaging things we can do is to murmur about one another, whether silently to ourselves or out loud to someone else. Benedict is adamant against grumbling:

> First and foremost, there must be no word or sign of the evil of grumbling, no manifestation of it for any reason at all (RB 34.6).

Grumbling in our hearts separates us from others. Murmuring puts a chink in the wall between ourselves and God. It is not constructive and destroys community.

The Tool

Simply replace grumbling with the words, "Lord, make me an instrument of your peace." This is the opening line of the Prayer of St. Francis that appears as the first tool in the Toolbox in chapter 7 on page 131. By saying these words whenever we catch ourselves grumbling aloud or in our hearts, we can stop our grumbling and make a space for God.

Tool #4: Give Up a Sin for Lent

Purpose of the Tool. To begin to "weed out" those things about ourselves that get in the way of our relationships with God, others, and even with ourselves.

Background of the Tool. One year I decided to give up anxiety for Lent. (Anxiety is a sin for it separates us from God.) I was plain tired of being anxious about this and that. The negative energy was draining me, attacking me in my prayer time, and getting in the way of my being a free agent for Christ. So I said, "I'm giving up anxiety for Lent." Then, whenever I felt anxious, I remembered that I'd given it up for Lent and gave the anxiety to the Lord. I'd say, "Lord, I gave this up for Lent. Please take it again." This technique really worked.

The Tool

What could you give up for Lent, or anytime, to make you a more energized and joyful person? What most gets in the way of your relationships with others?

Whatever it is, this behavior gets in the way of your relationship with God, too. It also compromises your relationship with yourself, for it blocks not only peace but also freedom of action in Christ. So the question for the third Lenten practice is this: What sin blocks me the most? Got it?

Now, give it up: give it to Jesus, hand it to God. Cleanse your heart and mind. Then, when you find yourself falling into the old pattern just say to Christ, "Lord, I gave that up. I give it to you again."

Tool #5: Give Alms

Purpose of the Tool. To share our God-given resources of time and/or money with others.

Background of the Tool. Giving alms is a time-honored Lenten tradition. As a mark of our repentance, we take steps to share with others the gifts that God has given to us, be they money or personal talents.

The Tool

The fifth Lenten tool is simply this: give alms. Using this tool we reach out to others in intentional and specific ways. We share our money with the needy or our time to a worthy cause. Do something that you have not done before. Reach out beyond your normal sphere of concern.

Tool #6: Give Up a Favorite Food, Drink, or Other Fun Pastime

Purpose of the Tool. To sharpen our spiritual minds by denying our bodies a pleasure.

Background of the Tool. I read somewhere a long time ago that, in the opinion of the monastic writer, the main challenge for those in the religious life was not chastity but abstinence. Denying self certain food and drink was more difficult. In chapter 49 of the Rule, Benedict encourages us to take on some "abstinence from food or drink" (49.5). He even expands this opportunity for denial to sleep, unnecessary talking, and offensive humor (49.7). By denying ourselves a pleasure, he says, we can then look forward to Easter with joy and spiritual desire.

The Tool

Is there a food or drink that you can give up for Lent? Or do you wish to try for unnecessary talking? Or maybe even giving up joking that may make fun of others? Is there a fun pastime that you could give up for a time? Decide what you will give up and write it here:

Offer this sacrifice to God with a humble and contrite heart. Ask for God's help in making it through the forty days of Lent or for the period of time you choose to practice this discipline.

In the time you gain by giving up food, drink, or a pastime, consider an offering of prayer or giving time to others through volunteering. It's meaningful for me when I'm on a fast from food to pray for the many people who live continually hungry. Combining prayer with abstinence helps God make our hearts more loving.

Tool #7: Devote Yourself to Prayer

Purpose of the Tool. To expand the time for prayer and to experience different types of prayer.

Background of the Tool. During Lent, Benedict instructs us to add additional time of prayer to our usual routine (49.5).

The Tool

Add ten to fifteen additional minutes of prayer time each day. Try a method of prayer that you don't normally use. For example, if you generally pray in words, try Centering Prayer, which is Tool #5 in chapter 5 on page 97. If you don't use Scripture as a resource, try *lectio divina.* The format for this prayer is Tool #1 in chapter 2 on page 36.

～ *Interlude* ～
Getting Back on the Wagon

This year at St. Peter's we were fortune indeed to have a Lenten resource written by members of the parish. Each day bought a new meditation on the scripture readings for that day. I found these daily reflections meaningful and thought-provoking. On the Saturday for the third week in Lent, an image grabbed my attention. The writer was reflecting on the challenge of keeping a Lenten discipline. "About this time during Lent, most of my resolve to observe a 'faithful' [Lent] is fading,"[4] the writer admitted. That resonated with me as I was already running along behind the wagon: it's *hard* to be faithful!

I'm a faithful and committed nibbler—nothing bad, mind you. I snack on things like raisins, peanuts, carrots-carrots-carrots, spears of Romaine lettuce tugged off the stalk, and my favorite—pieces of "homemade" granola bars from a local supermarket.

As a seasoned nibbler, I'm motivated to succumb to the habit through a number of different "outside conditions." Unlike the brother who is to readily admit his mistake in the liturgy (45.1) or during other work (46.1–3), I happily blame circumstances for my weakness. Stress will bring me to the pantry. Tiredness will, too. Anger as well as worry, boredom, or simply walking into the kitchen will activate the urge to munch. When any of these conditions are present, I'll gravitate to the source of comfort—chewing! I try not to do this. For a while I even had my husband, John, hide the peanuts. But, no problem—undeterred, I'd root around the house until I found them and then, without guilt or remorse, I'd happily munch away. The problem with all of this was that by mealtimes I wasn't hungry, which kept me from eating a healthy and balanced diet. Plus, overconsumption of certain foods had me wondering whether I should hop like a bunny or swing like a chimp. So for my Lenten discipline, I devised a plan to combine self-denial with almsgiving. When the nearly uncontrollable urge came to nibble, I'd refrain and instead place a dollar in an envelope. All monies were to be given to the Good Shepherd Home in Cameroon, a home for children orphaned by the ravages of AIDS.[5] In the first three days, I'd surged through twenty-five one-dollar bills!

Things were great for the first week or so. As I fixed dinner I would beat a path between kitchen and foyer where I'd stuff dollar after dollar into an envelope. But as the days and weeks of Lent trooped slowly by, my resolve weakened. I began to form "cleverly devised myths" (2 Peter 1:16) that the Romaine lettuce I "rabbitly" consumed before dinner didn't count, that the peanuts and raisins I munched after dinner while my husband and I did dishes were a part of the dessert that was to follow, that the granola bar pieces furtively consumed when under stress were a mental necessity, and that the bar munched after breakfast was, in truth, just "breakfast dessert." *Thud!* Clearly I had fallen off the "Lenten wagon." I needed a reminder—a wake-up call.

The Lenten reflection by a wise member of my parish reminded me that faithfulness and steadfastness were also a part of the promise that I'd made to God and not just abstinence. It's a tough change but Lent calls us to a change of heart, not just a change of habit. When we fall, or jump, off the Lenten wagon, it's a really slip in our faithfulness and our steadfastness. I needn't add that even when it's not Lent, you and I are jumping off wagons all the time. Lapses in our faithfulness to any number of things, and to God, are a year-round reality.

In his Rule, Benedict describes the process by which newcomers enter religious life. He stresses the importance of standing firm and persevering in keeping the Rule as evidence that the individual is committed enough to be received into the community (chapter 58). Faithfulness and steadfastness are a part of the vow of stability; a newcomer agrees to live in a particular community and remain steadfast to that community. It's also a promise to be faithful to living according to a Rule that puts Christ at the center of all things.

We make such promises to be faithful in our lives, too. We promise to remain committed to family, friends, religious or church community, the wider community, business relationships, and, first and foremost, to God. We promise to be faithful to our Baptismal Covenant, to seek and serve Christ in all persons, to respect the dignity of every human being, to proclaim the Good News by what we say and do. All these and our Lenten disciplines are outward signs of our inner commitment to God in Christ. They are evidence that we embrace, as best as we can, Benedictine stability. Our resolve to live a Gospel-directed, Christ-centered life every day of the year reflects this inner commitment. The grace is that when we aren't faithful, God will give us another chance. The writer of the Lenten reflection put it this way: "I know if I regress, I can always jump back on the 'Lenten wagon' and start again." With penitent hearts and renewed resolve, you and I can turn to Christ and his unconditional love, and humbly walk back to the wagon. What we'll find is the hand of the compassionate, forgiving Christ held out to us. We can put our hand in his and let him hoist us back onto the wagon where we can begin again to live as faithful and steadfast people of God.

Putting It Into Practice

Here are some questions to ponder:

- In what area of your life could you use the help of Christ to get back on the wagon?
- What might you do to be open to allowing him to help you begin again?

Here is a guided meditation: Find a time when you can be alone and undisturbed. Sit in a comfortable, straight-backed chair with your feet on the floor. Spend a few minutes breathing deeply to relax.

Now identify an area where you feel you've fallen off the wagon. Picture what you're doing instead of what you wish to do. Try to recall what you feel like when you're taking this action.

Now picture the action you desire. Be specific in your thoughts and mental pictures. Try to get a sense of what it feels like to do the action that you desire.

Now picture standing behind a beautiful wagon. Jesus is there in the wagon. Look at him. Then imagine his hand reaching out to you to help you back onto the wagon. Take his hand and let him lift you up back into the wagon.

Just take a few moments to sit beside him in the wagon and be thankful.

CHAPTER 9

The Holiness of Labor
Benedictine Work and Service

... so that God may be glorified in all things ...
—1 PETER 4:11 AND RULE 57.9

When we meet new people we don't get too far into the conversation before we ask, "What do you do?" We're curious about other people's jobs, and we place a high value on work. Our society especially honors hard work. We work hard to support our families. We work hard to further our careers. We work hard at our volunteer tasks. We work hard to provide a clean house and an ordered, secure life for our children. If we're not busy doing things at home or at our job outside the home, many of us feel that we're not accomplishing anything of value. Retirement can bring a crisis as we come face to face with the realization that our work has formed our self-image: "My work defines who I am." When that work is gone, we may wonder, "Who am I?"

"What is the value of work? What really is our work? Who are we as people who work?"

In this chapter we'll explore the Benedictine view of work and service. As you read, think about how Benedict's ideas about work connect with your own life, whether you're employed outside the home, work in the home, do volunteer work, or are retired. Then we'll explore how Benedict's ideas translate into the world of the twenty-first century.

Benedict's View of Work

The main work for the monastic was the *Opus Dei*, the Work of God. These were the eight prayer services that the monk attended, from the middle of the night, through the following day, and into the evening. Monks weren't idle the rest of the time, however. Benedict prescribed a day that was filled but balanced. When not in the chapel for prayer, the monks would be working, praying, reading, eating, or resting.

Work is an important component in the life of the monk. In a chapter on daily work, Benedict states that idleness is the soul's enemy. He specifies time for work with the hands as well as time for reading (48.1–2). Benedict believes in the importance of manual labor, stating that real monks are those who live by the "labor of their hands" (48.8). Here Benedict follows the example of Paul, who worked as a tentmaker (Acts 18:3), so that no one would need to provide him with daily necessities. Benedict desires that the monks be like their monastic fathers who also were self-sufficient.

One type of work isn't any more important than any other type of work. All labor has value because it enables people to serve one another. Monks work on the land, with the animals, in the kitchen, in the gardens, and, if they were literate, copying books. All types of work are equal and all are important. For example, in chapter 35, Benedict makes it clear that all would work in the kitchen unless ill or working on another task where they were of greater usefulness to the monastery. By serving one another, the brothers would promote feelings of love, not only in themselves but throughout the community (35.1–2).

In the Rule work is always an opportunity to help others. For example, the strong are to help the weak:

> Let those who are not strong have help so that they may serve without distress, and let everyone receive help as the size of the community or local conditions warrant. (RB 35.3).

Benedict also gives us a model in which the worker is respected and cared for. For example, the kitchen workers assigned for that week receive something to drink and some bread in addition to their regular portion an hour before they are to serve the meals. Thus the work is not be burdensome and can be done without grumbling or complaining (35.11–12).

Not only are workers respected, the tools used in the monastery are to be treated carefully, as carefully as the sacred vessels on the altar (31.10–11). For Benedict, everything is sacred and to be reverenced, from the humblest to the most glorious. The sacred pervades every part of life.

Work is also to be an occasion for prayer. The Rule frames the weekly change of shift in the kitchen with prayers for those leaving and for those coming into service (35.15–18). Work has a strong spiritual component for Benedict: it's a way to find God. In the Prologue he writes of the connection between prayer and work:

> First of all, every time you begin a good work, you must pray to him most earnestly to bring it to perfection (RB Prologue 4).

The emphasis on a life of continual prayer informs the work style of the monks. During work, monks are silent, repeating to themselves a word or a phrase that they would have taken from their *lectio divina*. At other times a monk might read while others worked. We tried this latter approach in a women's group at the church. While seven members worked in the kitchen one member read from Scripture. The experience would have been great except for a misfortunate choice of task—sorting silverware. The reader could hardly be heard above the clatter of spoons, knives, and forks! We suspended this holy labor when laughter took over, clearly failing the tenth step of humility (7.59), all of us being more than ready and quick to laugh!

Benedict knew the value of work but also knew that to define oneself by one's work was dangerous. Work is a means to glorify God. The skilled may practice their craft, but only with humility. Should they become conceited with their abilities or with the profit they brought to the monastery, their work would be stopped. Only with proper humility could the individual return to his or her craft (57.1–3).

Products of the monastery artisans may be sold but without fraud. "The evil of avarice must have no part in establishing prices" (RB 57.7). The prices were even to be a bit lower than found outside the monastery "so that in all things God may be glorified" (1 Pet 4:11 RB; RB 57.8–9).

Esther de Waal explains that for Benedict, work is "neither simply a means to an end nor something which has absolute intrinsic value."[1] She points out, however, that Benedict's emphasis on work had a tremendous effect on Western culture during the past fifteen centuries. Benedictine monasteries were highly successful in the Middle Ages. Author Arnold Toynbee sees them as "the grain of mustard seed from which the great tree of Western civilization has sprung."[2] But for Benedict, work was just part of the life of a monk, a life that was to be well-ordered and well-balanced with work, prayer, study, and rest.

Work and Benedictine Balance

Life under the Benedictine Rule is a balanced life. Benedict carefully prescribes daily activities in detail, with a balance between physical activity and rest, work, and prayer, time alone and time together, work with the mind and work with the body. There are specific times for rest during the day. Sundays are to be free of manual labor. The structure of life is formed by the Divine Hours. Stopping work to pray throughout the day is a way that Benedict places work in a specific perspective: not an end in itself or a way to self-fulfillment, but an offering to God to fulfill God's purpose.

In Benedict's time monasteries were rural and agrarian. The monks did the manual labor and had a balance of physical, intellectual, and spiritual work. After Benedict's death, invading armies destroyed many monasteries, forcing the monks to flee to Rome and the protection of the Church. This upset the balance of life that the Rule fostered, as manual labor came to be performed by lay brothers.[3] Another way that this balance was lost came through changes in the Divine Office itself. The liturgy became more involved in the Middle Ages, especially in the monasteries under the direction of a monastery in Cluny, France: the choir monks spent almost all day in the chapel singing the Office and did no manual labor or intellectual work, such as the reading that Benedict recommended. Many people today have the same lack of balance, with no or little physical activity: we can live in our heads and on our couches!

The Benedictine Ideal of Work in the Twenty-first Century

How do Benedict's ideas on work translate into contemporary American life? We learned that in Benedictine life, work is balanced. Manual labor, reading Scripture, corporate prayer, private prayer, meals, rest, and sleep are all important components of the balanced Benedictine life. Restoring a similar balance in our own lives would provide a way for us to live healthier, happier, and more productive days. Also, Benedict's Rule gives a model of community life for family, church, friendships, communities, and workplace in which members of a community all contribute. The strong help the weak instead of standing back and criticizing. There is no hierarchy of importance regarding the type of work: each person serves the other in love, and work is framed by each person's relationship to God.

Benedict would allow a tired mother or father to rest. He would encourage family members to take on some extra chores so that another's load might lighten. Benedictine work tells us that instead of complaining that someone can't do something that we can do, we can just offer to help. We can respect the contributions that each makes in the community.

The Benedictine view of work has a component of stewardship: we are stewards of the gifts, talents, and skills that have been given to us. Everything we've been given has been loaned to us by God and through our work we can find our way to God. Each of us has been blessed with talents or skills for which we can joyfully give thanks. Our work is a way that we can glorify God. At the end of his compositions, eighteenth-century composer Johann Sebastian Bach always wrote *Soli Deo Gloria*: "to God alone the glory."

As we use our gifts to help others, we can strive to keep our own lives in balance, allotting the time necessary for each task we have before us— no more, no less. We can keep in mind the importance of our work yet not let work determine the structure of our lives. We need to be good to others, we need to be good to ourselves. This means taking care of body, mind, and spirit, balancing not only our various activities but also what we do for others and what we do for ourselves. To serve others in Christ's name, we need to keep ourselves strong.

Work can also become a way to deepen our connection with God. Following the practice of the monastics, we can give our work to God and can pray through our work. Through our work we are co-creators with God.

Finally, members of our family, church, and workplace do not need to be defined by what they do. There are too many things that can destroy our work: layoffs, job cuts, illness, relocation, and so forth. Instead, we can define who we are on a higher level, beyond the reach of change. As an antidote to identity-by-job, I offer Rachel Hosmer's definition of a Christian. She wrote, "This is who I am: member of Christ, child of God, inheritor of the kingdom."[4] It's a definition of self rooted in our Baptism and connects our identity to Christ. With who we are secure in the hands of Christ, we can negotiate life's changes with peace and grace.

The Work Doldrums

We've all had them, no matter what jobs we do. Another name for these doldrums is *acedia*. (pronounced "eh-see'-dee-eh"). Acedia means apathy, or indifference—literally, "I don't care." Most of us have struggled with these feelings that drain us and can make it difficult even to get out of bed. Often called the "noonday demon," acedia is the opposite of mindfulness and attentiveness. This demon "tempts us to give up, whispers to us that what once seemed so full of promise is in fact going nowhere, that our efforts are in vain."[5] I can relate to a personal description of acedia from Kathleen Norris. Perhaps you can as well.

> I thought that I was merely tired and in need of rest at year's end, but it drags on, becoming the death-in-life that I know all too well, when my capacity for joy shrivels up, and, like drought-stricken grass, I die down to the roots to wait it out. The simplest acts demand a herculean effort, the pleasure I normally take in people and the world itself is lost to me.[6]

The noonday demon "suggests that whatever I'm doing, indeed my entire life of 'doings,' is not only meaningless but utterly useless."[7]

> This plunge into chill waters of pure realism is incapacitating, and the demon likes me this way. It suggests sleep when what I need most is to take a walk. It insists that I shut myself away when what I probably need is to be with other people. It mocks the rituals, routines, and work that normally fill my day; why do them, why do anything at all, it says, in the face of so vast an emptiness. Worst of all, even though I know that the ancient remedies—prayer, psalmody, scripture reading—would help to pull me out of the morass, I find myself incapable of acting on this knowledge.[8]

However the noonday demon attacks, the end result of acedia is spiritual: we become estranged from God, which is exactly what this demon wants. The noon liturgy of the Hours called "sext" focuses on the dangers of acedia and calls the monastic to renewed fervor and commitment.

Author Deborah Smith Douglas says that to defeat this sense of hopelessness, we can bring to our work an understanding that "our real work, no matter how we earn our livelihoods, engages us in saying yes to God" and that we must have "complete trust in God's presence and purposes."[9] You and I have a choice either to open ourselves to God or to close our fist around our life and risk falling into acedia, with its perilous lack of meaning. Smith writes that we must courageously choose the former and find meaning in our lives.

What can we do if we feel acedia creeping in? Through prayer we reach out to God. We can fully rely on God and have a profound trust in God's love and purposes for us to help reset our spiritual compasses to true north.[10] Often we need others to help us banish the feelings of hopelessness. They can pray for us. This can remind us of God's help and presence and point us in a direction where we can regain balance in our lives. We can try physical activity to refresh mind and body. We can seek help from a spiritual director. We can treat ourselves to an activity that brings us refreshment and joy. Finally, we can just hang in there. I've often found that a good meal and a good night's sleep does wonders!

Our Real Work

Most of us wear many work hats: we're parent, spouse, employee, employer, homeowner, church member, community member. We work at a job, we work as a volunteer. We work to help other members of our community or family by caring for children, for elderly parents, and for others. Every day we work at a myriad of tasks. We mow the lawn, clean the toilets, and make meals. We take children to school and to other activities, we do food shopping. We work at one job; then something happens and we lose that job. Layoffs, closings, business failures lead to loss of particular work. If we do all this work in so many different places, who *are* we? And when we lose our work or can no longer do what we had done before, *then who are we?*

Jesus wore many different hats, too. His occupation moved from carpentry to itinerant ministry. In this role Jesus taught the crowds, instructed his disciples, healed the sick, exorcized demons, debated with critical and jealous religious leadership, struggled to teach his disciples, who didn't really understand what he was all about, and endured humiliation. He gave his life for his work. Through all this work, Jesus had one purpose: he pointed to God. This is what grounded him and gave him stamina and energy. Whatever was required of him at the moment, this purpose enabled him to remain centered in God. His strength came from being rooted and grounded in God.

Benedict's Rule also points to God, to God in Christ, and those who follow his Rule are guided to a life that is centered in Christ. In chapter 1 of this book, I quoted this statement by Esther de Waal about the purpose of the Rule:

It is all about love.

It points me to Christ.

Ultimately the whole meaning and purpose of the Rule is simply, [in Benedict's own words] "Prefer nothing to the love of Christ."[11]

Preferring nothing to the love of Christ impacts the way we view our work regardless of where the work takes place or what it is. Our *real* work is to love one another and to point to Christ. This means that in our work we're not just to *do*. We are to *be*.

Tasks can change, jobs can change, the circumstances of our life can change. But under it all and through it all, we remain people who are all about love and who point to Christ. Our *real work* is to *be* as we show the presence of Christ in our daily life. Whatever our work is and if that work ever changes, we're still the same people when we recognize that *who we are* is more important than what we do. The real thing that defines us does *not* change: each of us is a child of God. Paul wrote that nothing could separate us from the love of Christ (Rom 8:39). Our stability is in Christ and not in the externals of our life.

And so we are to be people who are all about love and who point to Christ. We are people who are to remain centered in Christ and rooted in God. Then it no longer matters *what* we do. It's *how* we do the task before us that's important. The *how* is answered by the teaching of Jesus in the Gospels. The *how* is expanded by Paul in his letters, by other New Testament writings, and by the many spiritual writers through the ages who have sought to place Christ first in their lives. The *how* is explained by Benedict in the Rule. The *how* calls us to be people who love in whatever work God gives us to do.

Entering the Holiness of Work

Since our real work is to love and to point to Christ, no matter what our earthly and tangible work of the moment is, *all our work is a holy endeavor*. Work is a way we seek God. Work is the way we use our God-given gifts in service to others. Our work provides opportunities to be in relationship with others where we can let the light of God shine through us. All our work can be an occasion to praise God, whether we work in office, home, church, school, or outdoors. All our work can be infused with the presence of God. All our work can be an opportunity to listen for God each day.

Finally, what we do as our work is important; yet our true work is beyond what we do with our hands and our minds. John McQuiston II expresses this elegantly in his contemporary interpretation of the Rule of Benedict, titled *Always We Begin Again*.

> When we rise from sleep let us rise for the joy
> of the true Work that we will be about
> this day,
> and considerately cheer one another on.[12]

When you rise tomorrow, ask yourself, "What is the true Work I am to do today?"

Benedictine Work and the Baptismal Covenant

The Benedictine view of work is rooted in spirituality. Through our work we serve God by serving one another. In our work we use the gifts that God has given to us in a generous, responsible, and humble way. Work is important but it doesn't define who we are. Work is an occasion to "step aside" and let our actions glorify God. Through work we can exercise and hone our "Christian muscles." We can seek God as we do each task of the day.

Our true work as Christian people is to be Christ's Body here on earth, committed to the work of fulfilling the promises we make in our Baptismal Covenant: to proclaim by word and example the Good News of God in Christ, to seek and serve Christ in all persons, loving our neighbors as ourselves, and to strive for justice and peace among all people, respecting the dignity of every human being.

The Hands of Christ

On our last trip to Italy together, one day my husband, John, and my mother-in-law, Ruth, and I visited a particular church in a small town. In it there was a statue of Christ with arms outstretched. It was a beautiful and poignant statue. Jesus' face was calm yet somehow pleading. As I surveyed the statue I noticed that the hands were missing. "A victim of religious wars," I thought at the time, recalling the many defaced statues I'd seen in England. I turned to Ruth, who was standing next to me, and remarked, "The statue is beautiful, isn't it? Too bad the hands got lopped off." Ruth turned to me and explained patiently. "The statue is *supposed* to have no hands. *We're* his hands!"

You and I are his hands, blessed with countless gifts we can use to do God's work through our own work.

> Every activity is important in the *Rule*, important enough to do conscientiously and regularly. Work becomes, then, a way of glorifying God. Usually, when we think in these terms, we assume that God is glorified through our offering of "important," outwardly successful labor. While this is true, it is also true that dirty dishes washed well and in the presence of God also give glory. To do what needs to be done, humbly and simply, is enough.[13]

TOOLBOX
Work as a Holy Endeavor

In Benedictine spirituality, work is service to others and a holy endeavor. The most important work is the *Opus Dei*, the daily round of corporate prayers around which Benedict folds the rest of life. We all work, whether in home, community, or workplace. Work is a main branch of the tree of activities in our lives. Finding God's presence in our work is critical to retaining balance and joy in our lives. This section of the Toolbox will provide some ways to remain connected to God though our work.

Tool #1: **Ways to Bring Prayer and God's Presence into Your Work**

Purpose of the Tool. To give some suggestions on ways to infuse your work with the knowledge that God's presence is always with you.

Background on the Tool. Whether we work at home, as a volunteer, or at a paid job, it's easy to get caught up in the rush of tasks to be completed. This can easily lead to a frantic state of mind. Benedict asks that we have a balanced approached to life. This means that, as we work, we remain calm, yet focused. A way to do this is to always—or as much as possible—be aware that God is alongside us as we work, offering grace and help.

The Tool

Here are just a few suggestions to help you be aware of God's Presence as you work.

- **First thing in the morning, give your day to God.** Use whatever words you would like. Examples include: "This one is for you, Lord," or "God, I give you this day" or "Be with me and guide me. Help me bring your presence to others."
- **When you first sit down at your desk, pray once again.** Pray for God's presence throughout the day, for God's help in your tasks, and for the ability to be open to God's call.
- **Pray before you begin a task.** You can express your love to God and ask God to be with you in the task. When you finish a task, give thanks for God's help.
- **Imagine Jesus next to you as you work.** Envision his encourage-ment, support, and love.
- **Before a difficult conversation, pray.** Ask for God's guidance. Ask God to help you stay put (stability) and not flee either physically or emotionally. Ask to remain open to the other person and to really listen (obedience).

- **Send arrow prayers to God throughout the day.** See Tool #7 below entitled "Arrow Prayers" in this section of the Toolbox.
- **Repeat a short prayer or a Bible verse while you work.** This works especially well when the work of the moment is physical. Use your favorite Bible verse such as, "The Lord is my shepherd" or "Do not let your hearts be troubled" or "Be still, and know that I am God." Or use your own words.
- **Listen to a spiritual book or uplifting music while you work.** Even if you move around, you can do either of these via a portable tape or CD player fastened at your waist. No hard rock, heavy metal, or mystery novels, please. Try singing along with hymns or an inspiring choral work by Bach or Handel.
- **Pray the prayer of St. Francis each day.** As you say this prayer, envision yourself in the place where you work, be it at home or in an office or outside. Envision coworkers, family, or friends with you. This practice will prepare you to be Christ's presence during the day. See Tool #1 in the Toolbox for chapter 7 for this prayer.
- **Give thanks during the day.** If you cannot think of anything to be thankful for, try giving thanks for your senses: sight, hearing, smell, taste, touch.
- **Listen for God's voice in the voices of your coworkers, family, and friends.** Everyone and everything can become a channel through which God speaks. When you hear that voice, listen carefully and respond (obedience).
- **Remember that your work is holy.** Work gives you many opportunities to use the skills and talents God gave to you, to serve others, to be in close relationship with others, and to praise God. Underneath all the typewritten pages and through all the phone calls and all the vacuumed rugs, work is spiritual!
- **Jot down your own ways to remember God's presence as you work.**

Tool #2: Exploring My Work

Purpose of the Tool. To provide an opportunity to reflect on work.

Background on the Tool. Do we ever think about the work we do? Reflecting on our work can help us appreciate the role of work in our lives and lead us to make positive changes in our work or how we do our work.

The Tool

Here are some questions to help you think about your work.

- Describe your work. Work is not necessarily a job with a paycheck. Work is what you do, whatever that is. Do you work in the home? Do you work outside the home? Do you volunteer? Do you work in a religious community? You probably will be describing work in several different areas. Whatever your work is, be it one job or ten, describe it fully to yourself. Then continue with the following questions.

- Do I find my work fulfilling? Why or why not?
- Does my work energize me? Why or why not?
- What are some changes I might make my work more fulfilling and/or energizing?
- What makes me want to run away from my work? Do I? If you have run, either mentally or physically, next time, stay put and listen for what God may be asking you to do and be. This suggestion relates to Benedictine stability and obedience.
- Is there work I do that is physical? If the answer is yes, what is the impact of this work? If the answer is no, is there some physical work that I might do, even if it is gentle and light?
- Is work distributed fairly in my household? Who carries the heaviest load? Is there a way to make the workload more even? Talk to members of your family about this.
- What are the gifts I could share with others through volunteer activities? What might those activities be?

As you do your work be alert to the following: the gifts you use in your work, how you serve others in your work, and how God might be using you now in the situations that come up in your work.

Tool #3: God in My Work

Purpose of the Tool. To reflect on God's presence in your work.

Background on the Tool. God is always with us—in that we can trust. Yet God seems to be more present to us in some situations than in others. If we can identify where God seems close to us and why this is, we can look at the tasks and situations where we feel isolated. Then we can pray for guidance to recognize God's presence even in these tasks and situations.

The Tool

Here are some questions to help you reflect on your sense of God's presence in your work.

- How might God be present in my work?
- Are there some tasks in which God seems to be more present than in others? What are these tasks? How do I sense God's presence?
- What are the tasks in which God's presence seems absent?
  These may be situations where you are in conflict or frustration.

What are some ways I can recall God's presence in these tasks or situations?

- Have I ever considered that my work is holy? What work I do might lend itself to this way of thinking?

Try viewing this work or task as holy, then expand your thinking to other work.

Tool #4: Banishing Work Doldrums

Purpose of the Tool. To provide some ways to banish the "noonday demon."

Background on the Tool. Most all of us at one time or another have felt down about our work. We have days that crawl by with frustrating slowness, as we do the same tasks we did the day before and the day before that. Our work seems to have lost meaning. We become indifferent, inattentive, unmotivated, tired, sad, and bored. This is called *acedia*. This can happen with a job or even at certain times in life.

The Tool

This tool will first provide several questions to help you determine if you suffer from acedia, and then suggest steps to restore your energy for your work and your life.

ACEDIA ASSESSMENT

1. Read the paragraph above under "*Background on the Tool.*" When you think about your work, whatever that work is, do some of the characteristics describe how you feel about your work right now?
2. Does work that once seemed full of promise now seem unimportant or hopeless?

SOME SUGGESTIONS FOR ACEDIA SUFFERERS

Author Deborah Smith offers three ways that monastics dispel acedia: work, prayer, and humility.[14] These can be remedies for us as well. Each is rooted and grounded in trust in God.

Work

- *Choose* to respect yourself and the decisions you made that brought you to this work or to being where you are. Letting go of self-doubt can chase those demons away.
- *Choose* to stick with the job at hand and remain faithful to it. How? Give it to God and then take it one little step at a time. Write *this* letter, file *that* piece of paper, change *this* diaper, make *that* phone call. One moment at a time. Trust that God is with you.

Prayer

- *Choose* to reach out to God even if you are indifferent or discouraged. The biggest danger with acedia is that we cut ourselves off from God, the one resource that can extricate us from this dark place. So our first line of defense is to reestablish a trusting connection with God.
- *Pay attention* to God and to the world around you. Simone Weil, French philosopher, said that prayer is "the orientation of all the attention of which the soul is capable toward God."[15]

   A way of paying attention is through "arrow prayers." These are short prayers we can send to God throughout the day as a way to remain connected. Arrow prayers are described in Tool #7 of this Toolbox. We can also pay attention to the beauty around us, looking up at the clouds as we drive to work or pausing to enjoy the color and liveliness of the flowers outside our window.

Humility

For Benedict the first step of humility is fear of God, which is an awe-filled recognition of God's power and presence. Deborah Smith Douglas suggests two ways that humility can banish the noonday demons.[16]

- Look for and accept the ways that God is reaching out to you to help you. Reach out to others.
- Accept and come to terms with your own limitations, remembering that life is a process of continuing growth and change.

Another important suggestion I offer is to do some of the things that give you pleasure. This can help us to "lighten up."

Finally, take heart. God loves you and wants you to be a whole and joy-filled person. Henry Sloan Coffin, author and minister at Riverside Church in New York City, said, "The glory of God is a human being fully alive."[17] Trust God's love as you take one step at a time into the light once again.

Tool #5: The Tools of My Work

Purpose of the Tool. To help you embrace the Benedictine view that all the tools we use are to be treated as the sacred vessels of the altar.

Background on the Tool. In his instructions to the cellarer, the brother who dispenses the goods of the monastery, Benedict explains that the tools of the monastery are to be treated with the same reverence as the sacred vessels of the altar. Benedict asks us to see the holiness of all of life.

The Tool

Use the following questions to help you to explore the use of tools in your own life.

- What are the tools I use in my work?
- What do the tools allow me to accomplish both in the big picture and in the small?
- What might be worth reverencing about the tools and implements I use every day?
- Is it possible to give thanks for the computer, the vacuum cleaner, the lawn mower? How might this impact how I think about my work?

The next time you use a tool, try giving thanks for the tool, for the people who sold it to you or gave it to you, for the people who made the tool, for those who transported it to you, and for those who help you maintain it, for the people who invented it, and for you who have the strength to use it. Give God thanks.

Tool #6: Is My Life in Balance?

Purpose of the Tool. To identify whether or not your life has balance.

Background on the Tool. To live within Benedictine spirituality is to strive for a balance among the many kinds of activities that we do in a day.

The Tool

At the risk of sounding like Goldilocks, for each area in the chart please indicate whether you view the amount of time you spend on each activity as too much, too little, or just right.

THE ACTIVITY	TIME SPENT		
Physical activity	Too much	Too little	Just right
Sleep	Too much	Too little	Just right
Work	Too much	Too little	Just right
Relaxation	Too much	Too little	Just right
Prayer	Too much	Too little	Just right
Work that uses the mind	Too much	Too little	Just right
Work that uses the body	Too much	Too little	Just right
Time alone	Too much	Too little	Just right
Time with others	Too much	Too little	Just right

Now look at the chart as an overall picture of the way you structure your life and reflect on the following questions:

- Is there a balance of activities in my life, for example, between work and leisure, between things that I do with others and things that I do by myself, between physical work and mental activity, between time for myself and family, and time for God?
- What are the neglected areas?
- If I feel drained at the end of each day, does the picture of my life as shown in the chart give me a clue as to why that may be?
- What might I do to have a healthier balance in my life?

Tool #7: Arrow Prayers

Purpose of the Tool. To remind us that prayer is the key to unlocking the grace in our work.

Background on the Tool. While we may not be able to visit a monastery or convent to participate in the Divine Office, we can make a conscious effort to pray throughout the day. There are many ways to do this. This tool gives a simple way to connect to God and sanctify the day.

Remember that *prayer is relationship and communication with God.* Each time we pray, we are opening ourselves to God who calls us continually. We pray because God first places the prayer in our hearts.

The Tool

Arrow prayers are very brief prayers that can be said quickly and are easily remembered. They consist of a single word or phrase and come from Scripture, from spiritual writings, or are your own words. Here are some examples:

Lord, you are my shepherd. (Ps 23:1)
God, you are my light and my salvation. (Ps 27:1)
God, you are my refuge and strength. (Ps 46:1)
I will praise the Lord as long as I live. (Ps 146:2)
Come, Lord Jesus! (Rev 22:20)
Lord, I love you.
Help me.
Thank you for all.
Keep me steadfast, O God.

Notice in the first three examples I've changed the words of Scripture to address God directly. "The Lord is my shepherd" became "Lord, you are my shepherd." I find that this helps me feel more connected to God. Try it!

The bottom line is to use a word or phrase that comes from your heart, be it your own or Holy Scripture or from another source. Repeat these words throughout the day, or set your watch alarm for each hour. When the alarm rings, pray. Or, use the word or phrase before you answer each phone call or make a phone call. Pray at stoplights. Find other places to use your arrow prayer and do whatever works for you.

Throughout the day you'll have contact with God. In a sense, prayer will never cease and God's presence will sustain and support you as you share in Christ's work in the world.

Tool #8: Finding Prayers about Work

Purpose of the Tool. To encourage you to seek out prayers that will help you through your work.

Background on the Tool. In the preface to his book *Power Lines: Celtic Prayers about Work*, David Adam writes that we need to tune in to the power and peace of the presence of God that is always available and offered to us. To accomplish this, his book offers prayers that can undergird the structure of our lives. Resources such as this book can provide us with some excellent, ready prayers whose words can become our own.

The Tool

Here are two selections from *Power Lines.*

Power to Work

Lord you are
The love of my life
The light of my way
The peace of my mind
The Presence.
Help me
Strong One
To be a strength to the weak
Help me Caring One
To be a support to the sad

Help me
Saving One
To be a helper of the lost
Help me
Present One
To be a comfort to the lonely
Help me
Holy One
To Worship you now and evermore.[18]

Bringer of Peace

In busyness
Bring stillness,
In your work without cease
Your unending peace,

When things would harm
Your inner calm.[19]

Seek out other prayers that can speak for you as you prepare for work and as you work each day. Search your local library and bookstores. Talk to your priest or minister and your friends. Check the Internet. One site I found was www.jesuit.ie/prayer. Presented by the Irish Jesuits, this website guides us through reflection, Scripture, and prayer in a ten-minute session—a good morning or afternoon break from work.

May God continue to bless you and guide you in your prayer and in your work.

⌒ *Interlude* ⌒
Discovering the Holiness of Our Tools

These are some of the tools of my life. They are ordinary things: computer, pen, and dust rag, wooden spoon and cooking pan. Bits of metal and cast iron, electronics and chips, some wispy material to catch dust and wood formed into a handy utensil to sauté veggies.

Computer, pen, and dust rag, wooden spoon and cooking pan. With them I do my work at the church, my work at home, my work for the community, and my work for those in need. With these and other tools I do the work that I believe that God has given me to do.

What are the tools of your work? Calculator, hammer, lawn mower, telephone, or sewing thread? Vacuum cleaner, truck, or blackboard, paint brush or garden tool? We all work regardless of whether we receive a paycheck or whether we are even of working age. What are the tools of your work? Wrench, washing machine and drier, forms to fill out, or cell phone?

I invite you now to collect several tools of your work or, if you can't physically do this—your computer or your forklift might be tough to grab—just name the tools on a piece of paper and place it beside you as your continue on.

Benedict and Work

In his instructions to the cellarer, the brother who dispensed the goods of the monastery, Benedict explains that the tools of the monastery were to be treated with the same reverence as the sacred vessels of the altar (31.10). We might say that it was because Benedict wanted them to stay in good condition. There is more to it than all this, however, for Benedict sees the holy in *all* of life. It's through tools like these—computer, pen, and dust rag, wooden spoon and cooking pan—that I serve God. It's through the tools that you have right now that you serve God. I think that's why Benedict says that tools aren't to be taken lightly. Tools are the means by which we serve God by serving others through the many kinds of work that we do each day. The Benedictine view of work has a component of stewardship: we're stewards of the gifts and talents and skills we've been given. We're stewards of our ability to work and of the work we do.

The Holy in the Ordinary

In *Living with Contradiction: An Introduction to Benedictine Spirituality*, Esther de Waal explains that the Benedictine life shown in the Rule "is undramatic and unheroic; it simply consists in doing the ordinary things of daily life carefully and lovingly, with the attention and the reverence that can make of them a way of prayer, a way to God."[20] Making work a way of prayer? Most would think only a member of the clergy could do this, or that you could do this only through some form of outreach or community service. But the tools of our work can bring a greater awareness of God's presence and help us infuse our work with prayer.

One way to do this is to recognize that the way we view our tools can change the way we view our work. Consider the real wonder of our tools: they enable us to bear fruit as branches on the vine that is Christ (John 15:2). They enable us to share ourselves and our love and care for others as we prepare meals, answer telephone calls, and write letters, as we keep our homes tidy and our children's clothes clean, as we teach young children and allow the older ones to spread their wings and fly.

Look at the tools you have before you now. Who do you touch as you do your work with these tools? These people can be coworkers or members of your community or your family. They can also be people who use what you might create using the tools. How does your work connect with their lives and their work? When you do your work with thoroughness, love, and care, how does this impact their lives? How would your life be different without these tools? How might the lives of those you named in the first question above be different without you?

Know that God *is* working through you as you use these tools. This is pretty awesome if you think about your computer or your dust rag in this way! Let us give thanks for our tools!

Finally, tools themselves can become reminders for us to say prayers of blessing and thanksgiving. Before we use a tool, we can ask God to bless those who made it, those who transported it to us, and those who gave or sold it to us. When we finish a task, we can thank God for the tool. Each prayer will make us aware of God's presence and will bring a sense of the sacred to all we do.

The ordinary things of daily life are done with the ordinary tools of daily life—computer, pen, and dust rag, wooden spoon and cooking pan. These tools become holy when we do the tasks of our day simply, humbly, and well, aware of God's presence. Life becomes a way of prayer, a way that we serve others, a way that we can bring the love of God to others, a way that we share our gifts with others, and the way that you and I can cocreate a better world with God.

In your mind's eye, put your tools on the altar They are sacred vessels. Through them we bring Christ to others; through them we point to Christ.

Putting It into Practice

There are some questions about tools listed in the text of this Interlude. If you didn't think about your answers as you read the Interlude, return to these questions on page 170 and answer them. If you did answer them, take a moment to review your answers. Then continue.

One way we can discover God in our work is to say a prayer each time we begin a task. In the Prologue to the Rule, Benedict tells us to pray before we begin a "good work." We pray for God to help us complete and perfect the work. Unless it injures others or ourselves in some way, all work is good. Therefore, why not pray as we pick up a tool, whatever it is, to begin a task.

- Pick a task that you do every day.
- Make a mental (or written) note to pray in thanksgiving for the tool you use the next time you begin the task and to pray for God's help to complete the task.
- Next time the task comes up, put your resolve to pray into action.

CHAPTER 10

What Are You Looking For?
Developing a Rule of Life

> *The next day John again was standing with two*
> *of his disciples, and as he watched Jesus walk by,*
> *he exclaimed, "Look, here is the Lamb of God!"*
> *The two disciples heard him say this, and they*
> *followed Jesus. When Jesus turned and saw*
> *them following, he said to them, "What are*
> *you looking for?"*
>
> —JOHN 1:35–38

"What are you looking for?" In the Gospel of John, when two of John the Baptist's disciples began to follow him, Jesus asked them this question. The Greek text might translate better to, "What are you looking for *in life*?" No wonder they answered, "Rabbi . . . , where are you staying?" (See John 1:35–39.) Has anyone ever asked you what you were looking for in life? If so, did you respond immediately with a detailed explanation or did you instead comment on the weather?

The Challenge of Finding Meaning and Happiness

What are you looking for in life? What do you *really want* to make your life worthwhile and meaningful? These aren't easy questions to answer. Responsibilities and desires pull us in different directions, and we're faced with choice after choice. How should I spend my time? On what should I spend my money? Should I read this or should I read that? What really is important? The answers often are whatever is clamoring the most for attention—job, family, church, or community.

Priest and former abbot M. Basil Pennington explains that monks are happy because they know what they want and to some extent they already have it. "More important," he writes, "they know the way of life they are following will inevitably lead to enjoying it to the full."[1] Those of us who don't lead the life of a monk need to find ways to bring peace and order from within by creating our own rule of life. This rule can help us keep the bigger picture before our eyes. Otherwise we can find ourselves always doing the immediate and never doing the important."[2]

And so we are back to the original question that will help us focus on the important: What am I looking for in life? Once you've answered this, you can take steps to make what's important move from dream to reality.

A Rule as a Path to Meaning

Because we need routine to manage our daily lives, most of us have a "rule" of sorts already. In the morning when I get up, I feed the cats, then fix tea, have prayer, on most days exercise, get ready for work, eat breakfast (sometimes in the car—not good!), get to work, check messages, and so on throughout the day. My own routine fits this definition of a rule:

> A Rule is most often a chosen daily pattern of life and is arranged so that there are particular moments in the day when certain things are done.[3]

Although doing what we must do is necessary, life needs to be more than task accomplishment. But contemporary life pulls us toward accomplishment, from completing our required work to striving for success and recognition. This can leave us feeling empty, rushed, and unfulfilled, yearning for a better way to live.

Living life to the fullest is what the Rule of Benedict is all about. Early in the Prologue to the Rule, Benedict poses a question from Psalm 34: "*Is there anyone here who yearns for life and desires to see good days?*" (Ps 34:12 RB and RB Prologue 15) He then explains what to do:

> If you hear this and your answer is "I do," God then directs these words to you: If you desire true and eternal life, *keep your tongue free from vicious talk and your lips from all deceit; turn away from evil and do good; let peace be your quest and aim* (Ps 34:14–15 RB and RB Prologue 16–17).

In *Speaking of Silence: Christians and Buddhists on the Contemplative Way*, David Steindl-Rast states that the key question we need to ask to truly find life is this: "How can we put ourselves into a frame of mind that will lead us to live life in its fullness?"[4] To answer this question, we need to remember that we're baptized Christians. In Christ we have a way to reach this fullness of life—a way that will lift us beyond the limitations of our own desires into the bigger picture—to love God first, then to love neighbor as self. All our actions flow from this love. This is the way of Benedict who, in his deep love for the Lord, says in the Rule, "See how the Lord in his love shows us the way of life" (RB 49.4).

The Rule of Benedict as a Model for Daily Life

My hope and prayer is that through the pages of this book you've discovered that Benedict's Rule is a holy treasure trove of ways to be and to live as a Christian. The Rule is an aid to Gospel living with the goals of harmony for community and eternal life for the individual. The aim of the Rule is "to teach us to follow Christ and to follow Him through love."[5] Everything in the Rule points to Christ and to living a Christlike love. Every task can be infused with the presence and love of Christ. The Rule doesn't take us *out* of the world but lets us live fully *in* the world to be a transforming presence in the day-to-day ordinary tasks of life.

In his Rule Benedict gives some components that can be a part of our own rule as we follow Christ. He shows us a way to begin—we *stay put,* we *listen* to life around us and *respond* to what God is asking us to do, and we *remain open* to God's transforming work in our lives. In other words, we practice *stability, obedience,* and *conversion of life.* These Benedictine vows or values become the glue that holds our life together and keeps us on course with the Lord.

Benedict carefully details the Divine Office in the Rule, showing the importance he places on *intentional time with God.* Prayer is both communal and individual and is steeped in Scripture. Worship is a key component in the Benedictine way of life.

Benedict creates a *balance of daily activities* within the overall structure of the eight prayer services of the Divine Office. There is a balance between work and prayer, study and recreation, rest and activity, time alone and time together. Benedict recognized that an overemphasis in one area throws a person off balance. Although achieving balance in our life may not be completely possible, we can take Brian Taylor's advice:

> Those of us who work with our minds require exercise on a regular basis, or physical labor around the house. Those who make a living doing manual labor must find ways of stimulating the mind. All of us need to find ways of introducing prayer into our overworked lives. Without a balance of activities, we cannot become whole, as we are made to be as humans.[6]

Within the balance, *self-care* is an important component. To spend our time caring for others and neglecting our own physical and emotional health may leave us susceptible to exhaustion and resentment. Benedict recognizes this. Guests to the monastery are to be treated with the utmost hospitality and loving attention. Yet even with an influx of guests, he protects the routines of the brothers (chapter 53). The Rule keeps us from becoming consumed by our responsibilities.

On the other hand Benedict says—and much of the Rule indicates— that we're to *serve one another.* However we design a rule of life, that rule needs a component of outreach to others, near and far.

In the chapter on the Divine Office (chapter 6 of this book), we spoke of the importance of *clearly beginning* a task, *focusing on* the task, and *clearly ending* the task. We need to work in a *quiet, calm, and unhurried*

way. Our work, recreation, and service to others should show these characteristics. Technology conspires against this way of working. Some of us
become experts at multitasking as faxes, e-mails, and phone messages
seem to demand instant response. Sometimes they really do need prompt
attention, but often we just feel pressured unnecessarily. Just because
technology is instant doesn't mean our response must be instant.[7]

Benedict also stresses *moderation* in all areas of life. As you read the
following paragraphs about moderation, think about your own life.
Benedict encourages moderation in disciplining children. In the early
centuries of monasticism, it wasn't uncommon for people to dedicate
their children to religious life at an early age or to send them to the abbey
for education where they lived very much like monastics themselves.[8]
Treatment of children is to be appropriate and guided by their age and
how much they understand of the Rule (30.1). Boys to the age of fifteen
are to be supervised by everyone, but only with moderation and good
judgment (70.4–5); a monk would get into trouble for being angry or for
using poor judgment with the boys (70.6).

Benedict also stresses moderation in *food* for both practical and spiritual reasons: eating improperly can cause indigestion and can burden us
with the sin of overindulgence (39:7–9). In one of my favorite quotes
from the Rule, Benedict legislates moderation in drink as well:

> We read that monks should not drink wine at all, but since the monks of
> our day cannot be convinced of this, let us at least agree to drink moder-
> ately, and not to the point of excess, for *wine makes even wise men go astray.*
> (Sir 19:2 RB and RB 40:6–7)

For us, moderation with regards to food is not only a health and spiritual issue, it is a justice issue. Instead of overindulging in food, we must
share with those who are hungry.

In his discussion on *manual labor,* the nonprayer work of the monks,
he once again speaks of moderation and balance:

> Yet, all things are to be done with moderation on account of the fainthearted
> (RB 48:9).

Benedict emphasizes moderation in *conduct* and with *material possessions.* As the individual in charge of the goods of the monastery and their
distribution, the cellarer shouldn't be greedy, wasteful, or extravagant
(31:12). The abbot must show moderation in making work assignments
and exercising discipline (chapters 2, 27). These are all very good messages
for us in the twenty-first century—all in moderation and all in balance.

Two closing points. First, the basis of Benedictine spirituality is the
quality of *humility,* the quality that makes it possible to set aside our own
agenda and desires for those of another. The inner attitude of humility is

also what makes it possible to follow Benedict's Rule. Second, what also makes it possible to live Benedict's Rule is a *heart centered on Christ.* Benedict says to his listeners, "Let them prefer nothing whatever to Christ" (RB 72:11). With Benedict, we live fully in the world, doing our daily tasks, yet knowing that we are also fully connected to God.

> The Rule discloses . . . a life in which prayer and the constant awareness of the presence of God are never lived out at the expense of concern for the demands of ordinary daily life, of attention both to things and to people. This requires of me nothing less than holding on to a contemplative centre, a heart of prayer in the midst of my busy daily life.[9]

That contemplative center is the peace of Christ.

> As humans there are certain things we definitely want. Happiness begins with going to bed—for we will never be happy if we don't get enough sleep. And we need food, exercise, friends, intellectual stimulation, etc. But we are more than human. We have been baptized into Christ and so we also need the things of Christ-life: prayer, sacraments, Scripture, etc.[10]

Taking the Plunge! Bringing a Rule into Your Life

How do we bring a rule into our lives, so that we can live to the fullest as whole, healthy, strong, and Christ-centered people? Answer: one step at a time!

Just as a jigsaw puzzle is completed one piece at a time and a sweater is knitted one stitch at a time, so, too, our rule can develop one practice at a time. We can start with one thing, such as reading Scripture for ten minutes in the morning, or taking a vigorous walk by ourselves three times a week, or pausing at noon to give thanks to God, or creating a friendly space around ourselves to welcome others. We begin wherever we feel that God is leading us and wherever we feel we need the most peace. When we incorporate this practice into our life we can move on to the next step.

Since to love God is the first and most important commandment that Jesus identified, as we begin to develop and live a rule, we need to take time for God first. Then, since we have so many tasks to do in a given day, we also need to find ways to love God, self, and others through the tasks we must do. In short, we intentionally overlay our day with God. This overlay, whatever form it takes, becomes our "Rule" and gives meaning to our life.

We learn to see God and to live in God's presence in the ordinary tasks of daily living. We can do this because we grow better and better able to place ourselves in the presence of God who is always with us.

TOOLBOX
A Personal Rule of Life

Here are some steps you can take to begin to design a rule of life. Please realize that any rule takes time to follow. Start slowly and be flexible. Don't be too hard on yourself. Simply trying is important!

> Do not be daunted immediately by fear and run away from the road that leads to salvation. It is bound to be narrow at the outset. But as we progress in this way of life and in faith, we shall run on the path of God's commandments, our hearts overflowing with the inexpressible delight of love (RB Prologue 48–49).

Tool #1: A Sample Contemporary Rule as Model

In *Always We Begin Again*, John McQuiston gives a sample schedule that provides some guidelines for designing a Rule. He stresses the importance of repelling thoughts of "apprehension, melancholy and selfishness" and of taking control of our time so that we carefully spend it.[11] The elements included in his plan are the following:

1. *Reading and Meditation:* before breakfast and at the close of day
2. *Giving thanks throughout the day:* midmorning, noon, midafternoon, and at bedtime, as well as when you commute to and from work
3. *Mealtimes:* whenever possible, eat with family or friends and not alone
4. *Slow down:* when you feel yourself harried or racing
5. *Exercise:* evening or morning

McQuiston encourages us to turn off the television as a way to find new time and to try not to schedule meetings or work in the evenings. Spend time with family. He concludes with these meaningful suggestions:

> Each day we should expose ourselves to the inspiration of others. Thousands of saints and wise men and women have left us messages of hope and encouragement. Read what is honest. Read the scriptures and the commentaries. Read great literature and poetry. Read the psalms. Read that which expresses the anguish and the exhilaration of experience, and teaches us that we are not alone.[12]

A wise and hope-filled thought!

Now, using the elements that McQuiston provided, design your own Rule.

Tool #2: Designing Your Own Rule of Life

Purpose of the Tool. To give you a process to design a rule of life for yourself.

Background on the Tool. There are three key areas that are stressed in Benedict's Rule: (1) our connection with God, (2) our connection with others, and (3) balance among all aspects of life. It's difficult to devote the appropriate time to each of these without some intentionality on our part.

The Tool

The following is a process that you can use to design a rule of life. Again, start slowly, experiment, be flexible.

1. *In prayer, think about and then state what you want in life.* To do this, ask yourself these questions: What am I looking for in life? What's missing from my life now that would bring greater wholeness?

   What most people really want in life is beyond material concerns. Examples might include a good balance between work and family, more time for myself, more time for my family, more time for God, a deeper relationship with God or with another person.

2. *Decide if there's a particular area of the Rule of Benedict you wish to focus on.* You may be drawn to one of the three vows/values: stability (staying power), obedience (listening and responding), or conversion of life (openness to change). Or you may want to focus on work, prayer, balance, and so on.

3. *Determine the steps to take to achieve this goal.* Form a daily, weekly, monthly, or yearly plan. Use the resources in this book and in other books. One step could be to add a spiritual practice from the Benedictine Toolbox, but a step could also be to take something away or change something such as a negative attitude, the desire to control others, or the need to know exactly where I'm going.

   Talk to friends. Get ideas. Put them on paper.

4. *Implement your rule, one step at a time.* Start conservatively and be faithful. Add steps only when you're successful in the previous step.

5. *Be flexible.* You may need to change, drop, or add steps. You are a work in creation and so is your rule!

Tool #3: Some Inspiration

On of my favorite books on the Benedictine Rule is the contemporary paraphrase of the Rule *Always We Begin Again.* I've included the first two chapters of his paraphrase, for they may give you some ideas for your own rule of life. They are also rich resources daily for prayer and reflection.

The First Rule

Attend to these instructions,
Listen with the heart and the mind;
they are provided in a spirit of goodwill.

These words are addressed to anyone
who is willing to renounce the delusion
that the meaning of life can be learned;
whoever is ready
to take up the greater weapon of fidelity
to a way of living
that transcends understanding.

The first rule is simply this:

live this life
and do whatever is done,
in a spirit of Thanksgiving.

Abandon attempts to achieve security,
they are futile,

give up the search for wealth,
it is demeaning,

quit the search for salvation,
it is selfish,

and come to comfortable rest
in the certainty that those who
participate in this life
with an attitude of Thanksgiving
will receive its full promise.[13]

Each Day

At the beginning of each day,
after we open our eyes
to receive the light
of that day,

As we listen to the voices
and sounds
that surround us,

We must resolve to treat each hour
as the rarest of gifts,
and be grateful
for the consciousness
that allows us to experience it,

recalling in thanks
that our awareness is a present
from we know not where,
or how, or why.

When we rise from sleep let us rise for the joy
of the true Work that we will be about
this day,
and considerately cheer one another on.

Life will always provide matters for concern.
Each day, however, brings with it reasons for
joy.

Every day carries the potential
to bring the experience of heaven;
have the courage to expect good from it.

Be gentle with this life,
and use the light of life
to live fully in your time.[14]

⁓ Interlude ⁓
Spinning the Web

When we take the time to stop, open our eyes, and really look at the marvels of God's creation, they bless us with all their wonder and wisdom. One fall day as I was walking up the rectory sidewalk (the rectory is the house where the priest generally lives), I noticed a spiderweb. Three strong supporting threads formed the main framework. The center support stretched down from the overhang of the front porch, the right support was fastened to the top of a boxwood bush about four feet high, and the left stretched out to the front post of the porch. In between these three anchoring threads was a huge web nearly two feet from top to bottom and from side to side. This magnificent creation was home to a one very large brown spider!

Each time I went into the rectory I'd pause to see what the spider was doing, happy that there was a safe distance between her and me. The web seemed to be a very effective supermarket. Caught by the fine and sticky filaments of the web, unsuspecting insects were neatly packaged, ready to become tasty spider lunches and yummy spider dinners. I watched the spider deftly glide across her web, making sure dinner was secure or repairing a tear in her web and thought, "How wondrous is God's creation!"

Several days later after a heavy rain, I stopped once more to check on the spider and web and saw an amazing sight. The web was there but it was a tattered remnant of its former self. Many threads that supported the web and the circular threads that made the web had vanished. The remaining filaments were no longer tight and strong but sagged in loose loops weighed down by tiny drops of water that created a pattern like Swiss lace. Instead of catching insects, the web had caught hundreds of droplets of rain! Further stress was evident as the web blew gently in the breeze like a flag on a pole. That the web held together was remarkable. Somehow the center support held tight!

I found the spider at the very center of the web, curled in on herself, legs hidden, head hidden, body a brown nut on the remains of its web. As I looked at the spider, I thought, "This spider does what we do when hard times rain on us. When our lives are weighed down by a storm of hardship or drops of sadness, we curl up in order to survive!" There are many ways that we do this. I sometimes curl up in bed with comfort food or to sleep. Or we curl up with a book and lose ourselves in a world of fantasy and fiction. The best thing that we can do is to curl up in the arms of God and let God help us ride out the storm. The Psalms give us many examples of this "curling" in God's arms.

> I life up my eyes to the hills—
> from where will my help come?
> My help comes from the LORD,
> who made heaven and earth (Ps 121:1–2).

> In God, whose word I praise,
> in God I trust; I am not afraid;
> what can flesh do to me (Ps 56:4)?

Later that day when several of us left the rectory after a meeting, we stopped to look at the spider. The droplets of rain had fallen off and the breeze had stopped blowing. The spider had come alive and was intensely busy. In fascination we watched as she remade her web, going around and around, working from the outside to the inside, laying tiny filaments between the supporting threads of the web. It was then that I named her Martha because she was a picture of ceaseless work (see Luke 10:38–42). There was rhythm in her movements and a sure confidence in what she was doing. As the filament issued from the back of her body, she would grab it with her back foot (is it called a foot?) and push the filament into a support piece to secure it. She would then move her other legs in a certain order as she hurried to the next support to secure the next filament of the circular web. Around and around she went without stopping, laying these threads an eighth or even a sixteenth of an inch apart. The web was glorious.

I marveled at her single-minded attention to her task and her supreme skill at what she was doing. "If only I could live out my humanity the way Martha lives out her spiderhood," I mused. If I were a spider on Martha's web, enlisted to help her out, I can see it now: me wandering off somewhere trying to form the web from the center out or skipping support filaments as I worked or even spinning around in circles getting entwined in my own web-stuff. And Martha, stopping in her tracks, putting two of her inside legs on the "hips" of her body would say with exasperation, "Can't you get it right?"

No, not with ease. We humans so often don't get it right. We spend time spinning webs of work, webs of worry, webs of needless tasks, webs of achievement, success, or security and forget that our primary task is each other—our relationships. Over and over again life reminds us of this true priority. When a loved one gets sick, we drop everything that seemed so crucial before in order to tend to that person and our relationship. When a friend encounters trouble or hardship, we take the time to help. When our child hits a rough spot growing up, we set aside the wash or the dishes to hold tight, to listen, and to dry tears. These are reminders to us of what is really important in life.

Jesus gave us the commandment to love one another as he loved us (John 15:12). This is what our own "web work" should be about, at all times and not just in the crises. With the importance of relationships in our hearts and minds, our actions will form a neat web as we work toward the center that is Christ. There will be no straying, no falling into the trap of our own relentless agendas. With our energies on being love in whatever place we find ourselves, we'll know who we are to be and what we're to do in each situation. This is the work of our humanity. It is not easy. We'll need to try again and again. But, with God's help, we can find the rhythm and weave the web of love with the same sure confidence as Martha spinning her web.

Putting It into Practice

Here are a few questions for reflection.

- As you think about your life, what's your most important "web work?" Is this work a real priority in your life, or are you fitting it in among tasks that are less important but noisier in their demands?
- What steps could you take to reclaim the importance of this priority web work? How might you weave this priority web work into your own rule of life?

Living in the Present Moment

"Where shall I look for Enlightenment?" the disciples asked.

"Here," the elder said.

"When will it happen?" the disciple wanted to know.

"It is happening right now," the elder said.

"Then why don't I experience it?" the disciple asked.

And the elder answered, "Because you do not look."

"But what should I look for?" the disciple wanted to know.

And the elder smiled and answered, "Nothing. Just look."

"But at what?" the disciple insisted.

"Anything your eyes alight upon," the elder continued.

"Well, then, must I look in a special kind of way?" the disciple said.

"No," the elder said.

"Why ever not?" the disciple persisted.

And the elder said quietly, "Because to look you must be here. The problem is that you are mostly somewhere else."[1]

One of the most important tools in *St. Benedict's Toolbox* is to listen for God in our daily lives and to find God in the people and in the world around us. To do this we need to be present right where we are at any given moment. Benedict asks us to live in the present moment. He says, stay put (stability), listen to the people and to life around you and respond to who God is calling you to be and what God is asking you to do (obedience), and be open to the ways in which God will transform you as you live the Christian life (conversion of life). Benedict wants us to live in the present moment, fully alert to the now and ready to respond, whether we are at work, with our family, with friends, or with God in prayer.

How hard that is! Our thoughts race between yesterday, today, and tomorrow. As people speak to us, our own minds form silent words: words that we want to say in response, words that judge, words that love, words of mistrust, even words for our grocery list! We're often distracted by sounds around us. How difficult it is to be really present to the world that's right before our eyes and ears—a world brimming full of God's presence and light!

One of the best books on living in the present moment was written by a Jesuit priest named Jean-Pierre de Caussade entitled *The Sacrament of the Present Moment.* In this book, published in 1741, he explains that living in the present moment is a matter of letting ourselves fall in faith into the knowledge that God indeed *is* in *everything.* When we practice this belief, we grow in our ability to live in the present moment and to find God there. Yet even with this wisdom in heart and mind it's not easy. As I was looking over my copy of de Caussade's book, I saw a margin note that read, "It's easy to see this when I'm calm. How do I see this in the midst of chaos, boredom, or sickness?"

Like Benedict, de Cassuade believes we must accept where God has placed us in self-surrender, trust, and faith.[2] The key is to trust God, to give ourselves completely to whatever happens, and to work through it to the best of our abilities.

Echoing Benedict's call to obedience, de Caussade says that we're to offer no resistance to life.[3] He writes, "We can never achieve anything great except through surrendering ourselves; therefore let us think no more about it. Let us leave the care of our salvation to God."[4] To find the Divine Purpose, we are to love God in the present moment. But if our minds are somewhere else (lack of stability), we'll most likely miss God in the present moment (lack of obedience) and the gifts of growth and strength that God offers us (lack of conversion of life).

So, how do we live in the present moment?

When I was in seminary, I was often overwhelmed with the amount of work that needed to be done for school, in my position as seminarian at a parish and at home. One day I mentioned this to my homiletics professor, telling him that I was trying to take each day as it came, focusing on just the day, but that it wasn't working. I was still in a panic. He looked me in the eye and said gently and calmly, "Just focus on the moment. Concentrate on whatever you are doing right now. Just a moment at a time."[5] What great advice! If I was walking to class, I tried to focus my thoughts on that. "I am now walking to class; one step at a time. I won't get there any faster by wishing I were already there." If I was driving to church I thought, "Now I am driving to church. I won't get there any faster if I think that I should have been there ten minutes ago. Look at the clouds. They're beautiful, and the trees are, too. They're before me this moment." And so on. I found I grew calmer and better able to focus on whatever I was doing. By doing my best to always give whatever is before me my full attention, I am able to be in the present moment where I can absorb the grace that God sends to me.

Esther de Waal describes a "very simple" and wonderfully creative discipline that encourages her to see God in the present moment through the wonder of the tiniest things in God's creation. She carries a small magnifying glass with her. "Then," she explains, "whenever I can, I walk slowly and stop and look at whatever it may be, and I find a whole other world—in a leaf, in a small stone, in a twig. Time and again the glass has brought me a sharp shock of surprise, sometimes so intense that I have cried out in wonder and amazement. . . . I see patterns and configurations, endlessly delicate and different—a diversity of shape and form that carries a harmony and a relatedness of the parts of the whole. I see a glimpse of this mysterious inter-relatedness, a glimpse of the mystery at the heart of the universe."[6] By taking the time to really look at the beauty of the smallest things in our world, we hone our ability to really look at life and be aware of all that's around us. Such skills help us to live in the present moment, seeking God in everything.

Lack of acceptance can draw us away from living in the present moment. Something happens that's not to our liking, and we think about how much better things used to be. Something else happens and angry thoughts tumble about in our heads. Another unwelcome event occurs and we worry ourselves into the future. Whatever our response, lack of acceptance pulls us away from the present into a world of grumbling and negativity, both enemies of the present moment.

Benedict recognizes the importance of acceptance. When a task seems too difficult, a brother is to accept it, calmly and obediently. If it proves to be too much, the brother may explain to his superior why he can't do it but would still do the task if asked to, with trust in God's help and with love for the superior (68.1–5).

The truth is that we don't always know what's best for us. So, like the brothers, we can embrace all we're given and asked to do unless we're in physical or emotional danger. We can be thankful for every experience, the good and the bad. In a four-step process we can *accept* an experience, *decipher* what we must do, *reflect* on what that experience means to our life, and finally, we can *give thanks* for every experience, even the difficult and unpleasant ones.[7]

The last step, giving thanks, is pivotal to our spiritual health, as Anglican William Law explains.

> If anyone would tell you the shortest, surest way to all happiness, all perfection, he would tell you to make a rule to yourself to thank and praise God for *everything* that happens to you. For it is certain that whatever seeming calamity happens to you, if you thank and praise God for it, you turn it into a blessing. Could you therefore work miracles, you could not do more for yourself than by the thankful spirit, for it heals with a word spoken, and turns all that it touches into happiness.[8]

Esther de Waal describes the path of acceptance as saying "Yes."

> Yes means that we try to listen to God in all the ways that God is speaking
> to us. This means that I accept the present and do not try to run away
> from myself but remain where I am, firmly rooted and accepting of myself.
>   I pray Yes at the start of every day, accepting what lies ahead and hop-
> ing that I may, in all that happens, see and feel and know the presence of
> God. I pray Yes at the end of every day as I hand all that has happened
> over to God and ask his blessing on it. So that the Yes I say in prayer gradu-
> ally becomes my Yes to the whole of life. The Yes that holds everything
> together; that brings everything into focus and gives it meaning.[9]

Closing Thoughts

We began this journey into the Rule of Benedict with this question: "How
do we sit at the feet of our Lord so that we may fulfill the promises that
we make in our Baptismal Covenant and so that wholeness, meaning,
and peace may be increased in our lives?"

Through the pages of this book and in the various tools in the
Toolbox, we've explored ways to shape our actions, thoughts, and words
so that we can sit at Jesus' feet. We've explored ways to nurture our awareness of the presence of God. We've looked at ways to listen to God in
prayer and find God in the ordinary things of daily life. We've opened
ourselves to new spiritual practices and ways to find the holy in the daily
tasks we're called to do. We've considered the ways we need to reach out
to others both near and far. We've discovered ways that the Rule of
Benedict can bring meaning and depth to our relationships with God,
with ourselves, and with others.

We've explored how the Rule supports living into our Baptismal
Covenant. By keeping us centered in Christ, focused on the Scriptures,
and alert to ways to serve and to honor those around us, we listen for
how God asks us to fulfill the promises we make each time we renew this
Covenant. We've seen that the Rule is also deeply committed to providing ways we can live Jesus' Great Commandment (Mark 12:29–31):

> "Hear, O Israel: the Lord our God, the Lord is one; you shall love the Lord
> your God with all your heart, and with all your soul, and with all your
> mind, and with all your strength." The second is this, "You shall love your
> neighbor as yourself." There is no other commandment greater than these.

This book is just another step in a longer journey. Augustine said,
"Our souls are restless until they rest in Thee." We will always be on this
quest for God, for holiness, and for the Christian life. And so it's a blessed
gift indeed that we have a guide like St. Benedict, so full of wisdom, compassion, and practicality, who can give us the Rule and some wonderful

tools and point us in the right direction where we can learn to prefer Christ above all and find Christ in all. I close with a paraphrase of the last words of the Rule.

> Friend, whoever you are, hurrying to your heavenly home, with Christ's help carry through this little rule written for beginners. Then, strive for the heights of learning and virtue achieved by our spiritual fathers and mothers, and, with God's protection, you will reach them too.

God be with you.

Soli Deo Gloria
To God alone, the glory

A Listing of the Tools in the Toolbox

The following is a list by chapter of all the tools in the Toolbox.

Endnotes

Welcome to *St. Benedict's Toolbox*

1. This quote is found in chapter 66 of the Rule of Benedict. The translation is from *RB1980: The Rule of Benedict in English,* edited by Timothy Fry, O.S.B. and published by The Liturgical Press in 1981 (91). The structure of the Rule will be explained in chapter 1.

2. Prologue 9, 15–16.

Introduction

1. Sighard Kleiner, O.C. *In the Unity of the Holy Spirit: Spiritual Talks on the Rule of Saint Benedict.* (Kalamazoo: Cistercian Publications, 1989), 207–8.

2. The Book of Common Prayer of the Episcopal Church of the U.S.A. (New York: The Church Hymnal Corporation, 1979), 304–5.

3. Joan Chittister, O.S.B. *Wisdom Distilled from the Daily: Living the Rule of St. Benedict Today* (San Francisco: HarperSanFrancisco, 1991), 4.

4. David Steindl-Rast, with Sharon Lebell. *Music of Silence: A Sacred Journey through the Hours of the Days* (Berkeley, Calif.: Seastone, 1989), 23.

5. Joan Chittister, O.S.B. *The Rule of Benedict: Insights for the Ages* (New York: Crossroad, 1997), 13.

6. The Book of Common Prayer, 304–5.

7. Frederick Buechner, *Now and Then* (San Francisco: Harper & Row Publishers, 1983), 87.

8. Ibid.

9. Ibid.

10. John McQuiston II, *Always We Begin Again* (Harrisburg, Pa.: Morehouse Publishing, 1996), 17.

11. This gentle prayer method came through my spiritual director, Sr. Margaret Brackett, O.S.M.

1. The Rule of Benedict

1. Esther de Waal, *Living with Contradiction: An Introduction to Benedictine Spirituality* (Harrisburg, Pa.: Morehouse Publishing, 1997), 38–39.

2. Glenn W. Olsen, "The Benedictine Way of Life: Yesterday, Today and Tomorrow" *Communio-US* 11 (spring 1984): 35.

3. Heather M. Wallace, "The Road That Leads to Salvation: Benedictine Spirituality for Today," in George Demidowicz, ed., *Coventry's First Cathedral* (Stamford, England: Paul Watkins, 1994), 183.

4. Julian Stead, *St. Benedict: A Rule for Beginners* (New Rochelle, N.Y.: New City Press, 1993), 34.

5. Joan Chittister, O.S.B., *Living the Rule Today* (Erie, Penn.: Benet Press, 1982), 7–8.

6. From www.earlychurch.org.uk/pachomius.html, a website that provides information regarding influential persons and documents from the time of the early church.

7. Esther de Waal, *Seeking God: The Way of St. Benedict* (Collegeville, Minn.: The Liturgical Press, 1984), 29.

8. Esther de Waal, *Living with Contradiction: An Introduction to Benedictine Spirituality* (Harrisburg, Pa.: Morehouse Publishing, 1997), 38.

9. Quoted in de Waal, *Seeking God,* 30.

10. John Harriott, "A Benedictine Spirituality," in *Basil Hume,* ed. Tony Castle (London: Collins, 1986), 67–68.

11. See Robert Hale, "Discovering Consanguinity: The Monastic-Benedictine Spirit of Anglicanism," in *Canterbury and Rome: Sister Churches* (Ramsey, N.J.: Paulist Press, 1982), 97.

12. Ibid., 91.

13. Ibid., 97; italics in original.

14. Elizabeth J. Canham, "A School for the Lord's Service," *Weavings* 9 (January–February 1994): 12.

15. Will Derkse, *The Rule of Benedict for Beginners* (Collegeville, Minn.: The Liturgical Press, 2003), ix.

16. de Waal, *Living with Contradiction,* 41.

17. de Waal, *Seeking God,* 23.

18. Chittister, *Living the Rule Today,* 130.

19. Basil Cardinal Hume, *In Praise of Benedict* (London: Hodder and Stoughton, 1981), 47.

20. Ibid., 47.

21. Chittister, *Living the Rule Today,* 130.

22. Hume, *In Praise of Benedict,* 31.

23. Brian C. Taylor, *Spirituality for Everyday Living: An Adaptation of the Rule of St. Benedict* (Collegeville, Minn.: The Liturgical Press, 1989), 13.

24. Debra Farrington, "The Hearing Heart," *Alive Now* (January–February 2003): 16.

25. Ibid.

26. Ibid., 16–17.

27. Ibid., 17–18.

28. I thank Dr. Patricia Briegs for this helpful advice.

29. Ibid., 18.

30. Adapted from *The Rule of Saint Benedict,* trans. Abbot Parry, O.S.B. (Herefordshire, UK: Gracewing, 2000), 2.

2. The Prayer of *Lectio Divina*

1. M. Basil Pennington, *Lessons from the Monastery That Touch Your Life* (Mahwah, N.J.: Paulist Press, 1994), 30.

2. M. Basil Pennington, Lectio Divina: *Renewing the Ancient Practice of Praying the Scriptures* (New York: Crossroad, 1998), 88.

3. Luke Dysinger, "Accepting the Embrace of God: The Ancient Art of *Lectio Divina*," *Valyermo Benedictine* vol. 1, no. 1 (spring 1990): 2; from the O.S.B. website www.osb.org.

4. Ibid., 2.

5. Korneel Vermeiren, O.C.S.O., *Praying with Benedict: Prayer in the Rule of St. Benedict*, trans. Richard Yeo, O.S.B. (Kalamazoo, Mich.: Cistercian Publications, 1999), 90.

6. Quoted in Pennington, Lectio Divina, 88.

7. Thelma Hall, *Too Deep for Words: Rediscovering* Lectio Divina (Mahwah, N.J.: Paulist Press, 1988), 41; emphasis in original.

8. Dysinger, "Accepting the Embrace of God," 4–5.

9. Ibid., 6.

Part II: The Benedictine Vows

1. I am indebted to Sr. Shane Margaret Phelan of the Episcopal Convent of St. John Baptist in Mendham, New Jersey, who suggested the use of *value* for those of us who have not taken religious vows.

2. Esther de Waal, "The Benedictine Tradition and the Family," in *Journey to God: Anglican Essays on the Benedictine Way* (West Malling, Kent: Malling Abbey, 1980), 150.

3. A spiritual director is an individual with whom you can talk not only about your relationship with God but also about the things in your life that impact this relationship (i.e., relationships with others and with yourself, situations in your life, past and present, concerns for the future, distractions that impede wholeness and joy in living). A spiritual director can also guide you in the practice of prayer, meditation, and the reading of Scripture.

3. Stability

1. Elizabeth J. Canham, "A School for the Lord's Service," *Weavings* 9 (January–February 1994): 15.

2. Esther de Waal, *Seeking God: The Way of St. Benedict* (Collegeville, Minn.: The Liturgical Press, 1984), 64.

3. Jean Leclercq, OSB, "In Praise of Stability," *Monastic Studies* 13 (Montreal: The Benedictine Priory of Montreal, 1982), 92–93.

4. Quoted in Charles Cummings, *Monastic Practices* (Kalamazoo, Mich.: Cistercian Publications, 1986), 172; emphasis in original.

5. de Waal, *Seeking God*, 60.

6. Henri Nouwen, *The Genesee Diary: Report from a Trappist Monastery* (New York: Doubleday, 1981), 76.

7. Ibid., 77–78.

8. de Waal, *Seeking God*, 56.

9. Phyllis Thompson, "Living Stability in the Wake of Life's Changes," *The American Benedictine Review* (June 2001): 161.

10. Quoted in Michael Casey, O.C.S.O., "The Value of Stability," *Cistercian Studies Quarterly* 31, no. 3 (1996): 294.

11. Brian C. Taylor, *Spirituality for Everyday Living: An Adaptation of the Rule of St. Benedict* (Collegeville, Minn.: The Liturgical Press, 1989), 17.

12. Casey, "The Value of Stability," 295.

13. de Waal, *Seeking God*, 58.

14. Ibid., 64.

15. Cyprian Smith, O.S.B., *The Path of Life* (Leominster: Ampleforth Abbey Press, 1995), 21.

16. Ibid., 22.

17. Ibid., 23.

18. Ibid., 23–24.

19. Augustine Roberts, *Centered on Christ: An Introduction to Monastic Profession* (Still River, Mass.: St. Bede's Publications, 1979), 111.

20. Terrance G. Kardong, *Benedict's Rule: A Translation and Commentary* (Collegeville, Minn.: The Liturgical Press, 1996), 31.

4. Obedience

1. John McQuiston II, *Always We Begin Again* (Harrisburg, Pa.: Morehouse Publishing, 1996), 33.

2. Paschal G. Cheline, "Holiness of Heart and Mind: A Benedictine Perspective," *Asbury Theological Journal* (fall–spring 1995–96): 236.

3. Dom Leonard Vickers, "On a Human Notes," in *A Touch of God: Eight Monastic Journeys,* ed. Maria Boulding (Still River, Mass.: St. Bede's Publications, 1982), 134–35.

4. Quoted in Heather M. Wallace, "The Road That Leads to Salvation: Benedictine Spirituality for Today," *Coventry's First Cathedral* (Stamford, England: Paul Watkins, 1994), 185.

5. Basil Cardinal Hume, *Searching for God* (London: Hodder and Stoughton, 1977), 68.

6. David Stendl-Rast, "Standing on Holy Ground," in Susan Walker, ed., *Speaking of Silence: Christians and Buddhists on the Contemplative Way* (New York: Paulist Press, 1987), 26.

7. Cyprian Smith, O.S.B., *The Path of Life* (Leominster: Ampleforth Abbey Press, 1995), 4.

8. Ibid., 4, 5.

9. Steindl-Rast, "Standing on Holy Ground," 26.

10. Columba Stewart, O.S.B., *Prayer and Community: The Benedictine Tradition,* Traditions of Christian Spirituality Series (Maryknoll, N.Y.: Orbis Books, 1998), 64.

11. Joan Chittister, O.S.B., *Living the Rule Today* (Erie, Pa.: Benet Press, 1982), 54.

12. Smith, *The Path of Life,* 46.

13. Brian C. Taylor, *Spirituality for Everyday Living: An Adaptation of the Rule of St. Benedict* (Collegeville, Minn.: The Liturgical Press, 1989), 26.

14. Chittister, *Living the Rule Today,* 78.

15. David Adam, *Power Lines: Celtic Prayers about Work* (Harrisburg, Pa.: Morehouse Publishing, 1992), 13.

16. The Book of Common Prayer (New York: The Church Hymnal Corporation, 1979), 446–52.

17. Carol Bonomo, *Humble Pie: St. Benedict's Ladder of Humility* (Harrisburg, Pa.: Morehouse Publishing, 2003), 142.

18. Chittister, *Living the Rule Today*, 73.

19. Esther de Waal, "The Benedictine Tradition and the Family," in *Journey to God: Anglican Essays on the Benedictine Way* (West Malling, Kent: Malling Abbey, 1980), 160.

20. Smith, *The Path of Life*, 55.

21. Ibid.

22. Ibid., 55–56.

23. Esther de Waal, *Seeking God: The Way of St. Benedict* (Collegeville, Minn.: The Liturgical Press, 1984), 50.

24. Esther de Waal, *Living with Contradiction: An Introduction to Benedictine Spirituality* (Harrisburg, Pa.: Morehouse Publishing, 1997), 57.

5. Conversion of Life

1. Elizabeth Canham, "A School for the Lord's Service," *Weavings* 9 (January–February 1994): 15.

2. Sheila Garcia, "Stability and Change: What Benedict's Rule Can Teach Us," *American Benedictine Review* (March 1989): 74.

3. Thomas Merton, "*Conversatio Morum,*" *Cistercian Studies* (1966): 143.

4. Esther de Waal, *Seeking God: The Way of St. Benedict* (Collegeville, Minn.: The Liturgical Press, 1984), 70.

5. Ibid., 77.

6. Ibid., 77–78. This is a statement made by Sr. Joan Chittister to her own community.

7. Canham, "A School for the Lord's Service," 16.

8. de Waal, *Seeking God*, 78.

9. Garcia, "Stability and Change," 81.

10. Brian C. Taylor, *Spirituality for Everyday Living: An Adaptation of the Rule of St. Benedict* (Collegeville, Minn.: The Liturgical Press, 1989), 22–23.

11. The Book of Common Prayer of the Episcopal Church of the U.S.A. (New York: The Church Hymnal Corporation, 1979), 794.

12. Thomas Keating, *Open Mind, Open Heart* (Rockport, Mass.: Element, Inc, 1992), 44.

13. David Steindl-Rast, "Standing on Holy Ground," in Susan Walker, ed., *Speaking of Silence: Christians and Buddhists on the Contemplative Way* (New York: Paulist Press, 1987), 24.

14. Ibid., 26.

15. Joan Chittister, O.S.B., *Wisdom Distilled from the Daily: Living the Rule of St. Benedict Today* (San Francisco: HarperSanFrancisco, 1991), 162.

16. Steindl-Rast, "Standing on Holy Ground," 24.

17. Chittister, *Wisdom Distilled from the Daily*, 162.

18. Garcia, "Stability and Change," 75.

19. Brother Lawrence, *The Practice of the Presence of God*, trans. E. M. Blaiklock (London: Hodder and Stoughton, 1981), 76.

20. Ibid., 68.

21. M. Basil Pennington, *Lessons from the Monastery That Touch Your Life* (Mahwah, N.J.: Paulist Press, 1994), 40–41.

22. Ibid., 40.

23. Thomas Keating, *Open Mind, Open Heart* (Rockport, Mass.: Element, Inc, 1992), 43.

24. Ibid., 110.

25. William Johnston, ed., *The Cloud of the Unknowing* (New York: Doubleday, 1973), 48–56.

26. M. Basil Pennington, *Centering Prayer: Renewing an Ancient Christian Prayer Form* (New York: Doubleday, 1980), 76.

6. Walking through the Day with God

1. C. W. McPherson, *Grace at This Time: Praying the Daily Office* (Harrisburg, Pa.: Morehouse Publishing, 1999), 1.

2. Ibid., 2.

3. Byron David Stuhlman, "Redeeming the Day: The Celebration of Light at Morning and Evening Prayer," in *Redeeming the Time: An Historical and Theological Study of the Church's Rule of Prayer and the Regular Services of the Church* (New York: The Church Hymnal Corporation, 1992), 37.

4. Esther de Waal, "Attentiveness," *Weavings* 12, no. 4 (July–August 2002): 26.

5. Will Derkse, *The Rule of Benedict for Beginners*, trans. Martin Kessler (Collegeville, Minn.: The Liturgical Press, 2003), 74; emphasis in original.

6. Ibid., 76.

7. Ibid., 77.

8. Ibid., 78.

9. Ibid.

10. Brian C. Taylor, *Spirituality for Everyday Living: An Adaptation of the Rule of St. Benedict* (Collegeville, Minn.: The Liturgical Press, 1989), 34.

11. Corinne Ware, *Saint Benedict on the Freeway* (Nashville: Abingdon Press, 2001), 73.

12. Kathleen Norris, *The Cloister Walk* (New York: Riverhead Books, 1996), 351.

13. Ware, *Saint Benedict on the Freeway*, 73–76.

14. Norris, *The Cloister Walk*, 105; emphasis in original.

15. M. Basil Pennington, *Lessons from the Monastery That Touch Your Life* (Mahwah, N.J.: Paulist Press, 1994), 16.

16. Joan Chittister, *The Rule of Benedict: Insights for the Ages* (New York: The Crossroad Publishing Company, 1997), 126.

17. The Book of Common Prayer (New York: The Church Hymnal Corporation, 1979), 304.

18. Ware, *Saint Benedict on the Freeway*, 76.

19. The Book of Common Prayer, 137–40.

20. Taken from www.gratefulness.org.

21. Ware, *Saint Benedict on the Freeway*, 77.

22. Derkse, *The Rule of Benedict for Beginners*, 71–81.

23. This prayer was given to me by my spiritual director, Sr. Margaret Brackett O.S.M., who never tires of reminding me to live with this kind of trust in God.

7. Benedictine Hospitality

1. Fr. Daniel Homan, O.S.B., and Lonni Collins Pratt, *Benedict's Way: An Ancient Monk's Insights for a Balanced Life* (Brewster, Mass.: Paraclete Press, 2000), 69.

2. Elizabeth J. Canham, "A School for the Lord's Service," *Weavings* 9 (January–February 1994): 13.

3. Esther de Waal, *Seeking God: The Way of St. Benedict* (Collegeville, Minn.: The Liturgical Press, 1984), 121.

4. Brian C. Taylor, *Spirituality for Everyday Living: An Adaptation of the Rule of St. Benedict* (Collegeville, Minn.: The Liturgical Press, 1989), 54.

5. *Journey to God: Anglican Essays on the Benedictine Way* (West Malling, Kent: Malling Abbey, 1980), 51.

6. Dom David Knowles, *The Benedictines* (Saint Leo, Fl.: The Abbey Press, 1964), 34–35.

7. Henri Nouwen, *Reaching Out: The Three Movements of the Spiritual Life* (New York: Doubleday, 1975), 76.

8. Esther de Waal, *Living with Contradiction: An Introduction to Benedictine Spirituality* (Harrisburg, Pa.: Morehouse Publishing, 1997), 89.

9. Ibid., 104.

10. Ibid., 68.

11. Ibid., 65.

12. Dom Idesbalk Van Hourtyve, *Benedictine Peace,* trans. Leonard J. Doyle (Westminster, Md.: Newman Press, 1950), 99.

13. *The Rule of Saint Benedict,* trans. Abbot Parry O.S.B. (Herefordshire: Gracewing, 1990; reprint, 2000), 116.

14. Joan Chittister, O.S.B., *Wisdom Distilled from the Daily: Living the Rule of St. Benedict Today* (San Francisco: HarperSanFrancisco, 1991), 128–29.

15. Website of the Abbey of Saint Regina Laudis, Bethlehem, Conn., www.abbeyofreginalaudis.org.

16. Canham, "A School for the Lord's Service," 14.

17. Ibid., 19.

18. *The Holy Rule of St. Benedict: The 1949 Edition,* trans. Rev. Boniface Verheyen, O.S.B. (Atchison, Kans.: Abbey Student Press, 1949), Prologue 49. Available on the website of the Order of St. Benedict: www.osb.org.

19. The Book of Common Prayer (New York: The Church Hymnal Corporation, 1979), 833.

20. Homan and Pratt, *Benedict's Way,* 69.

21. Nouwen, *Reaching Out,* 71.

22. Ibid., 76.

23. Homan and Pratt, *Benedict's Way,* 69.

24. Joan Chittister, O.S.B., *Leader's Guide for Wisdom Distilled from The Daily: Living the Rule of St. Benedict Today* (San Francisco: HarperSanFrancisco, 1991), 28.

25. Ibid.

26. Ibid, 132.

27. Alexander McCall Smith, *The Full Cupboard of Life* (New York: Pantheon Books, 2003), 6.

28. I have found this prayer technique to be a powerful way to diffuse anger against another person. Here's how it works. "Susan's Father in heaven, hallowed be your name in Susan, your Kingdom come in Susan, your will be done in Susan. . . ." Adaptation of the contemporary version, The Book of Common Prayer, 97."

29. Adapted from Chittister, *Living the Rule Today* (Erie, Pa.: Benet Press, 1982), 98–99.

8. Keeping a Holy "Benedictine" Lent Anytime

1. The Book of Common Prayer (New York: The Church Hymnal Corporation, 1979), 265.

2. Ibid.

3. Timothy Fry, O.S.B., ed., *RB1980: The Rule of St. Benedict in English* (Collegeville, Minn.: The Liturgical Press, 1981), 251.

4. I thank Cynthia Brady for an on-target reflection.

5. This home was begun by Sr. Jane Mankaa who founded the Benedictine Sisters of Bethany in 2002, for the purpose of educating and caring for the children of the streets of Cameroon. Should you wish additional information, contact the Episcopal Convent of St. John Baptist at 973-543-4641 or at csjb@worldnet.att.net.

9. The Holiness of Labor

1. Esther de Waal, *Seeking God: The Way of St. Benedict* (Collegeville, Minn.: The Liturgical Press, 1984), 108.

2. Quoted in de Waal, *Seeking God*, 108–9.

3. Brian C. Taylor, *Spirituality for Everyday Living: An Adaptation of the Rule of St. Benedict* (Collegeville, Minn.: The Liturgical Press, 1989), 44.

4. Rachel Hosmer, *Gender and God* (Boston: Cowley, 1986), 2.

5. Deborah Smith Douglas, "Staying Awake," *Weavings* 17, no. 4 (July–August 2002): 39–40.

6. Kathleen Norris, *The Cloister Walk* (New York: Riverhead Books, 1996), 130–31.

7. Ibid., 131.

8. Ibid.

9. Douglas, "Staying Awake," 41–42.

10. Ibid., 43.

11. Esther de Waal, *Living with Contradiction: An Introduction to Benedictine Spirituality* (Harrisburg, Pa.: Morehouse Publishing, 1997), 38.

12. John McQuiston II, *Always We Begin Again* (Harrisburg, Pa.: Morehouse Publishing, 1996), 19.

13. Taylor, *Spirituality for Everyday Living*, 45.

14. Douglas, "Staying Awake," 40.

15. Quoted in Douglas, "Staying Awake," 43.

16. Douglas, "Staying Awake," 45.

17. I heard this quote on a recent PBS *Religion and Ethics NewsWeekly* program.

18. David Adam, *Power Lines: Celtic Prayers about Work* (Harrisburg, Pa.: Morehouse Publishing, 1992), 23.

19. Ibid., 36.

20. de Waal, *Living with Contradiction*, 71.

10. What Are You Looking For?

1. M. Basil Pennington, O.C.S.O., *Lessons from the Monastery That Touch Your Life* (Mahwah, N.J.: Paulist Press, 1994), 45.

2. Ibid.

3. Corinne Ware, *Saint Benedict on the Freeway* (Nashville: Abingdon Press, 2001), 43.

4. David Steindl-Rast, "Standing on Holy Ground," in Susan Walker, ed., *Speaking of Silence: Christians and Buddhists on the Contemplative Way* (New York: Paulist Press, 1987), 22–23.

5. Sighard Kleiner, O.C., *In the Unity of the Holy Spirit: Spiritual Talks on the Rule of Saint Benedict* (Kalamazoo, Mich.: Cistercian Publications, 1989), 207.

6. Brian C. Taylor, *Spirituality for Everyday Living: An Adaptation of the Rule of St. Benedict* (Collegeville, Minn.: The Liturgical Press, 1989), 30.

7. Will Derkse, *The Rule of Benedict for Beginners* (Collegeville, Minn.: The Liturgical Press, 2003), 78–79.

8. Joan Chittister, *The Rule of Benedict: Insights for the Ages* (New York: Crossroad Publishing Company, 1997), 103.

9. Esther de Waal, *Living with Contradiction: An Introduction to Benedictine Spirituality* (Harrisburg, Penn.: Morehouse Publishing, 1997), 36–37.

10. Pennington, *Lessons from the Monastery That Touch Your Life*, 47.

11. John McQuiston II, *Always We Begin Again* (Harrisburg, Pa.: Morehouse Publishing, 1996), 85.

12. Ibid., 86–88.

13. Ibid., 17–18.

14. Ibid., 19–20.

Conclusion: Living in the Present Moment

1. Joan Chittister, O.S.B., *Wisdom Distilled from the Daily: Living the Rule of St. Benedict Today* (San Francisco: HarperSanFrancisco, 1991), 201–2.

2. Jean-Pierre de Caussade, *The Sacrament of the Present Moment*, trans. Kitty Muggeridge (San Francisco: Harper Collins, 1982), 31.

3. Ibid., 44.

4. Ibid., 48.

5. I am grateful to the Reverend Dr. Charles Rice, my homiletics professor at Drew University, who gave me this advice that I have never forgotten and that I have shared with many people.

6. Esther de Waal, "Attentiveness," *Weavings* 12, no. 4 (July–August 2002): 27.

7. I thank Marge Dukes, a swimming friend, who shared this wisdom from a sermon that she had heard.

8. Esther de Waal, *Living with Contradiction: An Introduction to Benedictine Spirituality* (Harrisburg, Pa.: Morehouse Publishing, 1997), 141; emphasis in original.

9. Ibid., 140, 142.

Suggested Reading

The complete list of books used in *St. Benedict's Toolbox* may be found in the bibliography. This section gives some ideas for further reading and study on the Rule and on related topics.

Translations of the Rule

Fry, Timothy, O.S.B., ed. *RB 1980: The Rule of St. Benedict in English*. Collegeville, Minn.: The Liturgical Press, 1982.

> This is the translation that is most used in *St. Benedict's Toolbox*. The language is contemporary and can be readily understood.

McQuiston, John II. *Always We Begin Again*. Harrisburg, Pa.: Morehouse Publishing, 1996.

> A wonderful contemporary paraphrase of the Rule organized by topic. A good book to have for reflection and meditation.

Parry, Abbot, O.S.B., trans. *The Rule of Saint Benedict*. Herefordshire: Gracewing, 1990.

> Another translation of the Rule prepared for a general audience. Esther de Waal provides an excellent introduction to the Rule in the preface.

Books about the Rule

Benson, Robert. *A Good Life: Benedict's Guide to Everyday Joy*. Brewster, Mass.: Paraclete Press, 2004.

> This author reflects on longing for God, prayer, rest, community, and work to find a life of meaning and joy.

Canham, Elizabeth J. *Heart Whispers: Benedictine Wisdom for Today*. Nashville: Upper Room Books, 1999.

> An accessible interpretation of the Rule organized by topic. Each chapter includes a personal journal entry and prayer and closes with suggestions for reflection. A leader's guide is available for group work.

Chittister, Joan, O.S.B. *Illuminations*. San Francisco: HarperSanFrancisco, 1991.

> In an original format, Sister Joan presents key points of Benedictine spirituality organized by giving a word for every letter of the alphabet.

————. *Twelve Steps to Inner Freedom: Humility Revisited*. Erie, Pa.: Benetvision, 2003.
A contemporary presentation of Benedict's Twelve Steps of Humility by this noted Benedictine author.

————. *Wisdom Distilled from the Daily: Living the Rule of Benedict Today*. San Francisco: HarperSanFrancisco, 1991.
A beautifully written, thought-provoking book that brings the concepts of the Rule and Benedictine spirituality into deep meaning for everyday life. Each chapter covers a key concept in the Rule.

de Waal, Esther. *Living with Contradiction: An Introduction to Benedictine Spirituality*. Harrisburg, Pa.: Morehouse Publishing, 1997.
This excellent book focuses on the contradictions that this noted author sees in both Christianity and in the spirituality of the Rule of Benedict. She addresses the Rule in light of the relationships we have to God, self, others, and the world. She discusses the contradictions between solitude through prayer and the need for service in community, stressing how each is needed. At the end of each chapter, she gives some wonderful reflection questions.

————. *Seeking God: The Way of St. Benedict*. Collegeville, Minn.: The Liturgical Press, 1984; reprinted 2001.
A classic on the Rule of Benedict. Organized by topic, the book covers the key concepts of listening, stability, change, balance, material things, people, authority, and prayer. Dr. de Waal gives us not only thorough information and explanations but also beautifully written, reflective writing about the Rule. Republished in 2001, the book contains a preface by Kathleen Norris.

Homan, Fr. Daniel, O.S.B., and Lonni Collins Pratt. *Benedict's Way: An Ancient Monk's Insights for a Balanced Life*. Brewster, Mass.: Paraclete Press, 2000.
Presents brief chapters explaining various key points in the Rule. These include such topics as the vows, listening, prayer, humility, balance, conflict, community, joy, and leadership. Each chapter includes suggestions for reflection and application.

Hume, Basil. *In Praise of Benedict*. London: Hodder and Stoughton, 1981.
A collection of some of the talks that the cardinal, the former archbishop of Westminster, England, made on the anniversary year of Benedict's birth in 1980. In accessible language, Cardinal Hume reflects on various aspects of the Rule and its wisdom for contemporary life.

McCann, Abbot Justin, O.S.B. *Saint Benedict: The Story of the Man and His Work*. New York: Image Books, 1958.
An older but noted classic on the Rule of Benedict. Abbot Justin includes numerous stories about Benedict from Pope Gregory's biography of the saint.

Smith, Cyprian, O.S.B. *The Path of Life*. Leominster: Ampleforth Abbey Press, 1995.
The book includes chapters on listening, stability, conversion of life, obedience, silence, *lectio divina*, prayer, Eucharist, Liturgy of the Hours, private prayer, humility, and making life a unity. His chapters on the vows are excellent, each covering the outward and inward meanings of the three vows and what they mean for both monastic and nonmonastic.

Stewart, Columba, O.S. B. *Prayer and Community: The Benedictine Tradition*. Traditions of Christian Spirituality Series. Maryknoll, N.Y.: Orbis Books, 1998.

While the focus of the book seems to be for monastic communities, the author offers a thorough presentation of the Rule. Personally, I found many helpful insights.

Taylor, Brian C. *Spirituality for Everyday Living: An Adaptation of the Rule of St. Benedict.* Collegeville, Minn.: The Liturgical Press, 1989.

Here is an excellent book that gives good overviews of stability, conversion of life, and obedience along with practical applications of the Rule. The author discusses the important areas of prayer, work, and study and then addresses relationship to God, to others, and to things. Meditation or discussion questions are included.

The Benedictine Handbook. Collegeville, Minn.: The Liturgical Press, 2003.

Includes not only a translation of the Rule but also chapters about the Rule written by noted Benedictine authors, as well as a simple Daily Office for Morning and Evening Prayer. There is also a glossary of Benedictine words and thumbnail sketches of various Benedictine religious, i.e., noted monks and nuns in history.

Vest, Norvene. *Desiring Life: Benedict on Wisdom and the Good Life.* Boston: Cowley, 2000.

————. *Friend of the Soul: A Benedictine Spirituality of Work.* Boston: Cowley, 1997.

————. *No Moment Too Small: Rhythms of Silence, Prayer, and Holy Reading.* Kalamazoo, Mich.: Cistercian Publications, 1994.

Each of the three books offers an in-depth look at a specific area of the Rule.

Ware, Corinne. *Saint Benedict on the Freeway: A Rule of Life for the 21st Century.* Nashville: Abingdon Press, 2001.

I would buy this for the title alone! Ms. Ware provides us with a way to make our day a deeper sacrament by praying the hours in contemporary fashion and by having anchors in our life. She shares various ways to pray.

Reflections and Commentaries on the Rule

Each of these books presents the entire text of the Rule of Benedict with reflections on each part of the Rule by the author of the book.

Chittister, Joan, O.S.B. *The Rule of Benedict: Insights for the Ages.* New York: Crossroad, 1997.

"Insight" is an excellent word in the title of this book. Sister Joan offers many as she unpacks the meaning of the Rule for her readers. The Rule is divided into daily readings with Sister Joan's reflections on each. A great book!

de Waal, Esther. *A Life-Giving Way: A Commentary on the Rule of St. Benedict.* Collegeville, Minn.: The Liturgical Press, 1995.

This widely published author offers background, interpretation, and contemporary application of the Rule from her own experience. Filled with wonderful insights and points on which we can reflect.

Longenecker, Dwight. *Listen My Son: St Benedict for Fathers.* Harrisburg, Pa.: Morehouse Publishing, 1999.

In his commentary the author uses the Rule as a vehicle to help men become better parents. The Rule is broken into short daily readings and provides commentary to help strengthen men in their role as open-hearted, attentive, and intelligent fathers and husbands.

Kardong, Terrance G. *Benedict's Rule: A Translation and Commentary*. Collegeville, Minn.: The Liturgical Press, 1996.

In this book you'll find the Rule in both Latin and English plus a thorough verse-by-verse commentary by this noted Benedictine author. Father Kardong includes references to sources used by Benedict as well as his own interpretation of the Rule.

Prayer and Liturgy

Adam, David. *Power Lines: Celtic Prayers about Work*. Harrisburg, Pa.: Morehouse Publishing, 1992.

The author offers prayers for various times of the day, as well as for our various moods during our days.

Hall, Thelma, R.C. *Too Deep for Words: Rediscovering Lectio Divina*. Mahwah, N.J.: Paulist Press, 1988.

A classic text on the prayer form of *lectio divina*.

Keating, Thomas. *Open Mind, Open Heart*. Rockport, Mass.: Element, Inc, 1992.

Father Keating explains Centering Prayer and other spiritual disciplines that focus on a contemplative approach.

Pennington, M. Basil. *Centering Prayer: Renewing an Ancient Christian Prayer Form*. New York: Doubleday, 1980.

A classic text on Centering Prayer from one of the developers of its contemporary form.

Pennington, M. Basil. *Lessons from the Monastery That Touch Your Life*. Mahwah, N.J.: Paulist Press, 1994.

This book focuses on prayer in the Benedictine tradition. From the standpoint of the monastery, it covers *lectio*, Centering Prayer, the Daily Office, and work. The author explains what is done in the monastery and then gives suggestions for nonmonastics.

Steindl-Rast, David, with Sharon Lebell. *Music of Silence: A Sacred Journey through the Hours of the Days*. Berkeley, Calif.: Seastone, 1989.

A beautifully written, poetic explanation of the eight services of the Divine Office, the Benedictine *Opus Dei*, the work of God. The tone of each hour and how we can connect the teachings of that hour to our lives is described. The authors encourage us to adopt similar rhythms to our days.

Experiencing the Rule

The following books have been written by individuals who are oblates of a Benedictine monastery. These books present a contemporary application of the Rule of Benedict in daily life.

Bonomo, Carol. *The Abbey up the Hill: A Year in the Life of a Monastic Day-Tripper*. Harrisburg, Pa.: Morehouse Publishing, 2002.

Bonomo, Carol. *Humble Pie: St. Benedict's Ladder of Humility*. Harrisburg, Pa.: Morehouse Publishing, 2003.

Norris, Kathleen. *The Cloister Walk*. New York: Riverhead Books, 1987.

Bibliography

Adam, David. *Power Lines: Celtic Prayers about Work*. Harrisburg, Pa.: Morehouse Publishing, 1992.

Bonomo, Carol. *Humble Pie: St. Benedict's Ladder of Humility*. Harrisburg, Pa.: Morehouse Publishing, 2003.

The Book of Common Prayer of the Episcopal Church of the U.S.A. New York: The Church Hymnal Corporation, 1979.

Buechner, Frederick. *Now and Then*. San Francisco: Harper & Row Publishers, 1983.

Canham, Elizabeth J. "A School for the Lord's Service." *Weavings* 9 (January–February 1994): 11–20.

Casey, Michael, O.C.S.O. "The Value of Stability." *Cistercian Studies Quarterly* 31, no. 3. (1996): 287–301.

Cheline, Paschal G. "Holiness of Heart and Mind: a Benedictine Perspective." *Asbury Theological Journal* (fall–spring 1995–1996): 235–40.

Chittister, Joan, O.S.B. *Living the Rule Today*. Erie, Pa.: Benet Press, 1982.

———. *The Rule of Benedict: Insights for the Ages*. New York: Crossroad, 1997.

———. *Wisdom Distilled from the Daily: Living the Rule of St Benedict Today*. San Francisco: HarperSanFrancisco, 1991.

Cummings, Charles. *Monastic Practices*. Kalamazoo, Mich.: Cistercian Publications, 1986.

de Caussade, Jean-Pierre. *The Sacrament of the Present Moment*. Translated by Kitty Muggeridge. San Francisco: Harper Collins, 1982.

Derske, Will. *The Rule of Benedict for Beginners*. Collegeville, Minn.: The Liturgical Press, 2003.

de Waal, Esther. "Attentiveness." *Weavings* 12, no. 4 (July–August 2002): 21–27.

———. *Living with Contradiction: An Introduction to Benedictine Spirituality*. Harrisburg, Pa.: Morehouse Publishing, 1997.

———. *Seeking God: The Way of St. Benedict*. Collegeville, Minn.: The Liturgical Press, 1984. Reprinted 2001.

———. "The Benedictine Tradition and the Family." In *Journey to God: Anglican Essays on the Benedictine Way*, 147–68. West Malling, Kent: Malling Abbey, 1980.

Douglas, Deborah Smith. "Staying Awake." *Weavings* 17, no. 4 (July–August 2002): 38–46.

Dysinger, Luke. "Accepting the Embrace of God: The Ancient Art of *Lectio Divina*." *Valyermo Benedictine* 1, no. 1 (spring 1990); accessible via www.valyermo.com/ld-art.html.

Farrington, Debra. "The Hearing Heart." *Alive Now* (January–February 2003): 16–19.

Fry, Timothy, O.S.B., ed. *RB1980: The Rule of St. Benedict in English.* Collegeville, Minn.: The Liturgical Press, 1982.

———. *RB1980: The Rule of St. Benedict in Latin and English.* Collegeville, Minn.: The Liturgical Press, 1981.

Garcia, Sheila. "Stability and Change: What Benedict's Rule Can Teach Us." *American Benedictine Review* (March 1989): 71–81.

Hale, Robert. "Discovering Consanguinity: The Monastic-Benedictine Spirit of Anglicanism." In *Canterbury and Rome: Sister Churches: A Roman Catholic Monk Reflects upon Reunion in Diversity,* 80–104. Ramsey, N.J.: Paulist Press, 1982).

Hall, Thelma. *Too Deep for Words: Rediscovering Lectio Divina.* Mahwah, N.J.: Paulist Press, 1988.

Harriott, John. "A Benedictine Spirituality." In *Basil Hume,* edited by Tony Castle, 62–78. London: Collins, 1986.

Homan, Fr. Daniel, O.S.B., and Lonni Collins Pratt. *Benedict's Way: An Ancient Monk's Insights for a Balanced Life.* Brewster, Mass.: Paraclete Press, 2000.

Hosmer, Rachel. *Gender and God.* Boston: Cowley, 1986.

Hume, Cardinal Basil, O.S.B. *In Praise of Benedict.* London: Hodder and Stoughton, 1981.

———. *Searching for God.* London: Hodder and Stoughton, 1977.

Journey to God: Anglican Essays on the Benedictine Way. West Malling, Kent: Malling Abbey, 1980.

Johnston, William, ed. *The Cloud of the Unknowing.* New York: Doubleday, 1973.

Kardong, Terrance G. *Benedict's Rule: A Translation and Commentary.* Collegeville, Minn.: The Liturgical Press, 1996.

Keating, Thomas. *Open Mind, Open Heart.* Rockport, Mass.: Element, Inc, 1992.

Kleiner, Sighard, O.C. *In the Unity of the Holy Spirit: Spiritual Talks on the Rule of Saint Benedict.* Kalamazoo, Mich.: Cistercian Publications, 1989.

Knowles, Dom David. *The Benedictines.* Saint Leo, Fl.: The Abbey Press, 1964.

Lawrence, Brother. *The Practice of the Presence of God.* Translated by E. M. Blaiklock. London: Hodder and Stoughton, 1981.

Leclercq, Jean, O.S.B. "In Praise of Stability." In *Monastic Studies,* Volume 13, 89–98. Montreal: the Benedictine Priory of Montreal, 1982.

McCall Smith, Alexander. *The Full Cupboard of Life.* New York: Pantheon Books, 2003.

McPherson, C. W. *Grace at This Time: Praying the Daily Office.* Harrisburg, Pa.: Morehouse Publishing, 1999.

McQuiston, John II. *Always We Begin Again.* Harrisburg, Pa.: Morehouse Publishing, 1996.

Merton, Thomas. "Conversatio Morum." *Cistercian Studies* (1966): 130–44.

Norris, Kathleen. *The Cloister Walk.* New York: Riverhead Books, 1996.

Nouwen, Henri. *Reaching Out: The Three Movements of the Spiritual Life.* New York: Doubleday, 1975.

———. *The Genesee Diary: Report from a Trappist Monastery.* New York: Doubleday, 1981.

Olsen, Glenn W. "The Benedictine Way of Life: Yesterday, Today, and Tomorrow." *Communio-US* 11 (spring 1984): 35–45.

Parry, Abbot, O.S.B., trans. *The Rule of Saint Benedict*. Herefordshire, UK: Gracewing, 2000.

Pennington, M. Basil. *Centering Prayer: Renewing an Ancient Christian Prayer Form*. New York: Doubleday, 1980.

————. Lectio Divina: *Renewing the Ancient Practice of Praying the Scriptures*. New York: Crossroad, 1998.

————. *Lessons from the Monastery That Touch Your Life*. Mahwah, N.J.: Paulist Press, 1994.

Roberts, Augustine. *Centered on Christ: An Introduction to Monastic Profession*. Still River, Mass.: St. Bede's Publications, 1979.

Smith, Cyprian, O.S.B. *The Path of Life*. Leominster: Ampleforth Abbey Press, 1995.

Stead, Julian. *St. Benedict: A Rule for Beginners*. New Rochelle, N.Y.: New City Press, 1993.

Steindl-Rast, David, with Sharon Lebell. *Music of Silence: A Sacred Journey through the Hours of the Days*. Berkeley, Calif.: Seastone, 1989.

Steindl-Rast, David. "Standing on Holy Ground." In *Speaking of Silence: Christians and Buddhists on the Contemplative Way*, edited by Susan Walker, 22–29. New York: Paulist Press, 1987.

Stewart, Columba, O.S.B. *Prayer and Community: The Benedictine Tradition*. Traditions of Christian Spirituality Series. Maryknoll, N.Y.: Orbis Books, 1998.

Stuhlman, Byron David. "Redeeming the Day: The Celebration of Light at Morning and Evening Prayer." In *Redeeming the Time: An Historical and Theological Study of the Church's Rule of Prayer and the Regular Services of the Church*, 32–59. New York: The Church Hymnal Corporation, 1992.

Taylor, Brian C. *Spirituality for Everyday Living: An Adaptation of the Rule of St. Benedict*. Collegeville: The Liturgical Press, 1989.

Thompson, Phyllis. "Living Stability in the Wake of Life's Changes." *The American Benedictine Review* (June 2001): 156–70.

Van Hourtyve, Dom Idesbalk. *Benedictine Peace*. Translated by Leonard J. Doyle. Westminster, Md.: Newman Press, 1950.

Verheyen, Rev. Boniface, O.S.B., trans. *The Holy Rule of St. Benedict: The 1949 Edition*. Atchison, Kans.: Abbey Student Press, 1949. Available on the website of the Order of St. Benedict: www.osb.org.

Vermeiren, Korneel, O.C.S.O. *Praying with Benedict: Prayer in the Rule of St. Benedict*. Translated by Richard Yeo, O.S.B., Kalamazoo, Mich.: Cistercian Publications, 1999.

Vickers, Dom Leonard. "On a Human Note." In *A Touch of God: Eight Monastic Journeys*, edited by Maria Boulding, 120–36. Still River, Mass.: St Bede's Publications, 1982.

Wallace, Heather M. "The Road That Leads to Salvation: Benedictine Spirituality for Today." In *Coventry's First Cathedral*, edited by George Demidowicz, 181–89. Stamford, England: Paul Watkins, 1994.

Ware, Corinne. *Saint Benedict on the Freeway*. Nashville: Abingdon Press, 2001.